Identification & Value Guide To

SCOUTING
COLLECTIBLES

Edited by R. J. Sayers

BOOKS AMERICANA
INC

ISBN 0-89689-028-7

TABLE OF CONTENTS

INTRODUCTION

The collecting of Scouting items of all types has grown tremendously in the past few years. What began as a saving of memorabilia of personal significance in Scouting's early days, has now grown to be an important part of the burgeoning collectible industry in this country.

Values of many items have doubled, tripled and even quadrupled in some items in the past few years. Many items which were fairly common in 1978 are now rare in 1982.

This identification and value guide is intended, not as a bible covering every aspect of the hobby, but rather as a guide to assist the novice as well as the serious collector in identifying varieties of items and to give him some idea of the approximate value of a particular item.

Every user of this guide should bear in mind that values given in a guide such as this can only approximate the value of any given item on the national market. Certain items may vary considerably in different local markets. As a general rule, for example, very old items of local interest to your area will be more valuable there than to a collector in some other part of the country.

As with all collectibles, values are determined by supply and demand. In setting the values herein, we have disregarded those rare one-time sales where someone paid an unusually high price for a certain item he wanted badly. We have also disregarded the low price someone sold an item for because they didn't know the value. Values have been taken from the current market prices that items have been bringing in the Scouting Collectors marketplace.

We strongly recommend that anyone who has a serious interest in collecting Scout memorabilia subscribe to any of the newsletters covering his particular field of interest and contact one of the several professional dealers specializing in this area. The final chapter in this book has lists of most of them for your convenience.

We have included a special section of useful reference information for some of the more popular areas of collecting. We hope you find them useful.

As with any collectibles area where prices begin to reach substantial amounts, a few unscrupulous individuals will enter the scene and produce counterfeits. Unfortunately, this area of collectibles is also beginning to see this happen. We feel it only right to point out that to our knowledge only a few, if any of the individuals so involved, are now or ever have been registered members of a Scouting organization. Scouting and its members do not condone such activity, as one might expect. The Boy Scouts of America and the Girl Scouts of the USA both take great pains to control the manufacture and distribution of their awards, as well they should. A word of caution is in order, when buying and selling or trading Scout items, know who you're dealing with. The major dealers have National reputations and value that highly. The same is true with most of the major collectors in each field. They all know their business and they know Scouting.

To the newcomer to the hobby, I can only say that if you are not a Scout or Scout Leader, you soon will be. The people involved are really great and most willing to teach and help. One cannot collect Scout items without gaining a great respect for the organizations and the people, as well as the values and traditions they expouse. Welcome to the wonderful world of Scouting and its history through its memorabilia.

TERMINOLOGY USED

As with any hobby, each develops its own special terminology and abbreviations to help the individual better identify which specific item is being described. This hobby is no different. One striking difference from other hobbies is that it transcends its boundaries into other fields of collecting. Good examples of this are Scout coins or stamps. While collectors of Scouting memorabilia are most interested in these items, so are others in the numismatic or philatelic areas. Hence, while specific terminology and abbreviations are in use in the scouting area, so too are various abbreviations normally identified with other areas i.e. "bu" (numismatic) and "imperf" (philatelic). Thus, oftentimes descriptions of scout items will also contain non-scouting abbreviations.

Below are listed some of the more common and most popularly used abbreviations.

Type of Material:
c — chenille
f — felt
k — khaki
t — twill
w — woven

Edges:
(b) — bound
c-e — cut edge
(r) — ribbon (unbound)
r-e — rolled edge

Type of Embroidery:
fe — fully embroidered
f — twill background
s — fully embroidered

Type of Intern:
CP — Council Patch
CSP — Council Shoulder Patch
N/C — Neckerchief
NJ — National Jamboree
OA — Order of the Arrow
PM — Patrol Medallion
WJ — World Jamboree

Shapes:
A — Arrowhead
C — Circle
D — Dome
Dd — Diamond
H — Hat Shaped
O — Oval
Rec — Rectangle
S — Shield
Sq — Square
Tr — Triangle
X — Odd Shaped

TYPES OF PINS

Over the years, scouting has issued many different pins. As one might imagine, as technology has advanced and the economy fluctuated, different types of fasteners for these pins evolved. Generally speaking, the older the form of the fastener, the older the item is. One notable exception to this is that the Boy Scouts of America did use safety clasp pins on some of their items at their very beginning in 1910.

Top row (l-r)
Screwback Pin
Clutchback Pin

2nd Row (l-r)
Crude Type Clasp
Pin Shield Type Pin
Safety Pin Clasp

Bottom Row (l-r)
Bar Mount Safety Clasp
Folded Pins Type
Safety Clasp Pin

DEALERS

If you have items to sell or wish to purchase Scout collectibles, below are listed some of the larger dealers in the country.

Scout Collectors Shop
James W. Clough
7763 Elmwood Drive
South Glens Falls, New York 12801
(518) 793-4029

Douglas Bearce
P. O. Box 7081
Salem, Oregon 97303
(503) 363-1715

The Stevensons
90 West Thacker Street
Hoffman Estates, Illinois 60194
(312) 882-0421

Los Angeles Patch Exchange
12300 Hatteras Street
North Hollywood, California 91607
(213) 994-9090

Richard E. Shields, Jr.
The Carolina Trader
P. O. Box 26986
Charlotte, North Carolina 28213
(704) 597-9779

Scouting Memorabilia
R. J. Sayers
P. O. Box 246
Andrews, Texas 79714

Scouting Market Place
Elmer E. Fennert
3108 15th Avenue South
Apartment 2
Minneapolis, Minnesota 55407
(612) 724-0995

PUBLICATIONS ON SCOUT COLLECTIBLES

Scout Memorabilia (5 - Year)
Harry D. Thorsen, Jr.
7305 Bounty Drive
Sarasota, Florida 33581

Scouting Collectors Quarterly
806 East Scott Street
Tuscola, Illinois 61953

Badges Club Magazine (bi-monthly)
c/o Robert Haas
8151 Northwest 24th Street
Sunrise, Florida 33313

S.O.S.S.I. Journal (Monthly)
4304 South Hubert Avenue
Tampa, Florida 33611

In addition, most dealers will furnish their sales lists regularly on a subscription basis whether or not you purchase anything.

SCOUT COLLECTING ORGANIZATIONS

Badgers Club
c/o Robert Haas
8151 Northwest 24th Street
Sunrise, Florida 33313

National Scouting Collectors Society
c/o Ramond Lee, Jr.
806 East Scott Street
Tuscola, Illinois 61953

Scouts on Stamps Society International
4304 South Hubert Avenue
Tampa, Florida 33611

Western Traders Association
c/o Ken Witz
115 Jordan Street
San Rafael, California 94901

Southern California Association of Traders
c/o Jean S. Amster
5521 Saloma Avenue
Van Nuys, California 91411

HANDBOOKS, GUIDEBOOKS, PAMPHLETS

1910 BSA Official Manual (Original Edition)

Several variations of this are known to exist. Specific values will vary depending upon variation and condition.
   Paperback
   Hardbound (tan-brown print)
   Hardbound (green-gold print)

Price range from $180.00 - 250.00

Seton's Forester's Manual, 1912, 2nd series $155.00

NOTE: In 1910 there was printed a leather bound 1910 handbook signed by (5) — Seaton, Beard, Livingston, West and one other. Only 100 published. Value $500.00

NOTE: Autographed editions, West or Hillcourt, add $10 to $20. (Prices on handbooks are for very good to mint conditons.)

The Official Handbook For Boys (1st Edition)

1911 - June 13, (Proof) Black on Brown cover, interwoven with blank pages	$150.00
June 13, (Proof) Black on Brown cover, no blank pages	137.50
1911 - Aug. 13 Brown cover, also a proof but not marked as such	125.00
Nov. 29 Brown cover	110.00
Dec. 30 Dark, red cover	110.00
1912 - May 18 Black cover	100.00
May 18 Same, with red leather cover	110.00
July 29 Dark, red cover	110.00
— Same as the 7th printing (date unknown), cover page marked "4th edition"	110.00
1913 - Jan. 31 Red cover, marked "4th edition" and "1913" on title page	65.00
May 31 Red cover, same as the 9th printing but now has 416 pages .	65.00
Oct. 31 Orange cover	65.00
Dec. 31 Light green cover	65.00
1914 - Feb. 28 Dark red cover	60.00
Mar. 3 Dark red cover	60.00

Handbook For Boys (2nd Edition)

1914 - Oct. 31 Silver	80.00
Every Boys Library Edition of above	50.00
1915 - Jan. 27 Silver	55.00
Mar. 17 Silver	55.00
1916 - Apr. 11 Silver	50.00
June 30 Olive gray	50.00
Dec. Red	50.00
1917 - May Light Olive	45.00
Dec. Light Olive	45.00
1918 - May Light Olive	45.00
Dec. Light Olive	45.00
1919 - May Light Olive	40.00
Every Boys Library Edition of above	4.00
Dec. Light Olive	40.00
1920 - June White-Light Olive	38.00
1921 - Jan. Light Olive	38.00
June Dark Olive	38.00
1922 - Feb. Dark Olive	38.00
Aug. Dark Olive	30.00
1923 - April Dark Olive	30.00
May Dark Olive	30.00
1924 - Jan. Dark Olive	30.00
May Dark Olive	30.00
1925 - Jan. Dark Olive	30.00

May Dark Olive	30.00
Aug. Dark Olive	30.00
1926 - May Dark Olive	30.00
July Dark Olive	28.00
1927 - Mar. Dark Olive	28.00
May Dark Olive	28.00

Handbook For Boys (3rd Edition)
(Dr. H. W. Hurt, Editor)
Cover by Norman Rockwell - "Famous Americans"

1927 - Nov. 1st	25.00	1933 - Jul. 18th	15.00
Nov. 2nd	20.00	Dec. 19th	13.00
Dec. 3rd	20.00	1934 - Sep. 20th	13.00
1928 - Jan. 4th	20.00	1935 - Mar. 21st	13.00
Jan. 5th	20.00	Special Silver Cover edition	
Mar. 6th	20.00	with 4 page insert	100.00
Nov. 7th	20.00	Sept. 22nd	10.00
Nov. 8th	20.00	1936 - Mar. 23rd	10.00
1929 - Apr. 9th	18.00	Oct. 24th	10.00
Aug. 10th	18.00	Dec. 25th	10.00
1930 - Jan. 11th	15.00	1937 - Mar. 26th	10.00
Apr. 12th	15.00	Sept. 27th	10.00
Dec. 13th	15.00	1938 - Feb. 28th	10.00
1931 - Mar. 14th	15.00	Apr. 29th	10.00
Jun. 15th	15.00	Nov. 30th	10.00
1932 - Apr. 16th	15.00	1939 - Oct. 31st	10.00
Nov. 17th	15.00	1940 - May 32nd	10.00

Revised Handbook For Boys (4th Edition)
(First Edition) A Norman Rockwell cover depicting
a Cub Scout, Boy Scout, and Sea Scouts.

1940 - Dec. 33rd	7.50	1944 - Sept. 37th	6.00
1941 - Dec. 34th	7.50	1945 - Sept. 38th	6.00
1942 - Dec. 35th	7.50	1946 - Jun. 39th	6.00
1943 - Dec. 36th	7.50		

Handbook For Boys (5th Edition)
Cover by Don Ross depicting Hiking Scouts

1948 - Jan 1st says 420,000 printed	6.50	Jan. 1st says 840,000 in print	6.50
		1949 - Apr. 2nd	5.00

New cover by Don Ross depicting a campfire scene

1950 - Apr. 3rd	5.00	1956 - Jan. 9th	3.50
1951 - Jan. 4th	4.00	1957 - Jan. 10th	3.50
1952 - Jun. 5th	4.00	Oct. 11th	3.50
1953 - Jun. 6th	4.00	Special editon of above	
1954 - Jun. 7th	4.00	with 4 page insert	10.00
1955 - Feb. 8th	3.50	1958 - Sept. 12th	3.50

Boy Scout Handbook (6th Edition)
Cover by Norman Rockwell - a full color Scout
Color of cover: Green

```
1959 - Nov. 1st    ................  3.50
1960 - Aug. 2nd    ................  3.00
1961 - Aug. 3rd    ................  3.00
1962 - Sept. 4th   ................  3.00
1963 - Mar. 5th    ................  3.00
```
Special Edition printed
in language of the Ryukuyu
Islands
Cover; Oriental design .. 10.00
```
1964 - Jan. 6th    ................  3.00
1965 - Mar. 7th    ................  3.00
```

Boy Scout Handbook (7th Edition)
Cover by Don Lupo depicting hiking Scouts

```
1965 - Sept. 1st   ................  3.00
1966 - Apr. 2nd    ................  2.50
1967 - Jan. 3rd    ................  2.50
1968 - Feb. 4th    ................  2.50
1969 - Jan. 5th    ................  2.50
1970 - Feb. 6th    ................  2.50
1971 - Feb. 7th         ...
```

Scout Handbook (8th Edition)
Cover - two color green with drawing of Scouts observing the moon.

```
1972 - Jun. 1st    ................  2.50
1973 - Feb. 2nd    ................  2.00
1974 - Jan. 3rd    ................  2.00
```
New Cover by Csatari,
Author Frederick L. Hines
```
1976 - Jul. 4th    ................  2.00
1977 - Dec. 5th    ................  1.75
```

Official Boy Scout Handbook (9th Edition)
Cover - Norman Rockwell - picture of Scout Troop outdoors

1979 - Feb. 1st printing, Black
   Lettering 5.00
   2nd printing, Blue Lettering   3.00

Boy Scout of America Official Reprints

1970 - Oct. Hardbound reprint of 1911 Handbook 10.00

1971 - Softcover edition with brown cover published by Nashville Publishing Company with title, "The Very First Boy Scout Handbook" 7.50

1976 - Boy Scouts of America Reprint of 1911 Handbook to commemorate the Bicentennial, softbound with brown on white cover 6.50

BOY SCOUT REQUIREMENTS

To reduce the revisions to the Handbook, the Merit Badge requirements are published in an annually printed pamphlet. Catalog No. 3216, Flexiblecard

1960 - Feb. 100m - 93p - Green cover	1.25
1960 - Aug. 100m - 93p - MB arranged in subject groupings	1.00
1962	1.00
1963 - Sep. 185m - 96p	1.00
1964 - Jan. (1965) 160m - 102p	1.00
1965 - Nov. (1966) 225m - 108p	1.00
1966 - Dec. (1967) 220m	1.00
1967 - Sep. (1968) 220m - 113p	1.00
1969 - Jan 225m - 126p - Alphabetically arranged	1.00
1969 - Nov. 260m - 126p	1.00
1970 - Sep. 260m - 126p	1.00

Cover date in parenthesis

Change in Requirements Insert

1938 8p for 28th printing, 3rd Edition	.50
1946 12p for 39th print 4th Edition	.50
BSA Handbook Supplement copyright 1963	1.00
BSA Handbook Supplement in the language of the Ryukyu Islands ..	5.00

Handbook for Patrol Leaders
Author - William Hillcourt
Cover drawing by - Hy Hintermeister depicting a Scout camping
with imagined adventures of the future.

1929 - Jul. 1st	10.00	1938 - May 8th	5.00
Sept. 2nd	10.00	1939 - Jun. 9th	5.00
1931 - Jan. 3rd	8.00	1941 - Feb. 10th	4.00
1933 - Apr. 4th	8.00	1942 - Mar. 11th	4.00
Cover change - cover color		1943 - Mar. 12th	4.00
changed to Silver		1944 - Mar. 13th	4.00
1935 - Feb. 5th Marked "Silver		1945 - Mar. 14th	4.00
Jubilee Edition"	75.00	Nov. 15th	4.00
1936 - Jan. 6th	5.00	1946 - Mar. 16th	3.00
1937 - Jun. 7th	5.00	1948 - Dec. 17th	3.00
		1949 - Dec. 18th	3.00

Handbook For Patrol Leaders (2nd Edition)
Cover - depicting a Beckoning Scout
Called the World Brotherhood Edition

1950 - Dec. 1st printing	3.00	1964 - Dec. 16th	2.50
1952 - Jan. 2nd	3.00	1965 - Aug. 17th	2.50
Nov. 3rd	3.00	1965 - Dec. 18th	2.50
1953 - Dec. 4th	3.00	**Patrol Leader's Handbook**	
1954 - Sept. 5th	3.00	1967 - Sept. 1st	2.50
1955 - Sept. 6th	3.00	1968 - Dec. 2nd	2.50
1956 - Dec. 7th	3.00	1969 - Nov. 3rd	2.50
1957 - Dec. 8th	3.00	1970 - Oct. 4th	2.50
1959 - Jan. 9th	3.00	**Patrol and Troop Leadership**	
1961 - Feb. 11th	3.00	1972 - Jun	2.50
Dec. 12th	3.00	1975 - Feb.	2.50
1962 - Feb. 13th	3.00	1977 - Apr.	2.50
1963 - Feb. 14th	3.00		

1911 - 1st Edition Handbook 90.00

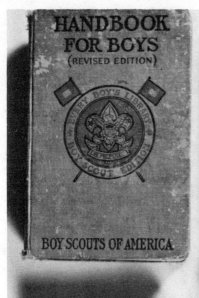

Top row (l-r)
1919 - Every Boy's Library Edition of the Handbook ... 40.00
1922 - 2nd Edition Handbook 30.00
Bottom row
1929 - 3rd Edition Handbook 18.00
1941 - 4th Edition Handbook 7.50

1973 Handbook	....	2.00
1977 Handbook	....	1.75
1979 Handbook	....	3.00

1971 Reprint of
1911 Handbook
.... 7.50

1970 Hardbound
Reprint of 1911
Handbook ..10.00

1976 Bicentennial
Reprint of 1911
Handbook ... 6.50

Handbook For Scoutmasters (1st Edition)

"Programs for Scout Masters of Boy Scouts of America" - green, soft cover

1912 - Proof, 203 pages. Contains Bertillon System of Identification ..	120.00
1912 - Proof 161 pages. Bertillon System dropped.	120.00
1912 - 161 pages. Not marked "proof" as were the previous two.	110.00

TITLE CHANGE

1913 - Proof 344 pages, not issued with a cover. Marked "proof". Title is "Handbook for Scout Masters, Boy Scouts of America" .	120.00

COVER CHANGE

Hardcover, tan, with black photo of Scout with staff and bugle.

c1913-1914 5th printing 352 pages. Editorial Board includes Jameson	50.00
c1913-1914 6th 352 pages. Editorial Board has Presbrey instead of Jameson	50.00
c1913-1914 7th 352 pages. A footnote appears on page 5.	50.00
c1913, 1914 & 1918 8th 404 pages. Marked "Eighth Reprint" on title page	40.00
c1913, 1914, 1918, & 1919 9th 404 pages. Marked "Nineth Reprint" on title page.	35.00

Handbook for Scoutmasters (2nd Edition)

Cover is fabricoid leather with gold title and First Class emblem.
Printing number is always shown on title page.

1920 - 1st 608 pages, Black cover	25.00
1920 - 2nd 615 pages, Black cover	25.00
1922 - 3rd 632 pages, Dark blue cover	35.00
1923 - 4th 632 pages, Brown cover	30.00
1923 - 5th 632 pages, Green cover	30.00
1924 - 6th 632 pages, Brown cover	28.00
1924 - 7th 668 pages, Dark Red cover. Cover remains dark red for the rest of this edition	22.00
1925 - 8th 668 pages, printed on thinner paper for the rest of this edition	20.00
1926 - 9th 668 pages	20.00
1926 - 10th 676 pages	20.00
1927 - 11th 676 pages	20.00
1927 - 12th 676 pages	20.00
1928 - 13th 676 pages	20.00
1929 - 14th 676 pages	20.00
1930 - 15th 676 pages	20.00
4-1932 - 16th 628 pages, 10,000 printed	20.00
6-1934 - 17th 628 pages, 3,500 printed	35.00
6-1934 - 18th 628 pages, 7,500 printed	20.00
12-1935 - 19th 628 pages, 7,500 printed	20.00

Third Edition - Volume I
Hardcover, tan, picturing a profile of a Scoutmaster holding a staff. Picture by Remington Schuyler. Title on cover is "Handbook for Scoutmasters, A Manual Of Leadership, Boy Scouts of America". Volume I is shown on the spine and title page.

1936 - Dec. 1st 501p, printing date listed as "Fall 1936" in book 15.00

1937 - Feb. 2nd 501p, printing date listed as "Spring 1937" in book. 12.00

1937 - Nov. 3rd 501p, printing date listed as "Winter 1938" in book. 12.00

1938 - Oct. 4th 501p 8.00

1939 - Mar. 5th 8.00
1940 - Nov. 6th 501p 8.00
1941 - May 7th 501p 8.00
1942 - Mar. 8th 501p, 15m 8.00
1943 - Feb. 9th 501p, 20m 8.00
1944 - July 10th 501p, 15m 8.00
1944 - Dec. 11th 498p, 10m 8.00
1945 - Mar. 12th 498p, 7m 8.00
1945 - Oct. 13th 498p, 20m 8.00

Third Edition - Volume II
Same cover as Volume I. Volume II is shown on spine and title page.

1937 - Mar. 1st 1150p, 25m , printing date is listed as "Spring 1937" in book 15.00

1938 - Mar. 2nd 1150p, 10m, printing date listed as "Winter 1938" in book 12.00

1938 - Dec. 3rd 1150p, 10m 8.00

1939 - Nov. 4th 1150p, 10m 8.00
1941 - Apr. 5th 1150p, 10m 8.00
1942 - Feb. 6th 1164p, 10m 8.00
1942 - Jul. 7th 1164p, 20m 8.00
1943 - Oct. 8th 1164p, 20m 8.00
1944 - Oct. 9th 1164p, 9m 8.00
1945 - Apr. 10th 1158p, 11m ... 8.00
1945 - Dec. 11th 1142p, 20m 8.00

Fourth Edition
Cover title is "Handbook for Scoutmasters, Boy Scouts of America"
Brown softcover picturing a Scoutmaster and a Scout.

1947 - Sep. 1st 512p, 40m Printings identified in each book 7.50
1948 - Feb. 2nd 512p, 25m 7.00
1948 - Oct. 3rd 512p, 50m 7.00
1950 - Jan. 4th 512p, 35m 7.00
1951 - Jun. 5th 512p, 35m 7.00
1951 - Sep. 6th 512p, 35m 7.00

1953 - Dec. 7th 512p, 35m, Overseas hats have replaced campaign hats on cover 6.50
1954 - Dec. 8th 512p, 35m 6.50
1955 - Dec. 9th 512p, 40m 6.50
1956 - Dec. 10th 512p, 45m 6.50
1957 - Dec. 11th 512p, 40m 6.50

Fifth Edition
Cover title is "Scoutmaster's Handbook, Boy Scouts of America".
Blue softcover with Norman Rockwell's picture "The Scoutmaster".

1959 - Jul. 1st 509p, 50m 6.50
1960 - Jul. 2nd 509p, 40m 5.00
1961 - Jun. 3rd 509p, 40m 5.00
1962 - Jun. 4th 509p, 40m 5.00
1963 - Jun. 5th 509p, 40m 5.00
1964 - Oct. 6Ath 509p Has "1963" on title page, in error 7.50

1964 - Oct. 6B 509p, 40m Has "1964" on title page 5.00
1965 - Nov. 7th 541p, 45m 5.00
1966 - Nov. 8th 541p, 45m 5.00
1967 - Oct. 9th 541p, 50m 5.00
1968 - Nov. 10th 541p, 75m 5.00
1970 - Aug. 11th 541p, 50m 5.00

Sixth Edition
Yellow softcover picturing a Scoutmaster and Scout. Title stays the same.

1972 - Jun. 1st 382p, 150m 3.50
1972 - Sep. 2nd 382p, 50m 3.00

1973 - Feb. 3rd 382p, 75m 3.00
1975 - Aug. 4th 382p, 24m 3.00

2nd Edition Scoutmaster's Handbook 25.00
3rd Editon Scoutmaster's Handbook 8.00
5th Edition Scoutmaster's Handbook 5.00

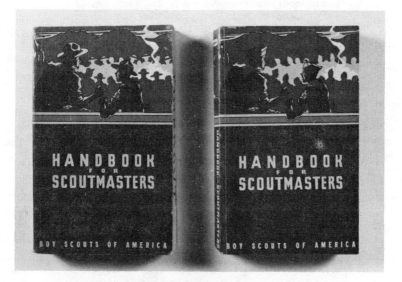

4th Edition Scoutmaster's Handbook
    Left: Early printings with Campaign Hats 7.00
    Right: Late printings with Garrison Hats 6.50

Fieldbook (First Edition)
Cover title is "Scout Field Book".
Softcover, brown, with a Don Ross picture of a Scout cooking.
Except for the 2nd printing, the printing dates are in the book.

1944 - Nov. 1st 540p, 500m Pebble-grain cover, requirements on back
cover 12.00
1947 - Nov. 2nd 540p, 50m Date in book still reads 11-44. Identified by
a smooth cover. Requirements on back cover 10.00
1948 - Oct. 3rd 540p, 50m Back cover overprinted blank 10.00
1949 - Dec. 4th 540p, 50m Back cover overprinted blank 10.00
1950 - Dec. 5th 540p, 50m Back cover overprinted blank 7.50
1951 - Jul. 6th 540p, 60m Back cover left blank 7.50
1952 - Oct. 7th 540p, 60m Back cover left blank 7.50
1953 - Jun. 8th 540p, 60m Back cover left blank 7.50
1954 - Sep. 9th 540p, 60m New requirements on back cover 7.50
1955 - May 10th 540p, 70m Requirements on back cover 7.50
1956 - May 11th 552p, 70m Requirements on back cover 7.50
1957 - Mar. 12th 552p, 75m Requirements on back cover, however,
copies exist with blank back cover 7.50
1958 - Apr. 13th 552p, 75m Requirements on back cover 7.50
1959 - Feb. 14th 552p, 60m Requirements on back cover 7.00

Second Edition
Title on cover is "Fieldbook for Boys and Men".
Green cover picturing Explorers hiking.

1967 - Apr. 1st 565p, 400m Some
copies with error on p. 306
Also exists in hardcover 5.00
1969 - Feb. 2nd 565p, 100m 4.50
1970 - Jul. 3rd 565p, 85m 4.50
1971 - Jun. 4th 565p, 40m 4.50
1972 - May 5th 565p, 80m 4.50

Third Edition
Green and yellow cover picturing a Camping Scout.
Title is now "Fieldbook".

1973 - Sep. 1st 565p, 80m 3.00
1975 - Jan. 2nd 565p, 70m 2.50
1976 - Jan. 3rd 565p, 70m 2.50
1977 - Dec. 4th 565p 2.50

1st Edition Fieldbook 7.50
2nd Edition Fieldbook 4.50

"How Book of Scouting" (First Edition)

1927 1st printing	....	7.00	1929 4th	.... 6.00
1928 2nd	....	7.00	1931 5th	.... 6.00
1928 3rd	....	7.00		

Second Edition

1934 1st 6.00
1935 - Oct. 2nd 6.00

Third Edition

1938 - Apr. 1st 6.00
1941 - Dec. 2nd 5.00
1942 - Jul 3rd 5.00

"Troop Activities"
Orange card cover.

1962 - Sep. 1st Blank spine 1.25
1962 - Dec. 2nd Title on spine .. 1.00
1963 4th 1.00
1965 .... 1.00

1966 .... 1.00
1969 - Jun 1.00
1970 - Aug. 1.00
1971 - Nov. 1.00

The Pine Tree Patrol
By J. A. Wilder

First Edition

1918 .... 12.00
1919 .... 10.00

Second Edition

1920 .... 10.00
1922 .... 9.00
1924 .... 8.00

1927 .... 6.00
1928 .... 6.00
1930 .... 6.00

Every Scout A Swimmer (First Edition)

1924 1st hardbound .... 10.00   1925 2nd 10.00

Swimming And Water Safety (Second Edition)

1927 1st 10.00

Third Edition   card cover in two colors, no title on spine.

1931 1st 7.50
1933 - Aug. 2nd 6.00
1936 - Feb. 3rd 6.00

Swimming, Water Sports, and Safety (4th Edition)
Card cover in three colors, title on spine

1938 - June 1st 8.00

Winter Camping

Proof Edition - brown paper cover
15.00

1927 Limited Edition - Flexible card brown cover with Camping Service Badge. 12.00

The Rally Book

1929 - Flexible card dark brown cover with green print, size: 5½" x 8" 7.50

Canoeing
by W. V. B. Claussen

1931 - Embossed card cover, blue green with orange print, .. 7.50

The Scout Circus

1934	....	8.00
1936	....	6.00

Boy Scout Games
By C. F. Smith, hardcover

1952 - Sep.	....	6.50	1956 - Nov.	.... 5.00
1955 - Aug.	....	5.00	1958 - Jan.	.... 5.00

Merit Badge Pamphlets

1st Edition - White paper cover	8.00
2nd Edition - Tan Kraft cover with 200 5th Avenue address	5.00
3rd Edition - Tan Kraft with 3 line 2 Park Avenue address	4.00
4th Edition - Tan Kraft with 2 line 2 Park Avenue address	4.00
5th Edition - Uniformed Scout on cover	2.50
6th Edition - Red and White card cover (wartime)	2.00
7th Edition - Red and White cover	1.50
8th Edition - Photo Top cover	1.00
9th Edition - Full Photo cover	.75
10th Edition - Green Band Area	.50

Hardbound these exist in practically all editions and are generally valued at about $2.00 than the edition therein.

Top row		Bottom row	
Tan cover edition	.... 5.00	Photo top cover edition	.... 1.00
Red and white cover edition	1.50	Full photo cover edition	..... .75

CUB SCOUT HANDBOOKS
The Boy's Cubbook
Three volumes comprise the Cubbook, one part for each rank.

Part I Wolf Rank
1st Edition
Brown cover - Indian drawing,
linen spine

1930	....	10.00
1931	....	9.00
1932 - Mar.	....	7.00
1933 128p	....	7.00
1934 - Apr.	....	6.00
Jun.	....	6.00
1935 - Mar	....	6.00

2nd Edition
Change in cover design
"Wolf and Cub" No title on spine

1936 - Nov.	....	5.00
1937 - May	....	5.00
1938 - Mar.	....	5.00
1939 - Mar-Nov.	....	5.00
1940 - Jun.	....	5.00
1941 - Feb-Nov.	....	5.00
1942 - Apr. 120m - Wolf on spine	....	5.00

3rd Edition
Same cover, color plates - 4 pages
in preface, Title on spine

1943 - Jun.	....	4.00
1944 - Apr.	....	4.00
Oct.	....	4.00
Dec. 100m 122p	....	4.00
1945 - Mar. 275m 122p	....	4.00
Oct. 150m 122p	....	4.00
1946 - Mar.	....	4.00

Wolf Cub Scout Book - 4th Edition
Red cover - Two color page printing

1948 - Jan.	....	2.50
1949 - Aug. 400m, 154p	....	2.00
Dec.	....	2.00
1951 - Sep.	....	2.00
1952 - Mar. 400m, 172p Revised		2.00
1953 - Jan. 460m, 172p	....	2.00

Wolf Cub Scout Book - 5th Edition
Drawing of a wolf on cover

1954 - Jul. 188p	....	1.75
1955 - Jan. 450m, 188p	....	1.50
Aug.	....	1.50
1956 - Sep.	....	1.50
1957 - Dec. 525m, 188p	....	1.50
1958 - Sep. 600m, 188p	....	1.50
1959 - Oct.	....	1.50
1960 - Nov.	....	1.50

1961 - Sep. 650m	....	1.50
1962 - Oct.	....	1.50
1963 - Sep. 650m, 188p	....	1.50
1964 - Oct. 650m, 188p	....	1.50
1965 - Aug.	....	1.50

Wolf Cub Scout Book - 6th Edition

1967 Parent's Supplement 30p	....	.50
1967 - Jul.	....	1.50
1968 - Mar.	....	1.25
1969 - Mar.	....	1.25
1970 - Feb.	....	1.25
1971 - Feb. 800m, 193p	....	1.25
1972 - Feb.	....	1.25
1973 - Mar. 1mm 193p	....	1.25
1974 - Aug.	....	1.25
1975 - Oct.	....	1.25
1976	....	1.25
1977	....	1.25
1978	....	1.25

THE BOYS CUB BOOK - 1st Edition
Part II Bear Rank
Green cover, linen spine

1930	....	10.00
1931	....	9.00
1932	....	7.00
1933	....	7.00
1934 136p	....	6.00
1935 - Aug. 136p	....	6.00
1936 - Oct.-Apr.	....	6.00
1937 - Mar.	....	6.00

2nd Edition
Change in cover drawing
Gold cover with BEAR on spine

1938 - Apr-Nov.	....	5.00
1939 - Apr.-Jul.	....	5.00
1940 - May	....	5.00
1941 - Mar.	....	5.00
1942 - Mar. 128p	....	5.00
Oct.	....	5.00

3rd Edition
Same cover, new title page
and color plates

1943 - Jun. 138p	....	4.00
1944 - Mar.	....	4.00
Dec. 50m, 122-p plus 8	......	4.00
1945 - Mar.	....	4.00
Oct.	....	4.00
1946 - Mar.	....	4.00
Apr. 138p	....	4.00

Bear Cub Scout Book - 4th Edition
Blue cover with title to denote
change in program name.

1948 - Mar. 156p	....	2.50
1949 - Mar.	....	2.00
Dec. 350m, 156p	....	2.00
1950 - Dec. 300m, 156p	....	2.00
1952 - Feb. 300m, 156p	....	2.00
1953 - Jan. 350m, 156p	....	2.00

Bear Cub Scout Book - 5th Edition
Drawing of a Bear on cover

1954 - Jun.	....	1.75
1955 - Jan. 320m, 156p	....	1.50
Sep.	....	1.50
1956 - Oct. 400m, 156p	....	1.50
1957 - Jul. 355m	....	1.50
1958 - Oct. 500m, 156p	....	1.50
1959 - Nov. 500m	....	1.50
1960 - Dec.	....	1.50
1961 - Oct.	....	1.50
1962 - Nov.	....	1.50
1963 - Dec. 490m, 156p	....	1.50
1964 - Dec. 500m, 156p	....	1.50
1965 - Dec. 460m, 156p	....	1.50

Bear Cub Scout Book - 6th Edition
1967 Parent's Supplement 31p
Catalog Nos. 3208, 3231

1967 - Jul. 750m, 202p	....	1.50
1968 - Mar.	....	1.25
1969 - Mar.	....	1.25
1970 - Feb. 202p	....	1.25
1971 - Feb. 650m, 202p	....	1.25
1972 - Feb.	....	1.25
1973 - Mar.	....	1.25
1974 - Sep.	....	1.25
1975	....	1.25
1976 - Feb.	....	1.25
1977	....	1.25
1978	....	1.25

Part III LION RANK
1st Edition
Blue cover Indian drawing,
linen spine

1930 144p	....	16.00
1931	....	14.00
1932	....	14.00
1933	....	14.00
1934	....	14.00
1935 - Jan.	....	14.00
1936 - Oct.	....	14.00
1937 - Mar.	....	14.00

Part III LION RANK
2nd Edition
Change in cover drawing. "Lion"
on spine - continued end paper
drawing & reddish cover color used.

1938 - Apr. 144p	....	6.00
1939 Jan-Jul.	....	6.00
1940 - May	....	6.00
1941 - Feb-Dec.	....	6.00
1942 - May red cover	....	6.00

3rd Edition
Same cover, new title page,
and color plates added

1943 - May 50m, 140p	....	5.00
1944 - Dec. 100m, 138p+9p	......	5.00
1944 - Mar.	....	5.00
1945 - Oct.	....	5.00
1946 - Mar.	....	5.00

LIon Cub Scout Book - 4th Edition
Black cover - bicolor page printing

1948 - Mar. 156p	....	2.00
1949 - Apr.	....	2.00
Dec. 250m, 156p	....	2.00
1950 - Dec.	....	2.00
1952 - Apr. 200m, 156p	....	2.00
1953 - Feb.	....	2.00

Lion Webelos Cub Scout Book
5th Edition
Drawing of a Lion on badge,
red cover

1954	....	2.25
1955 - Jan.	....	2.00
1955 - Nov. 320m, 180+4p	....	2.00
1957 - Feb. 200m, 188p	....	2.00
Dec. 275m, 188+4p	....	2.00
1958 - Aug. 400m, 188p	....	2.00
1959 - Sep. 400m, 188p	....	2.00
1960 - Oct.	....	2.00
1961 - Nov. 350m, 188p	....	2.00
1962 - Dec.	....	2.00
1963 - Nov. 350m, 188p	....	2.00
1964 - Feb-Dec.	....	2.00
1965 - Nov. 265m, 188p	....	2.00

WEBELOS SCOUT BOOK
6th Edition
Catalog Nos. 3209, 3232   Parent's
Supplement 15p c1967

1967 - Jun. 500m, 300p	....	1.50
1968 - Jan. 500m, 300p	....	1.25
1969 - Jan. 400m, 300p+ivPf	..	1.25
Nov. 500m, 300p+ivPf	....	1.25
1970 - Nov. 500m, 300p+ivPf	...	1.25

6th Edition (cont'd)

1972 - Jan.	....	1.25
1973 - May	....	1.25
1974 - Oct.	....	1.25
1975	....	1.25
1976	....	1.25
1977 - Jul. 330m, 284p	....	1.00
1978	....	1.00

THE DEN CHIEF'S DENBOOK
1st Edition
Blue cover, gold printing,
Catalog No. 3211

1932 Proof	....	10.00
1932 1st	....	5.00
1934 2nd	....	3.50
1935 - Aug. 3rd 5m, 154p+6Pf	..	3.00

2nd Edition
Blue cover, catalog no. 3211 c 1937,
Book size 4½ x 7

1937	....	2.75
1938 - Jan.	....	2.50
1939 - Apr.	....	2.50
1940 - Dec.	....	2.50
1941 - Mar.	....	2.50
Oct. 10m, 170p	....	2.50

3rd Edition
Revised text with Schuyler's illus-
trations, brown flexible cover. 1942
Proof copy "Denbook"

1942 - May 20m, 192p	....	2.50
1943 - Apr. 20m, 192p "Den Book"		
		2.25
1944 - May 24m, 176p	....	2.25
1945 - Apr. 176p	....	2.25
Dec.	....	2.25
1946 - Apr. 30m, 176p	....	2.25

4th Edition
1948 - Feb.	....	2.25
1949 - Oct. 35m, 176p	....	2.00
1950 - Jun.	....	2.00

5th Edition
1951 - Nov. 35m, 162p. Change in cover print style	....	2.00
1952 - Nov. 162p	....	1.75

6th Edition
New cover - Rockwell painting
Catalog No. 3211, same size,
Brown paper cover

1954 - May (Proof)	....	8.00
Sep.	....	3.50
1955 - Aug.	....	3.00
1957 - Aug.	....	3.00
1958 - Sep.	....	3.00
1959 - Dec.	....	3.00

Den Chief's Denbook - 7th Edition
Revised program text and cover.
Yellow cover, book size 5⅜ x 8

1963 - Jul 75m, 132p	....	1.50
1965 - Jan. 40m, 132p	....	1.25
Nov.	....	1.25
1966 - Oct.	....	1.25

8th Edition
Minor text revision, Orange cover

1968 - Feb. 75m, 156p	....	1.25
Aug.	....	1.00
1969 - Jul. 156p	....	1.00
1970 - Aug. 55m, 156p	....	1.00
1971 - Aug.	....	1.00
1973 - Aug.	....	1.00

Den Chief's Training Course Manual		
1940	....	1.25
Den Chief Training 1953	......	1.00
Den Chief Conference 1959	....	1.25
1960	....	1.00
1962	....	1.00
Den Chief Training Conference		
1964	....	1.00
The Den Chief; A Troop Officer		
1955	....	1.25
1960	....	1.00
How To Become A Den Chief	..	1.00

2nd Edition Cub Scout Handbooks
Wolf Cubbook 10.00
Bear Cubbook 10.00
Lion Cubbook 11.00

1948 (4th) Edition Cub Scout Handbooks
Wolf 2.00
Bear 2.00
Lion 2.50

DEN MOTHER'S DENBOOK
1st Edition
Blue cover - gold print

1937 200p	5.00
1938 - Jun.	3.00
1939	3.00
1940 - Apr.	3.00
1941 - Feb.	3.00
Apr. Red cover	3.00

Red linen cover

1942 - Jun.	2.25
1943 - Aug.	2.00
1944 - Apr. Red card cover	1.75
Dec. Red card cover	1.75
1945 - May	1.75
Oct-Dec.	1.75
1946 - Apr. 30m	1.75
1947 - Sep. 30m	1.75
1948 - Oct. 35m	1.75
1949 - Nov.	1.75
1950 - Mar.	1.75

Den Mother's Denbook - 2nd Edition
Multicolor cover, title added
to spine 1964

1951 - Aug.	1.75
1952 - June	1.50
1953 - Sep.	1.50
1954 - Nov. 70m	1.50
1955 - Oct.	1.50
1956 - Sept.	1.50
1957	1.50
1958 - Aug.	1.50
1959 - Dec.	1.50
1961 - Feb.	1.50
1962	1.50
1963 - Feb.	1.50
1964 - Aug.	1.50

Den Mother's Denbook - 3rd Edition

1967 - Jul	1.50
1968	1.25
1969 - Mar.	1.25
1970	1.25
1971	1.25
1972	1.25
1973	1.25

DEN LEADERS BOOK
(Title changed)
4th Edition

1967	1.25
1968	1.00
1969	1.00
1970 124m, 200p	1.00
1971 - Aug. 110m	1.00

1972 - Dec. 105m	1.00
1973	1.00
1977 - Nov. 55m, 201p	1.00

OTHER LEADER HANDBOOKS
DEN LEADER COACH

1967	1.25

WEBELOS DEN LEADER'S BOOK

1967 - Jul.	1.25
1968 - Mar.	1.00
1969 - Mar.	1.00
1973	1.00

CUB SCOUT SONG BOOK

1947	2.00
1950 Blue cover	1.50
1951 Red cover	1.25
1952 Grey cover	1.25
1955 Red cover	1.25
1956	1.00
1957	1.00
1960	1.00
1962 Blue cover	1.00
1966 Pink cover	1.00
1969	1.00

Cubber's Pow Wow, 1948	2.00
Pow Wow Guidebook, 1949	2.00
Pow Wow Guides, 1951	1.50
1949 Handicrafts	1.25
Ceremonies	1.25
Games	1.25
Stunts and Skits	1.25
Pack Administration	1.25
Webelos Day	1.25
Crafts for Cub Scouts	1.00
Webelos Den Activities	1.00
Skits and Puppets	1.00
Games for Cub Scouts	1.00

Pow Wow Guide

1958	1.00
1963	1.00
1968	1.00
Pack Administration, 1958	1.00
Games 1955	1.00
1963	1.00
Handicraft 1955	1.00
Crafts for Cub Scouts 1963	1.00
Skits, Puppets and Ceremonies	
1963	1.00
1965	1.00
Summer Program for Cubs	
1940	2.00
1947	1.00
Parents' Cub Scout Book, 1965	1.00
Ten Steps to Organize a Pack	
1963	1.00

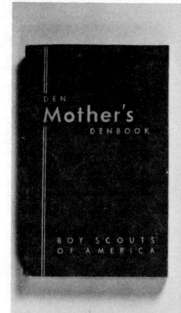

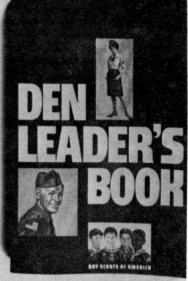

1943 Den Mother's Denbook 2.00
1968 Den Mother's Den-Book 1.25
Bottom
1952 Den Mother's Den-Book 1.50
1968 Den Leader's Book 1.00

Involving Handicapped Cub Scouts 1.00
Cub Scout Family Book c1975 .. 1.00
Cub Scout Magic
  1960 .... 1.00
  1969 .... 1.00
Webelos Day Guidebook, 1956 . 1.00
The Pack Meeting 1.00
Cub Scout Ceremonies, 1948 ... 2.00
Parent's Cub Book
  1930 .... 4.00
  1936 .... 3.00
Parent's Cub Scout Book
  1951 .... 1.00
  1954 .... 1.00
  1956 .... 1.00
  1960 .... 1.00
Cub Leader's Round Table Equipment Catalog, 1940 .... 2.50
The Cubbing Guide Book
  1939 .... 2.00
  1940 .... 1.50
  1942 .... 1.50
Cub Scouting Guide Book, 1944 . 2.00
Cub Scout Guide Book, 1956 ... 1.25
  1962 .... 1.00
Guidebook to Cub Scouting
  1967 .... 1.25
Temporary Outlines for Cub Leaders, 1929 .... 10.00
Indian Stone, 1929 .... 7.50
Information Book of the Cub Program, 1930 .... 10.00
  1935 .... 7.50
National Policies of the Cub Movement 1932 .... 3.00
  1934 .... 2.00
Ten Steps - How to Organize a Cub Pack, 1941 .... 1.50
  1948 .... 1.00
Cub Program - How It Works
  1936 .... 6.00
  1938 .... 5.00
  1939 .... 5.00
Cub Pack Organization Manual
  1935 .... 8.00
Cub Scout Fundamentals 1.00
Your Boy, 1941 .... 2.00
  1948 .... 1.50
Den Mother - Den Chief Relationships 1.00
Program Planning 1.00
Purpose of the Cub Scout Achievement Plan, 1951 .... 1.00

The Packs First Two Months
  1956 .... 1.00
  1972 .... 1.00
Den Meeting 1.00
Den Meeting Place 1.00
The Pack Committee, 1956 .... 1.00
  1959 .... 1.00
  1965 .... 1.00
  1967 .... 1.00
  1978 .... 1.00
The Webelos Den, 1955 .... 1.00
  1956 .... 1.00
  1960 .... 1.00
The Achievement Plan, 1954 ... 1.00
The Cub Scout Program 1.00
Organizing a Cub Scout Pack
  1967 .... 1.00
  1969 .... 1.00
Cub Scout Activities, 1970 ..... 1.00
  1978 .... 1.00
Ceremonies, 1968 .... 1.00
  1970 .... 1.00
Cub Scout Fun Book, 1956 ..... 2.00
  1957 .... 2.00
  1962 .... 1.50
  1977 .... 1.00
Back Yard USA, 1953 .... 1.00
Cub Scout Water Fun, 1955 .... 1.00
  1958 .... 1.00
  1977 .... 1.00

EXPLORER MANUALS

ADVENTURING FOR SENIOR SCOUTS
Edited by W. H. Hurt - Basic manual for older boy program, describing Sea Scouting, Rover Scouting and Air Scouting. Hard cover with drawing of Senior and Sea Scouts in blue on orange background. Rounded page corners. Book size: 4½ x 6¾.

1938 Proof 15.00	1944 - Jun. 5m, 687p red cover,
1st 692p+10p preface 15.00	Square corner pages 8.00
1939 - Apr. 2nd, 10m 10.00	1945 - Apr. 6m, 687p + 8p. New cover
1942 - May 10.00	tan on red background with an
Jun. 5m, 692p revised Second	Air Scout 7.00
printing 8.00	1946 - Jan. 5m, 686p+8p. 7.00

EXPLORER SCOUT MANUAL
By Carl D. Lane
A new manual for older boy units based on inland scouting with a new uniform, Program and advancement. Cover is flexible with a light green mountain scene on dark green. Booksize: 4½ x 7.

First Edition
1946 - Oct. 1st 6.00
1947 - Aug. 6.00

EXPLORER MANUAL
By Ted S. Holstein
2nd Edition
Manual enlarged, program and badge revisions. Same cover used with word "Scout" omitted from title. Booksize: 7 x 4½

1950 - Jan. 1st printing, 15m, 380 +4 pf 7.00	Nov. 2nd printing, 50m, 380 + 4 pf 6.50

3rd Edition		4th Edition	
1952 - Mar. 50m 4.00		1956 - May 4.00
1953 - Apr. 50m, 380+4Pf 4.00		1957 - Mar 4.00
1954 - Apr. 50m, 380+4 Pf 4.00		1958 - Jan. 4.00
Aug. 60m, 380+4 Pf 4.00			

EXPLORING
By Ted S. Holstein
New manuscript for a revised older youth program. The manual has a full color preface and flexible cover. Booksize 7 x 4½

1958 - Aug. 1st printing, 200m, 317+ 34Pf 2.00	1959 - Jan. 2nd printing, 200m, 317+ 34 Pf 2.00
	1966 - Sep. 60m, 317+34Pf 2.50

NEW SPECIAL INTEREST EXPLORING HANDBOOK
Medical Exploring
1973 - May 10m, 257p 2.50
1976 - Feb. 3m, 256p revised ... 2.00

Top row
1947 Explorer Scout Manual 6.00
1956 Explorer Manual 4.00
Bottom row
1959 Exploring Manual 2.00
Medical Exploring Manual 2.25

Other Senior Scouting-Exploring Literature

First Aid 1919 .... 10.00
   1922 .... 9.00
Signal Emergency Units, 1919 10.00
Scout Emergency - First Aid
   Unit, 1925 .... 8.00
Scout Emergency - Signaling
   Unit, 1924 .... 8.00
   1925 .... 7.50
Scout Emergency Units, 1926 .. 7.50
   1930 .... 6.50
Emergency Service Training
   Plan, 1940 .... 2.50
   1941 .... 2.00
Training for Mobilization, 1940 2.50
Pre-Ranger Training Program
   1943 .... 3.50
Emergency Preparedness, BSA,
   1964 .... 1.00
Emergency Service, 1971 ..... 1.00
A Guide for Starting Senior
   Scouting 3.00
Guide Book of Senior Scouting
   1935 .... 3.00
   1937 .... 4.00
   1938 .... 4.00
   1941 .... 3.50
Senior Scouting Guide Book
   1942 .... 6.00
   1946 .... 5.00
Manual for Course Leader's and
   Members, 1945 .... 2.00
Hints on Senior Scout Leadership
   1947 .... 5.00
   1948 .... 4.00
   1949 .... 3.50
New Explorer Plan and
   Recognitions, 1949 .... 3.50
Hints on Explorer Leadership
   1954 .... 2.25
   1955 .... 2.00
   1957 .... 2.00
Exploring at Work in Your Troop
   1950 .... 1.00
Council and District Explorer
   Activities, 1951 .... 1.00
Organizing an Explorer Unit
   1958 .... 1.00
   1961 .... 1.00
Council and District Exploring
   Guidebook, 1969 .... 1.00
Explorer Member's Guide
   1969 .... 1.00
Explorer Leaders Reference
   Book, 1969 .... 1.00

Post Committee Guide, 1969 ... 1.00
Organizing an Explorer Post .. 1.00
New Explorer Plan, 1949 ...... 1.50
   1951 .... 1.25
Explorer Blue Ribbon Events
   1954 .... 1.00
Explorer Recognitions and Awards
   1954 .... 1.00
Explorer Cabinet Guidebook
   1963 .... 1.00
Blue Ribbon Events of Explorers
   in Action, 1956 .... 1.00
   1957 .... 1.00
Explorer Parent's and Leader's
   Guidebook, 1958 .... 1.00
   1965 .... 1.00
Exploring Sales and
   Organizations 1.00
Exploring Techniques - Post
   Organizations 1.00
Explorer Leader Development
   Experience 1.00
Your Ticket To Popularity
   1950 .... 2.00
Inner City-Rural Post
   Action Ideas 1.00
Explorer Officer's Workbook
   1970 .... 1.00
Secretary's Record 1.00
Explorer Leader Development 1.00
Explorer Treasurer's Record . 1.00
Explorer Advisor's First
   6 Meetings 1.00
Explorer Reference Book 1.00
Council and District Explorer
   Activities 1.00
Explorer Techniques
   (6 pamphlets) 5.00

AIR SCOUT MANUAL

By H. W. Hurt and Lorne W. Barclay. Soft cover with a two engine propellor airplane on blue. Booksize: 4½ x 7 Catalog No. 3648

1942 - Feb. Pre-proof printing   12.00
  Nov. Pre-proof printing 10.00
  Dec. 1st printing, 10m, Title
  page states "proof" 10.00
1943 - Jan. 2nd printing, 10m .. 10.00
  Feb. 3rd printing, 25m 10.00

Feb. 4th printing, 25m, 442p +
  viii preface 10.00
Apr. 5th printing, 25m, 442p   10.00
Oct. 6th printing, 50m, 440p
  "proof" dropped 10.00

AIR EXPLORER MANUAL

New manual edited by Ted S. Holstein. Paper cover with green and dark blue depicts a jet plane. Booksize 4½ x 7, photo section

1st Edition
1951 - Feb. Proof printing 8.00
1953 - Dec. 10m, 224p 7.50
1954 - Aug. 7.50

2nd Edition
1955 - Jul 7.50
1957 - Dec. 6m 7.00
1958 - May 8m 7.00

AIR SCOUTING LITERATURE

1941 Program Development
Literature
Air Scouting Development .. 5.00
Scouting and Aviation 5.00
Tentative Program Proposals
    5.00
Hints to Squadron Leaders
  1942 .... 12.00
  1943 .... 11.00
Air Scout Contests 8.00
Air Scouting (pamphlet)
  1942 .... 10.00

Air Scouts, 1943, 16p 7.50
Air Explorer Advancement
  Requirements 6.50

Special Merit Badge Pamphlets
for Air Scouting
(blue cover)
Aeronautics 12.00
Airplane Structure 12.00
Aerodynamics 12.00
Airplane Design 12.00

Air Scout Manual 10.00-15.00
Air Explorer Manual 7.00-8.00

Cruising For Sea Scouts
By A.A. Carey

1st Edition

1912 .... 150.00

2nd Edition

1913 .... 100.00

3rd Edition

1914 .... 75.00

The Seascout Manual - 4th Edition
By J. A. Wilder

1920	1st	35.00
1922	2nd	30.00
1923	3rd	20.00
1923	4th	20.00
1923	5th	20.00

The Seascout Manual - 5th Edition
By Reisenberg

1925	1st	15.00
1926	2nd	15.00
1927	3rd	15.00
1928	4th	15.00
1929	5th	12.00
	6th	12.00
1932 - Apr.	7th	10.00
	8th	10.00
1933 - Nov.	9th	10.00
1934 - Sept.	10th	10.00
1935 - Jun.	11th	10.00
1936 - Jul.	12th	10.00
1937 - Apr.	13th	10.00
1938 - Apr.	14th	10.00

The Sea Scout Manual - 6th Edition
By Carl Langenbacher

Flexible cover in blue with white lettering and drawing of seafarers equipment. Text has bouys and signal flags in color. Booksize: 4⅝ x 7

1939 - May 1st printing, 50m, 698p
+10p preface, no spine title . 8.00
1941 - May 2nd 50m, 698p 8.00
1942 - May 3rd 6.00
1943 - Mar. 4th 20m 6.00
Oct. 5th 25m, 698p+10p preface
Title on spine 6.00
1944 - Mar. 6th 5.00
1945 - May 7th 5.00
Nov. 8th 5.00
1947 - Apr. 9th 25m 5.00
1949 - Apr. 10th 15m, 698p+10p
preface 5.00

Sea Explorer Manual - 7th Edition

Revised edition, dark blue cover, catalog no. 3229, booksize: 4⅝ x 7

1950 - Oct. 1st printing, 540p + 4p
preface 5.00
1952 - Sep. 2nd 4.00
1954 - Sep. 20m, 640p + 4p preface
.... 4.00
1956 - Dec. 15m, 640p + 4p preface
.... 4.00
1958 - Aug. 20m, 640p + 4p preface
.... 4.00
1960 - Mar. 15m, 640p + 4p preface
.... 4.00
1961 - Aug. 15m, 640p+ 4p preface
.... 4.00
1963 .... 4.00

Sea Exploring Manual - 8th Edition

New manuscript bound in flexible cover in sea blue with picture of sailing yacht. Booksize: 5⅜ x 8

1966 - Apr. 1st printing, 30m,
442p 4.00
2nd printing 3.50
1970 - Sep. 3rd 9m, 442p 3.50
1972 - Jan. 7m 3.50
1976 - Jun. 6th 4m 3.50
1977 - Sep. 7th 5m 3.50

Handbook for Crew Leaders
1st Edition
By Carl Lane

Blue flexible cover. Booksize 4½ x 7

1941 - Nov. 1st printing, 5m,
228p 10.00
1942 - Mar. 2nd 5m, 228p 8.00

2nd Edition

1946 - Apr. 1st 5m, 502p +4p
preface 5.00

Handbook For Skippers
1st Edition
By W. C. Menninger

Hardcover book, blue cover with silver seascout badge, rounded page corners. Booksize: 4½ x 7

1934 1st printing, 280p+index . 12.00
1935 - Apr. 2nd 3m, 280p + index
.... 10.00
1936 .... 10.90

Top row
4th Edition Sea Scout Manual 35.00
5th Edition Sea Scout Manual 15.00
Bottom row
7th Edition Explorer Manual 5.00
8th Edition Sea Exploring Manual 4.00

Handbook For Skippers

2nd Edition
Square page corners,
Skipper stripes added to cover
1939 - May 1st 5m, 431p+8p .. 6.00
1940 - Oct. 2nd 4m, 436p+8p ... 5.00
1942 - May 3rd 3m, 440p + 8p
   Star and bar replaces stripes 5.00
1945 - Apr. 4th 2.5m, 400p+ 6p

Wartime print, black cover . 4.00
1947 - Sep. 5m, 314p + 6p
   Revised 3.00

3rd Edition
Revised manuscript, Booksize:
5¼ x 8

1971 - Aug. 10m, 224p Blue picture
   card cover 3.50

LONE SCOUT HANDBOOKS

LONE SCOUTS OF AMERICA
Founded 1915, LSA Publications

1915 Handbook of Lone Scouts of America 25.00
1915 Lone Scout Degree - First - Book 1 .... 12.00
1915 Lone Scout Degree - Second - Book 2 .... 12.00
1915 Teepee Lodge Book, 1st, 2nd, 3rd Degrees 18.00
1918 Official Handbook of the Lone Scouts 20.00
1918 Tepee Lodge Book, Book 1, 1st, 2nd, 3rd Degrees 12.00
1918 Totem Pole Lodge Book, Book 2, 4th, 5th, 6th Degrees 10.00
1918 Sagamore Lodge Book, Book 3, 7th Degree 10.00
1920 Tepee Lodge, 3 separate books 10.00
1920 Totem Pole Lodge, 3 separate books 10.00
1920 Sagamore Lodge, 1 book 10.00

LONE SCOUT PROGRAM - 1924
Official Handbook of the
Lone Scouts of America
Degree Library —

Tepee Lodge First Degree ... 13.00
   Second Degree 13.00
   Third Degree 13.00
Totem Lodge Fourth Degree . 13.00
   Fifth Degree 13.00
   Sixth Degree 13.00

Sagamore Lodge
   Seventh Degree 20.00
Note: Reprints of these 3 books are
known to exist and generally sell for
about $10.00 each in fine condition.
1927 Lone Scout Trail 10.00
1965 Lone Scout Plan 3.00

ORDER OF THE ARROW
Order of the Arrow Handbook

1st Edition
1948 Proof, Pub. R. Newberry,
Charleston S.C. 45.00
1948 Hardbound 15.00
1948 Soft cover with "handbook"
   at top 15.00

2nd Edition
softcover without "handbook" at top
1950 - Mar 5.00
1951 - Jan. 4.00
1952 - Apr. 4.00
1955 - Oct. 3.00
1956 - Aug. 3.00
1959 - Mar 2.50
1960 - Oct. 2.50

3rd Edition
1961 - Jul. 2.00
1963 - Apr. 2.00
1964 - Feb. 2.00

4th Edition
1965 - Jul. 50th Anniversary Issue,
   Norman Rockwell print insert
               4.50
Aug. 2nd 50th Anniversary
   printing 4.00
1968 - Feb. 2.00
1970 - Aug. 10m 2.00

5th Edition
1973 - Aug. 100m 1.75

1977 .... 1.50
1978 - Mar. 1.50

Other Order of the Arrow Handbooks
1940 National Lodge Constitution
and Bylaws 8.00
1946 Local Lodge Manual 6.00
Order of Arrow information for
New Members, red cover ... 1.50
Order of Arrow information for
New Members, blue cover .. 1.00
1948 How to Organize an Order of
the Arrow Lodge 8.00
Indian Ritual Costumes 4.50
Spirit of the Arrow 1.00
1949 Area Leader's Manual ... 5.00
1954 Handbook for Lodge Officials
and Members 2.00
Order of the Arrow Training
Manual 2.00
1968 Order of the Arrow 1.50
1940 25th Anniversary Meeting,
Book of Minutes 15.00

O.A. Ceremony Booklets
Pre-1935 Ordeal (First) Degree ....
15.00
1935 - May Ordeal (First) Honor ..
10.00

1948 - Jul. Ordeal Honor 4.00
1960 Ordeal Ceremony 2.00
1968 - Mar. Ordeal Ceremony .. 1.75
1971 - Sep. Ordeal Ceremony .. 1.50
1977 - May Ordeal Ceremony .. 1.25

Pre-1936 Brotherhood (Second
Degree 20.00
1936 - Feb. Brotherhood (Second)
Honor 12.00
1949 - Aug. Brotherhood Honor . 4.50
1960 Brotherhood Ceremony .. 2.25
1968 - Oct. Brotherhood Ceremony .
2.00
1971 - Sep. Brotherhood Ceremony .
1.75
1977 - May Brotherhood Ceremony .
1.50

Pre-1940 Vigil (Third) Degree ....
25.00
1940 - Jan. Vigil (Third) Honor ....
15.00
1949 - Aug. Vigil Honor 5.00
1962? Vigil Honor 2.50
1968 - Oct. Vigil Honor Ceremony ..
2.25
1971 - Sep. Vigil Honor Ceremony ..
2.00
1977 - May Vigil Honor Ceremony ..
1.75

CHAPTER 3

SCOUT COINS

Over the years, the Boy Scouts of America has issued many coin type tokens and medallions as have the Girl Scouts. Keep in mind that values shown are for fine condition items. Items showing obvious wear, etc. will be worth less.

The following special abbreviations have been used:

al. - Aluminum
bt. - Bright
Cn. - Council
H - Hole for Chain
O - Obverse side
Oxid. - Oxidized
R - Reverse side
unk. - Unknown date
w - With

1910 - Baden-Powell Battle of Mafeking Commemortive medallion, steel, minted by Spink and Son, England 100.00
    Caution: A counterfeit of this is known to exist

1910 - Excelsior Shoe Company Medallions

Most have a cowboy on horseback. The original group is dated "July 1910". The reverse sides show either: 1) The Excelsior Shoe Company seal, 2) A group of good luck symbols which includes the old Indian good luck sign (which resembles the Nazi Germany emblem), or 3) same as above with legend "Membership Emblem of the Boy Scouts Club".

The standard Levy Adams numbering system is used for Excelsior Shoe Company Coins. All are priced $9.00-14.00 unless otherwise noted.

Type 1 - Dated "July 1910" - Company Seal on Reverse

(1A) (1) - Brass O: "BOY SCOUT" with inverted first quote (" ")
(1A) (2) - Same as (1A) (1), but on markedly thinner planchet 18.00
(1B) (1) - Brass (date - 13mm long) O: "BOY SCOUTS" with inverted first quote
(1B) (2) - Brass (Date - 15mm long) O: "BOY SCOUTS" with inverted first quote
(1B) (3) - Brass (Date - 12mm long) O: same as (1B) (1) R: Capital "O" of "CO."
(1B) (4) - Brass (date - 12mm long) O: Same as (1B) (1) R: Small "o" of "Co.", with "o" underlined
(1C) - Brass O: "BOY SCOUTS" with reversed first quote (" ")
(1D) - Brass O: "WORLD SCOUTS" with normal quotes (")

TYPE 2 - Dated "July 1910" - Good Luck Symbols on R
(Words 'Good Luck' at top)

(2A) - Brass O: "BOY SCOUT" with inverted 1st quote R: Maker: "Schwaab Milwaukee"
(2B) - Brass O: "BOY SCOUTS" w. normal quotes and 2 reins on horse R: Same
(2C) - Brass O: "BOY SCOUTS" w. normal quotes and 3 reins on horse R: Same

(2D) - **Brass** O: "BOY SCOUTS" w. reversed quotes (3 reins on horse)
   R: Same
(2E) - **Brass** O: "BOY SCOU~S" w. normal quotes (3 reins on horse
   R: No maker
           TYPE 3 - No Date - Good Luck Symbols on R with words
"Membership Emblem of the Boy Scouts Club" (Words 'Good Luck' at bottom)
(3A) - **Brass** O: "BOY SCOUTS" w. normal quotes R: Maker: "Schwaab
   Milwaukee"
(3B) - **Brass** O: "BOY SCOUTS" w. normal quotes   R: Maker: "The
   Whitehead & Hoag Co. Newark N J" (Approx. 15mm long)
(3C) - **Brass** O: Same as (3B) R: Same, but name of maker approx.
   18mm long
(3D) - **Brass** O: "BOY SCOUTS" w. inverted first quote R: Maker: "The
   Whitehead & Hoag Co. Newark N J" (Approx. 21mm long)
(3E) - **Brass** O: "BOY SCOUTS" w. inverted last quote R: Same as (3D)
(3F) - **Silver color metal** O: and R: Same as (3C) except for metal 15.00
(3G) - **Copper** O: "BOY SCOUTS" with normal quotes R: No maker
(3H) - **Copper** O: "BOY SCOUTS" w. inverted 1st quote R: No maker
(3I) - **Brass** O: "BOY SCOUTS" w. reversed 1st quote R: No maker
(3J) - **Brass** O: "BOY SCOUTS" w. **Indian** on horseback and one rein
   R; Maker: "The Whitehead & Hoag Co. Neward N J" in straight line
   under words 'Good Luck'

   TYPE 4 - No Date (O has legend: 'The Original "Boy Scouts" Army Shoe-
                Munson Last') - Company Seal on Reverse
(4A) - (1) Brass   (2) Gold-Plated Brass
   O: "BOY SCOUTS" w. normal quotes (3 reins on horse) R: No Maker 30.00
NOTE: There is another type in several variations which has reference to
Scouts and is not considered a Scout coin.
Date (L A number) **Event** - Sponsor (Extra notes)
   (L A letter) Type, size - Description

1924 (1) **Annual Fathers & Sons Banquet** - Milwaukee Boy Scouts (Wisc.)
   (a) bronze, 32mm O: Wording R: Lincoln Bust (facing right)
   (b) silver

1926 (1) **Lincoln Trail Hike** - Abraham Lincoln Council (Ill.)
   bronze, 31mm O: Lincoln Bust R: Wording

1924 (1) **Annual Fathers & Sons Banquet** - Milwaukee Boy Scouts (Wisc.)
   (a) bronze, 32mm O: Wording R: Lincoln Bust (facing right) 7.50
   (b) silver 9.50
1926 (1) **Lincoln Trail Hike** - Abraham Lincoln Council (Ill.)
   bronze, 31mm O: Lincoln Bust R: Wording 15.00
1937 (1) **1st National Jamboree** - Western Cartridge Company
   brass, 25mm 45.00
(Note: No official medallion issued. See L A U.S. 1973 (2-9).)
1937 (2) **25th Anniversary of Troop** - Troop 2, Wilkinsburg, Penna.
   white metal, 36mm O: First Class Badge R: Wording 5.00
1941 (1) **Boyce Memorial** - Starved Rock Council (Ill.)
   bt. bronze, 37mm O: "Sloppy Socks" Statue R: Wording 10.00
1947 (1) **Region 7, WEL-A-KA-HOW** - Hoosier Hills Council (Wisc.)
   silver-coated lead, 45mm O: Wording R: Wording 5.50
1948 (1) **I Joined Scouting in 1948** - Greater Cleveland Council (Ohio)
   al, 32mm O: Scout Badge R: Wording 4.00

1950 (1) 2nd National Jamboree - Official (Boy Scouts) (held at Valley Forge, Pa.) bt. bronze, 36mm O: Washington Kneeling R: Wording ...... 28.00 (See Footnote 1)

1950 (2) 2nd National Jamboree - Texas Traders, Concho Valley Council al., 32mm O: Washington Kneeling R: Bronco & Rider 12.00

1950 (3) Bay Shore Cn. at Jamboree - General Electric River Works (Lynn, Mass.) copper painted red, 48mm O: Scout Badge R: Name of Sponsor .. 10.00

1950 (4) Cleveland Cn. at Jamboree - Firestone Tire Co. (also used as neckerchief slide) steel, 65mm, w. two large H O: Tire Edges Design R: Blank 10.00

1950 (5) 2nd National Jamboree - Bruder Dairy, Cleveland, Ohio al., 32mm O: Washington Kneeling R: Good Luck Symbols 15.00

1950 (6) 25th Anniversary National Convention - Alpha Phi Omega Fraternity silver, 28mm H O: Fraternity Crest R: Wording 22.00

1952 (1) BSA Vote Campaign - Freedoms Foundation, Inc. (Valley Forge, Pa.)
(a) silver plastic on cardboard, 32mm O: Wash. at Prayer R: Small badge . 5.00
(b) gold plastic on cardboard (rare) (Designed by Dan Heilman) ... 30.00

1952 (2) Youth of the Scout World - Society of Medalists (Medal No. 46)
(a) bronze relief, 72mm O: Scouts Signaling R: American eagle 15.00
(b) .999 silver (Produced by Medallic Art Co., NYC; Sculptor - Karl Gruppe) (Only two believed to have been minted of silver) 30.00

1953 (1) 3rd National Jamboree - Official (Boy Scouts) (Irvine Ranch, Calif.) bt. bronze, 36mm O: Covered Wagon R: Wording (see Footnote 1) .. 20.00

1953 (2) 3rd National Jamboree - Region 4 al., 17mm O: Wording R: Map of Ohio 12.00

1953 (3) 3rd National Jamboree - Plymouth Automobile Corp. bt. bronze, 31mm O: Scout Badge R: Plymouth Flag 11.00

1953 (4) 3rd National Jamboree - al., 44mm O: Bucking Bronco R: Blank 10.00

1953 (5) 40th Anniversary of Mormon Scouts - Salt Lake City Mormon Scouts dull white metal, 29mm O: Mormon Temple R: Wording (Achievement Recognition) 10.00

1955 (1) 9th Annual Camporee - Greenville, South Carolina Scouts bt. bronze, 16mm O: Wording R: "On My Honor I Will Do My Best" .. 3.50

1956 (1) Girl Scout Senior Roundup - gold color O: Wording R: Wagon & Minneapolis Skyline 5.00

1957 (1) 4th National Jamboree - Official (Boy Scouts) (Valley Forge, Pa.) bt. bronze, 36mm O: Washington Kneeling R: Wording .... 10.00 (see Footnote 1)

1957 (2) Erection of Scout Tower at Valley Forge - Official (Boy Scouts) bronze, 32mm O: Washington at Prayer in Woods R: Wording 12.00

1957 (3) **Centennial Roundup** - Greater Cleveland Council (Ohio)
gold color, 36mm O: Baden-Powell Bust on Scout Badge R: Wording   3.25

1960 (1) **50th Anniversary of BSA** - Official (Boy Scouts) (Pocket Piece)
bt. bronze, 26mm O: 50th Anniversary Insignia R: Scout Oath 5.00

1960 (2) **50th Anniversary of BSA** - Official Anniversary Medallion (Boy
Scouts) thick bronze relief, 63mm O: Scout Badge R: Scout Oath Plaque .
10.00

1960 (3) **50th Anniversary of BSA** - Heraldic Art Company, Cleveland Ohio
(a) .925 silver, 30mm O: Scout Standing R: Scout Badge 100.00
(b) 22k gold (Issued: 6,400 silver, envelope numbered; 50 gold) 300.00

1960 (4) **5th National Jamboree** - Official (Boy Scouts) (Colorado Springs,
Colo.) bronze, 36mm O: 50th Anniversary Insignia R: Three Scenic Views
(see Footnote 1) 8.00

1960 (5) **50th Anniv. & 5th National Jamboree** - Troop 107, Erie, Pa. (Trading
Coin) copper, O: Map of Penna. R: Map of Erie, Penna. 4.50

1961 (1) **Scout Conference at Reed College** - Region 11 Northwesters
(Portland, Ore.) bt. bronze, 28mm O: Explorer Symbol R: Axe in Log ...
6.50

1961 (2) **Scouting Exposition** - Greater New York Council (N.Y.) (Held at
Coliseum) bt. bronze, 26x18mm oval O: Scout Badge R: Blank 3.00

1962 (1) **International Camporee** (Camp Sequassen) - Quinnipiac Council
bt. bronze, 36mm O: Compass & World Symbol R: Flower & Wreath . 6.00

1962 (2) **50th Anniversary of Girl Scouts** - Official (Girl Scouts)
(a) bt. bronze, 26mm O: 50th Anniversary Insignia R: Girl Scout
Promise 5.00
(b) w. lucite case, H 7.50

1962 (3) **50th Anniversary of Girl Scouts** - Heraldic Art Company, Cleveland,
Ohio (a) .925 silver, 30mm O: Girl Scout & Leader R: Girl Scout Trefoil .
95.00
(b) 22k gold (Issued: 6,400 silver in number packets; 50 gold) 400.00

1962 (4) **Start of Cadette Group** - Official (Cadettes) (Green and red design)
clear lucite, 28mm, H O: Cadette Badge R: Blank 8.50

1963 (1) **Camp Salmen Slidell, Louisiana** - New Orleans Area Cn. (La.)
(a) bronze, 38mm, reeded edge O: Camp Cabin & Scene R: Scroll .,. 2.50
(b) antique silver, 39mm, plain edge 10.00
(c) .999 silver (25 issued) (Intaglio die by H. Alvin Sharpe) 35.00

1964 (1) **6th National Jamboree** - Official (Boy Scouts) (Valley Forge, Pa.)
(a) bronze, 36mm O: Washington Kneeling R: Three American Scenes ..
5.00
(b) oxid. silver (see Footnote 1) 8.00

1964 (2) **6th National Jamboree** - Official (Boy Scouts) (Replica of Continental
Curr.) al., 39mm O: Sun Dial & Rays R: Linked Circle Chain 4.00

1964 (3) **New York World's Fair** - Official (Boy Scouts) (Sold at Scouting
Exhibit)
bt. bronze, 35mm O: Universal Boy Scout Emblem R: Unisphere 2.50

1964 (4) **Explorer Fitness Program** - AMF Inc. & Official (Boy Scouts)
bronze, 39mm O: Bowler and "I Played Dick Weber" R: Wording (Same
for all) 4.00

1964 (5) Same as (4), except O: Bowler and "I Beat Dick Weber" 4.00

1964 (6) Same as (4), except O: Golfer and "I Played Ben Hogan" 4.00

1964 (7) Same as (4), except O: Golfer and "I Beat Ben Hogan" 4.00

1964 (8) Same as (4), except O: Swimmer and "I Qualified for Swim Tests" ..
4.00

1964 (9) Same as (4), except O: Exerciser and "I Passed the Fitness Tests" .
4.00

(Financed from extra 1c charged for Monorail Ride at 1964-5 World's Fair)

1962 (10) **6th National Jamboree** - The Bunker Hill Co., Kellogg, Idaho
crudely done lead, 57mm O: 6th National Jamboree R: Region XI .. 12.50

1967 (1) **12th World Jamboree** - Official (Boy Scouts) (Farragut Park, Idaho)
(a) bronze, 35mm O: World Scout Badge R: Scout Sign & Hemisphere 6.00
(b) oxid. silver 8.00

1967 (2) **12th World Jamboree** - Private (Maynard Craig Enterprises,
Dishman, Wash.)
(a) bt. bronze, 39mm (2,500) O: Scouts Marching R: Map of Idaho 6.50
(b) oxid. bronze (2,500 minted) 6.50
(c) oxid. silver (1,000 minted) 8.00
(d) .999 silver (500 minted) 18.00

1967 (3) **12th World Jamboree** - Region 11 Scouts
white metal O: "For Friendship" R: Region 11 design 7.50

1967 (4) **12th World Jamboree**
white plastic, 45mm O: Jamboree Insignia in red R: "I am Indian Tea" 4.00

1967 (5) **12th World Jamboree Friendship Award** - Transatlantic Cn (Heidel-
berg, Germany)
bt. bronze, 36mm O: Hands Shaking R: Scout Badge 5.00

1967 (6) **Fare to Camp Alexander** - Official (Boy Scouts) (Colorado Springs,
Colo.) bt. bronze, 24mm O: Wording R: Scout Badge Outline (500 but
never used) 2.00

1967 (7) **Golden Jubilee** - Nassau County Council (N.Y.)
bronzed potmetal, 45mm O: Teddy Roosevelt R: Blank 4.50

1967 (8) **POW-WOW** - New Orleans Council (La.)
(a) bt. al., 39mm O: Clouds and Wording R: Scout Badge Outline ... 1.00
(b) blue-coated al. 1.00
(c) bt. bronze 1.25
(d) oxid. bronze 1.25

1967 (9) **Nat'l Cn. Meeting** - U.S. Steel Co., Pittsburgh, Pa.
steel, 51mm O: Wording with Emblem Design R: U.S. Steel Design &
Wording 10.00

1968 (1) **Official Boy Scouts of America Pocket Piece**
oxid. bronze, 39mm O: Scout Law & World Emblem R: Scout Oath . 3.00

1968 (2) **Promotional Coin** - BSA National Supply Service (Medallic Art. Co.
NYC) bt. bronze, 38mm O: "Pedro" the Donkey R: Horseshoes 3.50

1968 (3) **Scout-O-Rama** - Los Angeles Area Council (Calif.)
al., 39mm O: Four Hemisphere Sections R: Wording 1.00

1968 (4) **50th Anniversary of Council** - S.E. Louisiana Girl Scout Council (1917-
1967) bt. al., 39mm O: Girl Scout Trefoil R: Wording 3.00

1969 (1) 7th National Jamboree - Official (Boy Scouts) (Farragut Park, Idaho)
   (a) bronze, 34mm O: Jamboree Emblem R: Map of Idaho 5.00
   (b) oxid. silver (see Footnote 1) 8.00
1969 (2) 7th National Jamboree - New Jersey Council
   thick lead, 35mm O: Jamboree Emblem R: Blank 3.50
1969 (3) 7th National Jamboree - Troop 10, Peninsula Council (Va.)
   bt. bronze, 39mm O: Map of Virginia & Badge R: Wording 3.00
1969 (4) 7th National Jamboree - Troop 70, Mt. Ranier Council (Wash.)
   bt. bronze, 34mm O: Friendship Tower R: Mt. Ranier 3.00
1969 (5) 7th National Jamboree - Great Northern Railway
   bt. bronze, 34mm O: Scout Badge R: Mountain Goat 4.50
1969 (6) 7th National Jamboree - Kaiser Aluminum Company
   al, 39mm O: Maps of Idaho & Washington R: Hands Clasping 3.25
1969 (7) 7th National Jamboree - Washington Wheat Growers Association
   al., 36mm O: Tenderfoot Badge R: Modernistic Wheat 3.25
1969 (10) Boy Power '69 - Pike's Peak Council (Colo.) (Made in Italy)
   (a) gold anodized al., 39mm (1,000) O: Scout Seal R: Seal of Colorado 1.00
   (b) silver finished nickel (500 minted) 3.50
1970 (4) Boy Power Roundup - New Orleans Council (La.)
   (a) gold anodized al., 39mm O: Scout Badge R: Pelican 1.00
   (b) gold anodized al. (cull 1.00
1970 (5) Promotional Coin - U.S. Steel Co. (Given to delegates at Region 3 Meeting)
   steel, 50mm O: Scout Center, Pittsburgh, Pa. R: New U.S. Steel Bldg . 4.00
1970 (6) Juliette Gordon Low - Societe Commem. de Femmes Celebres
   (Issue No. 24) (3,223 produced by Franklin Mint)
   sterling silver proof, 38mm O: Low Bust R: Trefoil & Flags 22.50
1970 (7) 45th Anniversary National Convention - Alpha Phi Omega Fraternity
   (a) al., 39mm O: Fraternity Crest R: Wording 3.00
   (b) oxid. bronze (2,000 minted) 6.00
   (c) .999 silver (100 serially numbered) 18.00-30.00
1971 (1) Official 13th World Jamboree
   (a) copper in plastic case 6.50
   (b) gold in case 150.00
1971 (2) 13th World Jamboree Contingent - Official (BSA) (Given free in envel.)
   oxid. bronze, 32mm O: Scout Badge R: Statue of Liberty 7.50
1971 (3) 13th World Jamboree - Washington Trail Council (Pa.)
   al., 35mm O: Washington Bust R: Mt. Fuji ("Asagiri Heights" misspelled) 5.00
1971 (5) 13th World Jamboree - Philadelphia and Lancaster Councils (Pa.)
   al., 39mm O: Region 3 Emblem R: Jamboree Emblem 4.00
1971 (6) Boy Power - Man Power Program - Official (Boy Scouts)
   (a) silver color, 38mm O: Boy Power Insignia R: Scout Oath 4.00
   (b) bronze color 3.00

1971 (7) **Project SOAR** - Official (Boy Scouts) (Save Our American Resources project)
bronze-copper finish, 38mm O: SOAR Emblem R: Boy & Man Power Emblem 6.00

1971 (8) **Recycling Conservation Project** - Reynolds Aluminum Co. (magnetic inside)
olive colored rubber, 41mm O: Scout Badge (raised red print) R: Blank 3.00

1971 (11) **Region 3 Annual Meeting** - Official (Boy Scouts) (Pittsburgh, Pa.)
steel, 52mm O: Steel Triangle Building R: BSA Flag Plaza 5.00

1972 (1-12) **"Spirit of Scouting"** - Franklin Mint, Franklin Center, Pa. (BSA approved)
sterling silver, 39mm O: 12 Pictures of Scout Law R: 12 Scout Laws
(12 Official Medals designed by Norman Rockwell - Sold initially for $117
275.00 set

1972 (14) **U.S. Grant Sesquicentennial Pilgrimage** - Blackhawk Cn. (Ill.)
thick bronze, 44mm O: President Grant Bust R: Stage Coach 7.50

1972 (17) **60th Anniversary of Girl Scouts** - Official (Girl Scouts)
oxid. bronze, 32mm O: Juliette Low Birthplace R: Scout Badge Outline ...
3.00

1972 (18) **Official Cub Scout Pocket Piece** - (Square Medallion)
bt. bronze, 32mm O: Wolf Face & "Help Other People" R: Cub Promise ..
1.50

1973 (1) **8th National Jamboree** - Official (Boy Scouts) (E - Moraine; W - Farragut)
(a) goldine, 39mm (175,000) O: Map of U.S.A. R: Jamboree Emblem 2.00
(b) oxid. silver (15,000 minted) 4.00

1973 (2-9) **8th National Jamobree** - Official (Boy Scouts) (No. 9) is the same as (1a)
goldine, 39mm O: Replicas of 8 Jambo coins R: Emblems of 8 Jamborees
(set of 8 - one from each National Jamboree) (20,000 encased sets issued) ...
10.00

1973 (11) **8th National Jamboree** - Long's Peak Cn. (Wyo.) (Friendship token) (troope 3)
al., 39mm O: "Friendship Token" R: "Good For One Friend" 3.50

1973 (14) **Bicentennial Coin** - Official (Boy Scouts) (GIFT- Get Involved For Them)
oxid. bronze, 39mm O: Grand Union Flag R: Wording 2.00

1973 (15) **"The Big Parade"** - Franklin Mint, Franklin Center, Pa. (Serially numbered)
sterling silver proof, 2"x2½" rectangular O: Scout w. flag. R: Wording
(Picture "The Big Parade" reproduced from Norman Rockwell's Fondest Memories) 35.00

1974 (2-13) **"The Scout Oath"** - Official B.S.A. Medallic Series (Wittnauer Mint)

(a) bronze, 40mm O: 12 pictures of Scout Oath, Motto & Slogan R: Scout Sign & Wording .... 100.00 set

(b) .999 silver (Medals conceived by Joseph Csatari, BSA Art .. 225.00 set

(c) gold on sterling Director and all are numbered on the edge) 400.00 set

unk. (1) **Honoring Boy Scouts** - (Made by Whitehead & Hoag Co.)
bt. bronze, 32mm H O: Scout with Staff R: Words "BOY SCOUT" ... 7.00

unk. (2) **Hikers Shoes for Boys** - Peters Shoe Co., St. Louis, Mo.
bronze, 32mm O: Scout w. Staff R: Membership Emblem of Hikers Club ...
10.00

unk. (3) **Civic Good Turn Token** - (Made by Whitehead & Hoag - No. 255)
silver, 29mm O: Tenderfoot Badge R: No. & Maker (w. 10 border holes)

unk. (4) **Lincoln Trail Hike** - Abraham Lincoln Council (Springfield, Ill.; ca. 1950s
bronze, O: Lincoln Bust (diff from 1926 (1)) R: Wording 8.50

unk. (5) **Gen. MacArthur Award, B.S.A.** - Nat'l Victory Garden Institute (30,000 made)

(a) satin finished bronze, 32mm O: MacArthur Bust R: Fleur-de-Lis 20.00

(b) Same, except R: Wording "Boy Scouts of America" in raised letters ...
20.00

unk (6) **MacArthur Garden Award, B.S.A.** - Nat'l Victory Garden Institute
bronze, 32mm O: MacArthur Bust & "Boy Scouts of America" R: Wording
15.00

unk. (7) **Girl Scout Souvenir** - Official (Girl Scouts) (Free from G.S. Supply Dept.)
bronze, trefoil shape, H O: "GS" on Trefoil R: Wording 1.00

unk. (8) **Good Turn Pocket Piece** - Official (Boy Scouts) (Varieties in diff. years)
bt. bronze, 36mm O: First Class Badge R: Good Turn Wording 3.50

unk. (9) **Good Turn Pocket Piece** - Official (Boy Scouts) (Varieties in diff. years)
bt. bronze, 37mm O: Tenderfoot Badge R: Good Turn Wording ....:. 1.50

unk. (10) **Key Chain Piece** - Official (Cub Scouts) (Square Medallion) (1940s?)
bt. bronze, 32mm round H O: Wolf Face & "Cubs BSA" R: Cub Promise 4.00

unk. (11) **Key Chain Piece** - Official (Cub Scouts) (Square Medallion) (1950s?)
bt. bronze, 32mm, round H O: Wolf Face & "Cub Scouts BSA"
R: Cub Promise 2.00

unk. (12) **Pocket Piece** - Official (Girl Scouts)
bronze, 35mm O: Girl Scout Trefoil R: Girl Scout Promise 2.00

unk. (13) **Presentation Medallion** - Official (Boy Scouts) (For Cn. special service)
oxid. bronze, 76mm O: World Emblem w. Wreath R: Blank (for engraving) 5.00

Footnote 1: Reproduction in Brass of 1950 (1) made officially in 1973 by Boy Scouts of America. The original is easily distinguishable from the reproduction, but the difference is difficult to describe.

unk. **(14)** **Presentation Medallion** - Official (Boy Scouts)
bronze, 67mm O: World Emblem w. Wreath R: Blank (for engraving
name) 5.00

unk **(15)** **5th Annual BSA Vacation Training Camp** - (At Catalina Is., Calif.)
al., 33mm, H 1.50

In addition, numerous wooden tokens have been issued by Councils and
individuals. Some examples are:

Roger Nazeley Wooden Dollar 1.00
World Jamboree Staff Photographer Wooden Nickel 1.00
Wooden Nickels by Scouting Organizations .... .50
Wooden Nickels by Individuals .... .25
Jamboree Related Wooden Nickels 50-3.00

B.S.A. BICENTENNIAL COINS
Set of 5 .... 10.00
Individually 2.00

42

NORMAN ROCKWELL
SPIRIT OF SCOUTING MEDALLIONS
Sterling Silver Set 275.00
Individually 25.00

Top row
Gilwell Woodbadge Reunion Wooden Nickel .... .50
1952 Freedom Foundation Get Out The Vote Coin - gold color
                                                                    50.00
    Same - silver color 5.00
Bottom
Girl Scout Promise Coin (reverse shown) 2.00

REPRO SET

Reissues by Boy Scouts of America for Souvenirs

1937 Washington, D.C. 3.50
1950 Valley Forge 3.50
1953 Irvine Ranch 3.50
1957 Valley Forge 3.50
1960 Colorado Springs 3.50
1964 Valley Forge 3.50
1969 Farragut State Park 3.50

1973 Farragut State Park 3.50
    Moraine State Park 3.50
1977 Moraine State Park 3.50

Privately made by Max Silber - cast metal of all National Jamboree and some World Jamboree, finely done
                                          7.50 each

Top row (l-r)
Tenderfood Emblem Good Turn Pocket Piece 1.50
1st Class Emblem Good Turn Pocket Piece 3.50
World World of Scouting Coin 2.50
1973 National Jamboree Brass Coin 2.00
W.D. Boyce Memorial Coin 12.00
Scout Oath-Law Pocket Piece 2.00
2nd row, 1977 National Jamboree Brass Coin 2.00
1964 National Jamboree Continental Currency Coin 4.00
1971 Project Soar Coin 4.00
1977 National Jamboree Black Hawk Area Council Medallion
                                                      5.00
1960 National Jamboree Bronze Coin 7.00
1964 National Jamboree Bronze Coin 5.00
3rd row; Explorer's Fitness "I Qualified For Swim Tests"
    Coin 4.00
Explorer Fitness "I Passed The Fitness Tests" Coin ... 4.00
1967 World Jamboree Bronze Coin 5.00
1969 National Jamboree Bronze Coin 5.00
1971 World Jamboree Copper Coin 6.50
1969 National Jamboree Ox Silver Coin 8.00
Bottom row; 1967 World Jamboree Ox Silver Coin 10.00
1981 National Jamboree William J. Fortier Wooden Nickel .50
1975 World Jamboree Wooden Nickel 1.00
1973 National Jamboree Ox Silver Coin 6.00
1973 National Jamboree Wooden Nickel .... .50
BSA 1960 50th Anniversary Coin 5.00

CLOTHING

BELTS

Tan Web, no buckle 2.00	Leather, including standard
Blue Web, Air Exp. 5.00	leather belt buckle 3.50
Khaki Web 1.00	3 piece leather 3.50
White Web, 3 exploring branches ...	Schiff scout reservation (tooled) ...
1.50	10.00
	Philmont Scout ranch (tooled) . 5.00

JAMBOREE BELTS

3 piece leather - 1969 standard type 2 piece Jamboree Buckle 7.00
3 piece leather - 1973 standard type 2 piece Jamboree Buckle 5.00
3 piece leather - 1979 standard type 2 piece Jamboree Buckle 4.00

Girl Scout

Girl Scout Tan Web, ca. 1919 ... 7.50
G.S. Green patent, red lining ... 2.00
G.S. Green elastic type 1.50
Brownie cloth belt 2.50
Brownie cloth with grommets all
  around 1.50
Lady Cubbers, 1" Dacron-Polyester
  (blue belt for dress) 1.00
Lady Scouter, 1" Khaki Dacron-
  polyester belt for dress 1.00

Buckles - For Web Belts
1st large steel, 1st class emblem
  (long hanging knot) 6.50
2nd large steel, 1st class emblem
  (normal hanging knot) 5.00
Black with 1st class 4.00
Brass with 1st class 3.50
Brass - tenderfoot 1.00

Brass - 50's explorer emblem .. 4.50
Brass - 60's explorer emblem .. 3.00

Cub - For Web Belts
Black with emblem "CUBS BSA"
  pawprint 6.00
Brass with emblem "CUBS BSA"
  pawprint 4.00
Brass with emblem "CUB SCOUTS"
  BSA pawprint 1.25
Brass with emblem "CUB SCOUTS"
  BSA tenderfoot emblem 1.00
Brass, Webelos ends (no wording) ..
  1.00

"Tooth of Time" "Philmont",
  Rectangular shape, bronze ... 7.50
"Tooth of Time" "Philmont",
  Rectangular shape, silver ... 12.00
Oval Bronze - Bull (Philmont) . 4.50

G.S. Buckle for elastic belt, pebbled green metal with emblem 1.75
ca. 1919, emblem with "Be Prepared", black, for web belt 15.00
Standard Brass (Web) buckles with council issue - Jamboree related emblems
  exist and are valued .... 3.50 to 6.00

Jamboree Buckles

1967 World Jamboree Cast bronze
  alloy (Limited edition), Made by
  Roger Mazeley for Philadelphia
  Council 15.00
1967 World Jamboree Official
  Buckle 8.00

1969 National Jamboree Official
  Buckle 8.00
1973 National Jamboree Official
  Buckle 6.00
1977 National Jamboree Official
  Buckle 5.00

Wool Jacket-shirt
    blue for cub 25.00
    green for explorer 30.00
    red for all others 15.00
Red nylon jacket 2.00
Red poplin jacket 2.50
Red timberline jacket (padded) 2.00
Poncho (orange) 2.00
Poncho (green) vinyl, zippered
    hood 1.50
Vinyl Ponch green - zippered hood ..
    1.50

Professional Scouters Uniform Coat
3 button (ring type, metal), 4
pocket (with flaps, 2 are patch
type), single vent, wood-polyester
If label reads New York, Chicago or
San Francisco it is before 1954 ....
    35.00
If label reads New Brunswick,
Chicago, San Francisco it is 1954
or later 25.00

Mackinaw (1939)
    All wool plaid, "Bi-swing" back, double breasted no belt model, 2 button
    down side flap pockets, 2 slash pockets, adjustable cuffs, no visible Boy
    Scout of America markings, see label 15.00
Same with black plaid for professionals - RARE 50.00
Lumberjack (1939)
    All wool plaid mackinaw cloth, 2 large side pockets, knitted elastic waist
    band, no visible Boy Scout of America markings, see label 12.00
    Sweater, heather color, all worsted sweater, crew neck in pullover style,
    Boy Scout monogram on left breast 15.00
Bombazine Raincoat
    Full double breasted military style with raglan sleeves shoulders, converti-
    ble collar, all around belt, olive drab 7.50
Work Jacket
    ca. 1937, Explorer fatigue work jacket, light blue (5 buttons), side tabs with
    4 back buttons, slant cut pockets, without strips 15.00
Work Jacket
    ca. 1937, Explorer fatigue work jacket, light blue (5 buttons), side tabs with
    4 back buttons, slant cut pockets, without strips 12.00
    with strip patches (Blue on light blue; strip says "Senior Scouts BSA" 20.00
        "Sea Scouts BSA" 20.00
        "Air Scouts BSA" 15.00
        "Explorer Scouts BSA" 15.00

GIRL SCOUT DRESSES (UNIFORMS)
Leaders
1919 issue - tan, long skirt, inner band, 2 patch pockets with buttons, elastic back, side open, matching bush jacket, matching hat, wide brim 75.00
Girls
1919 - tan long skirt set on waistband, front opening, 2 patch pockets-buttons, matching tailored military style jacket, 2 pockets in front 50.00-110.00

1919 tan dress, buttons all the way, self belt, decorated buttons, 4 patch pockets, self belt 50.00-110.00

✳depending upon condition and patches affixed

1927 - long coat dress style of khaki-colored cotton jean, stamped on back with trefoil trademark three times to yard. Official buttons, embroidered insignia; patch pockets, belt. 40.00

1927 - Short coat and skirt. Same style, material and workmanship as long coat dress. Coat made with patch pockets, belt, official buttons and insignia. Skirt made with belt or patch pockets. 40.00

Girl Scout Middy, of official khaki with long sleeves, patch pocket and sailor collar embroidered with the letters "G.S." in squares 15.00

Bloomers plaited into belt. 10.00

Knee-band bloomer of official khaki. 10.00

Khaki hat 10.00

Norfolk Uniform of excellent olive drab serge; Norfolk jacket; patch pockets; notched collar, official buttons. 30.00

Same as above in khaki. 25.00

Officers hat of olive drab serge. Rolled, stitched brim with band embroidered in black trefoil insignia. Narrow brim. 15.00

Officer's hat, dark brown felt with roll brim, stitched edge and high crown. Officer's insignia attached by pin. 15.00

Norfolk Uniform of olive drab serge; Norfolk jacket; patch pockets; notch collar, official buttons. 35.00

Officer's leather belt with rings and hooks for attaching knife and whistle. ..

Officer's shirts, white English broadcloth. 2.50

Officer's black tie (four-in-hand) 2.00

Slip-over sweater in brown and heather color mixture of all-wool and knit in popular shaker stitch. 7.50

Lumberjack of all wool brown and green checkered fabric. Roll turn down collar and deep slope pockets 7.50

Sweater in heather mixture of green and brown in two models 7.50
Leaders
40's and 50's - Long sleeve green shirt waist dress, button down collar, 2 patch pockets, matching hat with grosgrain ribbon trim. 20.00

60's - Half belted princess jacket button lapels, button collar, front opening, A-line skirt, roll up short sleeve, green beret 8.00
Girls
40's and 50's - Girls is the same as leaders but buttons all the way with 3 patch pockets, button down lapel, green felt beret, yellow girl scout scarf ... 10.00

60's - Short sleeve shirt waist dress, 3 patch pockets, yellow bow tie with insignia, green beret with round insignia 6.00

Late 60's - Cadet uniform, A-line skirt, side zipper, side tab with insignia to waistband, white blouse, one pocket, short sleeve, embroidered insignia on pocket band, green cross tie, beret, insignia with pleated ruffle (green, white, copper) 5.00

Late 60's - Pullover, V-neck, short sleeve shirt, one patch pocket, pocket has band with insignia, matching bloomer shorts with elastic leg bands ... 5.00

Brownies

Ca. 50's - Shirtwaist dress opens to waist, short sleeve, side opening under arm, one patch pocket with dancing elf, belted, rust brown felt hat with dancing elf on pocket 15.00

60's - A line shirt waist, buttons to waist, short sleeve, breast pocket, band on pocket has a "Girl Scouts USA", dark brown felt hat with embroidered dancing elf on patch 6.00

70's - Elastic waist, straight leg pants, matching princess A line jumper, zipper front opening, side, slash pockets, ribbon patch embroidered "GIRL SCOUTS USA", Blouse - peter pan collar, 1 breast pocket, white with brown design stripes (featuring girl scout emblem), felt dark brown hat, patch with elf 4.00

GIRL SCOUT (MARINER)

Late 50's to early 60's - Royal blue dress, shirtwaist style, sailor flap on back, white piping with neckerchief, blue seaman's hat with white piping. .. 15.00

Early 60's - Royal blue skirt (A line), white blouse, blue felt beret with mariner emblem (trefoil on ship's wheel) 10.00

CUB

1930 - 1st issue - Blue knickers (or shorts), V neck shirt, short sleeves, (or long sleeves with collar), ring back buttons that say "CUB BSA" paw print, 2 flap button pockets above right pocket a strip says "CUB BSA", beanie, dark navy wool, yellow piping, dark navy wool socks (ribbed with cuff with two yellow bands), navy webbed belt, black buckle 35.00

1940 - heavy blue twill shirt in collar and collarless, long or short sleeves, blue long pants, heavy blue twill hat, yellow piping, webbed belt 20.00

50's - Blue twill pants with button flap on pockets with yellow piping; shirts - short and long sleeve, V neck and with collar, shirt pockets had pleats, strip above right pocket had "CUB SCOUTS BSA" 8.00

1967 - 70's - Cotton-polyester short and long sleeve, V neck and collar, pleated pocket, shirt had strip saying "CUB SCOUTS BSA"; Pants, button flap pocket, yellow piping 4.50

Late 70's - Same as above, no pleat on pocket, no flap on pants pocket, strip says "CUB SCOUT & EMBLEM" 3.00

A new uniform was issued in August, 1980.

DEN LEADERS

1930's - Blue shirtwaist, overlap belt, skirt has 2 patch pockets with piping, 1 breast pocket with piping, collar and cuffs have piping, collar points have embroidered emblem; Hat, brick orange red felt with brim 50.00

UNIFORMS FOR SCOUT LEADERS

1916 - Uniforms of coat and breeches, canvas leggings; coat with breeches and spiral puttees or leather leggings; Norfolk coat and long trousers 50.00-85.00

1916 - Scoutmaster's Hat of fur felt 25.00

1916 - Scoutmaster leather puttees .... 15.00 pr.

1916 - Scoutmaster's coat, olive drab or wool 35.00

1916 - Scoutmaster's Mackinaws 30.00

UNIFORMS FOR SCOUT LEADERS (1916)

$150.00

$125.00

Scoutmasters
Hat 35.00
Left: Norfolk
Coat 45.00
Right: Patrick
Mackinaw .. 40.00

BOY SCOUT UNIFORMS - 1916

Scout Coat 50.00

Regulation Scout Hat, olive drab felt, ventilated crown, silk band, detachable ties 20.00

Scout Leggings of extra heavy olive drab canvas and provided with new style lacing 10.00

Patrick Scout Mackinaw, olive drab, all wool, big rolling collar, four pockets and belted at waist. 30.00

Scout Breeches 20.00

Scout Knickerbockers 22.00

Scout Shorts 12.00

Scout belt of olive drab webbing with gunmetal fittings, including snap hooks for attaching equipment 8.00

Scout shirts 7.50

Water-Proof Cape, olive khaki, extra light weight, unlined, fitted with flannel-lined collars and patent clasps ...

1935 - Boy Scout Outfit, official Boy Scout hat, medium weight cotton shirt, heavy cotton breeches, official cotton stockings, neckerchief and slide, official belt 20.00

1935 - Boy Scout Outfit, official Boy Scout hat, medium weight cotton shirt, heavy cotton shorts, official cotton stockings, neckerchief and slide, official belt 22.50

1935 - Official Boy Scout Hat, well made from selected fur felt and shaped to keep appearance, low crown, wide brim, ventilated, silk band embroidered with the official Boy Scout insignia. 19.00

1935 - Heavy cotton shirt of heavyweight khaki material. Has loosely fitting roll collar. Stanley patch pockets with flaps to button; embroidered "Boy Scouts of America" sewed over the right breast pocket. Equipped with "Official" detachable buttons. 7.50

1935 - Medium weight cotton shirt of summer weight khaki material. Same as above 7.00

1935 - Heavy cotton breeches of standard khaki material. Has belt loops, two front, two hip pockets with flaps and buttons and one watch pocket, laces on legs 12.00

1935 - Wool breeches of 20 oz. olive drab melton. Same as above. 15.00

1935 - Wool shorts of 20 oz. olive drab Melton. Has two front, one hip pocket without flap and one watch pocket. 8.50

1935 - Heavy cotton shorts of heavy weight khaki material. Has two front, two hip pockets with flaps and buttons and one watch pocket. 7.50

1935 - Outdoor service shorts of lightweight khaki material. Has two front, one hip pocket without flap and one watch pocket. 7.50

1935 - Official woolen stockings from pure wool, olive drab yarn, re-enforced heels and toes. In good condition 1.00

1935 - Official cotton stockings. In good condition 1.00

1935 - Khaki anklets intended for camp use only, with elastic top. In good condition 1.00

1935 - Woolen garters for Scouts and Scouters - knitted from pure wool into a band 1¼ inch wide. Has tabs which will show below stockings. ..... 2.00 pr.

1935 - Official Boy Scout poncho of special lightweight process material absolutely waterproof. Contains no rubber. Opening in center for the head; closes with a ball and socket fastening. 5.00

BOY SCOUT UNIFORMS

Winter Shirt, 1916 .. 7.50

Scout Coat, 1916   .. 50.00

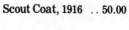

'20.00

Patrick Mackinaw, 1916
.... 40.00

Shorts, 1916 .... 8.00   Knickers, 1916 .... 15.00   Breeches, 1916 .... 15.00

1911 Boy Scout Uniform Coat
Note short, stubby collar and accordion patch pockets.
Buttons are ring back type. With this insignia affixed   150.00

1935 - Official Lumberjack shirt of all-wool plaid material with a double-knitted, snug fitting elastic bottom in colors similar to the shirt itself. Has two breast pockets with flaps to button. Cuffs of plaid material to button. Convertible collar. 7.00

··1935 - Sweat shirt of high grade cotton with crew neck, snug fitting bottom and wristlets. Brown tweed pattern. 4.50

Official Swimming Suits

1920-35, wool, dark blue 12.00

1935 - Tank suit style. One piece dark blue worsted swimming suit with Boy Scout emblem. Made of medium weight pure worsted. 10.00

1935 - Camp Trunks, white, made of cotton and will not stretch and get out of shape 2.00

1935 - Swimming trunks, high waisted style. All wool worsted. Furnished with white belt. 2.50

MERIT BADGE SASHES

Boy Scout

Tan - wide 4.50

Tan - narrow 4.00

Khaki - wide 1.25

Khaki - narrow 1.00

Explorer

Green 3.50

Air Scout

Light Blue 7.50

Brownie Scout

Brown, felt 1.50

Light brown, cloth 1.00

Girl Scout

Tan 5.00

Green and white fleck 1.50

Dark Green 1.00

The above prices are for merit badge sashes without badges affixed.

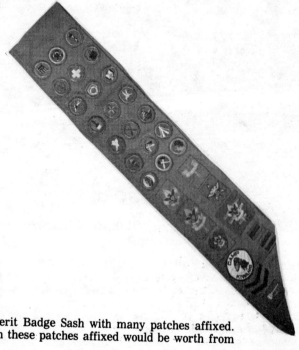

A wide tan Merit Badge Sash with many patches affixed. This sash with these patches affixed would be worth from 35.00 to 60.00.

ORDER OF THE ARROW SASHES

Honor Award Level	Band	Arrow	Comments
1915 Ordeal	Black	W	Felt arrow sewn to felt band.
1915 Vigil	Black	W	Triangle: embroidered or felt arrows counter-clockwise.
1918 Ordeal	White	R	Sateen arrow sewn to sateen band
1918 Vigil	White	R	Triangle: embroidered arrows clockwise
1924 ✸ Ordeal	White	R	Felt arrow sewn to felt band
1924 Vigil	White	R	Triangle: Embroidered or felt arrows; counter-clockwise
1934 Vigil	White	—	Triangle sewn to band; no arrow

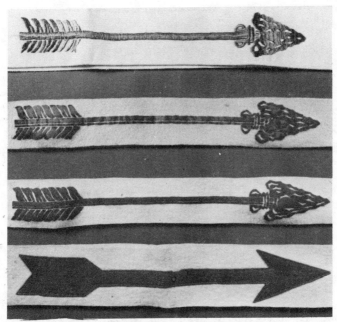

Order of the Arrow Sashes

Top to bottom
1924 Ordeal Sash 45.00
1930 era, flocked Brotherhood sash, 2 varieties 30.00
1930 era, flocked, Vigil sash, 3 variations, narrow or wide
.... 100.00
1948 Ordeal Sash 20.00
1948 Brotherhood Sash (This is an ordeal sash with red silk
bands sewn on upon elevation to Brotherhood) 15.00
1974 Ordeal Sash 2.50

1948 ✹ Ordeal	White	R	Flocked arrow on felt band
1948 ✹ Brotherhood	White	R	Flocked arrow and bars on felt band
1948 Vigil	White	R	Triangle: arrows counter-clockwise
1955 Ordeal	White	R	Embroidered arrow; cotton band, white double-line stitching up sides of band; cotton is heavy-weight thickness. Triangle: arrows counter-clockwise
1955 Brotherhood	White	R	Same as above
1955 Vigil	White	R	Same as above
1960 Ordeal	White	R	Light-weight cotton; double-line stitching used along edges of band in '55 is not used. Triangles: arrows counter-clockwise
1960 Brotherhood	White	R	Same as above
1960 Vigil	White	R	Same as above
1974 ✹ Ordeal	White	R	Cotton band 8.0cm wide; earlier issues were only 6.5 cm wide
1974 Brotherhood	White	R	
1974 Vigil	White	R	Triangle: arrows counter-clockwise

✹ illustrated on next page

NECKERCHIEFS
Boy Scout Standard Issue Neckerchiefs

1st Issue Scout seal type emblem on square cloth .... 10.00+

2nd Issue Scout tenderfoot emblem in a square on square cotton cloth, various colors 3.50

3rd Issue Scout tenderfoot emblem in a box with border bands on square cotton cloth, various color combinations, various colors 3.00

4th Issue Same design as 2nd issue except on triangle cotton cloth, various colors 1.50

5th Issue Same design as 3rd issue except on triangle cotton cloth, various colors 1.25

6th Issue Scout tenderfoot emblem embroidered on triangle cotton-polyester cloth with embroidered border, various colors 1.00

Cub Scout Standard Issue Neckerchiefs

1st Issue "Cubs" emblem, blue on golden yellow square cotton cloth 8.00

2nd Issue "Cub Scouts" and Paw Print, blue on golden yellow square cotton cloth 3.50

3rd Issue "Cub Scouts and Paw Print", blue on golden yellow triangle cotton cloth 1.50

4th Issue "Cub Scouts and Tenderfoot emblem", blue on golden yellow triangle cotton cloth 1.00

5th Issue Webelos emblem patch on green and red plaid triangle cotton cloth (for Webelos Scouts only) 1.00

6th Issue Cub Scouts and Tenderfoot Emblem, dark blue on light blue triangle cotton cloth (for Bear Rank Cub Scouts only) 1.00

Leader Yellow Wolf's head and "Cub Scout Leader" on dark blue cotton-polyester with yellow piping border 1.25

Left to right
BSA Issue Eagle Scout Neckerchief 10.00
National Eagle Scout Association Neckerchief 5.00

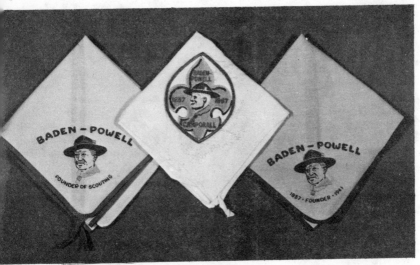

Left to right
Baden-Powell Neckerchief (type 1) 5.00
Baden-Powell Camporall Neckerchief 2.50
Baden-Powell Neckerchief (type 2) 5.00

Left to right
Schiff National Training School Neckerchief 12.00
BSA 1959 Scout-O-Rama Neckerchief 3.00
Sea Explorer Neckerchief 5.00

Left to right
Region 4 Buckskin Men Neckerchief (maroon) 15.00
1937 National Jamboree Boy Scout Neckerchief (red) 65.00
1950 National Jamboree Silk Neckerchief ...., 27.00

Sea Explorer Standard Issue Neckerchiefs

1st Issue Sea Scout Emblem, white on square navy blue cotton 8.50
2nd Issue Sea Scout emblem in white on triangle navy blue cotton (this is known to exist with 2 minor variations to the emblem design) 5.00

SPECIAL NECKERCHIEFS

Knights of Danamus (KD) neckerchief 10.00
National Eagle Scout Association Neckerchief, small NESA patch on white cotton 5.00
  a. National issue as pictured large eagle patch on blue silk with red, white and blue border, ... 8.00
  b. Various other types issued by same councils 6.00

Region Neckerchiefs

  a. Old 12 numbered region neckerchief and each region issued many neckerchiefs over the years. Some issues were highly restricted and others were not 8.00-35.00
  b. New geographic region neckerchiefs 4.00- 8.00
Baden-Powell Neckerchiefs 5.00
B.S.A. issue council activity neckerchiefs 1.00-3.00

National Base Neckerchiefs

Schiff

Schiff N.T.S. neckerchief 18.00
Schiff N.J.L.I.T.C. neckerchief 12.00
Schiff neckerchief, Schiff Shield emblem on red, white & blue 6.00
Schiff neckerchief - Schiff Shield emblem on light blue 4.00
Schiff - Conservation Training Camp neckerchief 15.00
Schiff - National Troop Leader Development neckerchief ... 13.00

Philmont

Philmont Volunteer Training Center neckerchief, red and yellow ... 5.00
Philmont Scout Ranch neckerchief, on yellow 4.00

Philmont Scout Ranch neckerchief, on white 3.00
Special Philmont neckerchief (various) .... 8.00+

Other National Bases

Land Between the Lakes neckerchief 15.00
Maine National High Adventure Base neckerchief 12.00
Region Seven Explorer Canoe Base neckerchief
  a. Regular on plain white 8.00
  b. White with printed map of base 10.00
Charles L. Semmers Wilderness Canoe Base neckerchief 10.00

National Jamboree Neckerchiefs

1935 - Boys neckerchief, white Jamboree emblem on blue square 100.00
  Boys neckerchief, white Jamboree emblem on red square 85.00
  Leaders neckerchief, white dome above scout emblem on blue square 120.00
  Leaders neckerchief, white dome above scout emblem on red square . 120.00
  National Staff neckerchief, orange dome above emblem on purple square .. 220.00

1937 - Boys neckerchief, white Jamboree emblem & stripe on blue square 85.00
  Boys neckerchief, white Jamboree emblem & stripe on red square ... 65.00
  Leaders neckerchief, white monument above emblem on blue square 110.00
  Leaders neckerchief, white monument above emblem on red square . 110.00
  200.00

1950 - Jamboree emblem on cotton triangle 22.00
  Jamboree emblem on rayon (silk) triangle 28.00
1953 - Covered Wagon Jamboree emblem on cotton 18.00

1957 - Jamboree Emblem on red, white and blue cotton triangle
   a. thick lettering 15.00
   b. thin lettering (4 varieties)................................. 15.00
1960 - Anniversary Jamboree Emblem on golden yellow cotton triangle . 10.00
1964 - Jamboree Emblem on red, white and blue cotton triangle
   a. thick letters 8.00
   b. thin letters 9.00
1969 - Jamboree deer emblem on yellow cotton triangle 6.00
   Souvenir neckerchief, red, white and blue cotton triangle printed with
   emblems of all jamborees to that time 5.00
   Trading Post A neckerchief, Jamboree emblem above A on blue cotton 20.00
   Trading Post B neckerchief, Jamboree emblem above B on blue cotton 20.00
   Trading Post C neckerchief, Jamboree emblem above C on blue cotton 20.00
   Trading Post D neckerchief, Jamboree emblem above D on blue cotton 20.00
1973 - Jamboree Emblem on blue cotton 2.00
   Order of the Arrow Service Corps neckerchief, "8th National Jamboree
   Service Corps WWW" printed in blue on yellow cotton 22.00
   Trading Post A neckerchief, Jamboree emblem above A 18.00
   Trading Post B neckerchief, Jamboree emblem above B 18.00
   Trading Post C neckerchief, Jamboree emblem above C 18.00
   Trading Post D neckerchief, Jamboree emblem above D 18.00
   Trading Post Staff neckerchief, Jamboree emblem above "Staff" 22.00
1977 - Jamboree emblem on red, blue and yellow cotton (4 varieties) 2.00
1981 - Jamboree emblem on cotton (3 varieties)...................... 3.00

NATIONAL ORDER OF THE ARROW CONFERENCE NECKERCHIEFS
1940 - Regular - Red "WWW" above "CTE" above "40" on gray 110.00
   Staff - Red "Anicus" above "CTE" above "40" on gray 150.00
1956 - Black 41st anniversary conference WWW on red arrowhead on white
   cotton 60.00
1958 - Conference emblem on yellow cotton with white piping 40.00
1961 - Regular - Conference emblem on white cotton with red piping 40.00
   Staff - Conference emblem on white above "Host" and red arrows along
   edge, cotton 60.00
   Committee - Red arrow through 3 chain links with "National Conference
   Committee, 46th Anniversary" on white cotton with red piping 50.00
1963 - Regular - Conference emblem on white cotton with red piping 28.00
   Committee - Conference emblem above "Conference Committee" on red
   cotton with white piping 35.00
1965 - Regular - Conference emblem on golden yellow with red piping ... 22.00
   Committee - Conference emblem on white with "Conference Committee" in
   red and with red piping 29.00
1967 - Regular - Conference emblem on tan cotton 15.00
   Band - Conference emblem on blue cotton with red piping 22.00
   Chorus - Conference emblem on yellow cotton with red piping 22.00
   Committee - Conference emblem with "Conference Committee" on white
   cotton with red piping 28.00
1969 - Regular - Conference emblem on white cotton 12.00
   Staff - Conference emblem and black "Staff" on blue cotton 20.00
1971 - Regular - Conference emblem on blue cotton 11.00
   Chorus - Conference emblem and red "Brotherhood Chorus" on blue cotton
   18.00

Committee - Conference emblem and red "Conference Committee" on blue cotton 15.00

1973 - Regular - Conference emblem on red cotton 6.00
    Chorus-Band - Conference emblem on purple cotton with white piping . 12.00

1975 - Conference emblem on white 5.00

1977 - Conference emblem on golden yellow 4.00

Please note: Fakes of many of these National Order of the Arrow Neckerchiefs are known to exist. Most are simply silk-screened logos on plain cotton.

Other Neckerchiefs

World Scouting Neckerchief - white on purple with white piping 7.50

Lone Scout Neckerchief - Lone Scouting emblem on yellow cotton, triangle, ca. 1980 .... 5.00

Foreign Scout Neckerchief - Neckerchief from foreign scout organizations can vary considerably depending upon nation, age, etc. 2.00-5.00

World Jamboree Neckerchief - Neckerchiefs have been issued for almost all World Jamborees and Special Contingent Neckerchiefs have been issued by countries attending for their own Scouts as well. Prices can range from around 5.00 to 300.00 or 400.00.

Council Issue Neckerchiefs - All councils have at one time or another issued their own neckerchiefs for the council, camp, shows, roundups, etc. Prices on these can vary from 1.00 to as much as 15.00+ for a council neckerchief from a merged council.

Other Order of the Arrow Neckerchiefs

Most all Order of the Arrow lodges have issued their own neckerchiefs. These can vary in value from about 3.00 to 100+ for an old one from a merged lodge. Likewise, the subunits of Lodges, called chapters, have in some cases issued neckerchiefs. These will also vary considerably in value.

Also, there are many regional and area Order of the Arrow activities as well as local lodge activities for which neckerchiefs have been issued. Again, keep in mind that values can vary greatly depending upon the lodge and-or event.

PINS, MEDALS AND JEWELRY

Descriptions of pins and clasps

1. Crude type clasp - single wire hook for pin to latch under.
2. Double loop crude type clasp - same except hook is a double loop of wire.
3. Solid hook type - clasp hook is a small solid piece of metal for the pin to latch under.

4. Pin shield type - hook is a piece of metal with what would appear to be a shield on it, one piece mold.
5. Safety pin clasp - a clasp which appears almost as a normal safety pin.
6. Safety clasp pin (bar mounted) - safety clasp is mounted on a bar which is then affixed to the badge.
7. Safety clasp pin (plain) - a safety clasp type pin where swivel and latch are two separate pieces affixed separately to the badge.

A variation of this has a square cut out of the bar which a "bump" protrudes. Some have the square cut with no protruding bump.

PINS
BOY SCOUTS
Attendance - 1st Issue, all gold color

Teens, 20's, 100 percent Duty Badge, round celluloid pin, white background with tenderfoot emblem and lettering "BOY SCOUTS OF AMERICA" - "100 PERCENT DUTY" (blue) - "1 MONTH" (red) 12.00
100 Percent Duty Shield, tenderfoot emblem over stars and stripes shield, gold plated, bar above has lettering "100 Percent DUTY" 15.00

100 Percent Bar Pin - Maltese cross with tenderfoot emblem, lettering "100 Percent DUTY" bars attach at top for each year (pin on back of each bar)10.00
Attendance - 2nd Issue
ca. '30s gold colored Maltese cross with tenderfoot emblem, no "100 Percent Duty", bars attach at top with pin on back 8.00
Attendance - 3rd Issue
late '40s - '60s - gold colored Maltese cross with tenderfoot emblem, no "100 Percent DUTY", pin on badge and bars hang below 3.00
1960 - same as the badge of the '40s' - '60s but badge has clutch back pin ... 1.00

AWARD - BOY SCOUTS
Thanks Badge - gold colored tenderfoot emblem with red, white, blue enameled square extending below with gold lettering "THANKS" in the blue bar, safety clasp pin 4.00
Same with clutch back pin 1.50
GIRL SCOUTS - Thanks Badge Pin, same as above but with clutch safety clasp 1.00
Order of Arrow Vigil Honor Pin, triangle shape, white enamel fill, three gold colored arrows, gold outline, 1st issue - screw back 12.00
2nd issue - clutch back 3.50
SEA EXPLORER - Pewter Bar Pin - 2 types, one has lettering "Qualified Seaman", other has lettering "Small Boat Handler", both have 1st class emblem over anchor and have double clutch back pins. .... 6.00 ea.
Cub Scout - round sunburst design, lettering "NATIONAL SUMMERTIME AWARD - CUB SCOUTING", clutch back .... .50

Cub Scouts - Weblos Activity Badge Pins; they are all silver colored, clutch back:

Aquanaut, swimmer	.50	Geologist, mountain	.50
Artist (1st type) horse head	1.00	Naturalist, stylized bird	.50
Artist (2nd type), artist palette	.50	Outdoorsman, flying duck	.50
Athlete, runner	.50	Scouter, diploma with bow	.50
Citizen, scroll	.50	Showman, hand puppet	.50
Craftsman, hammer	.50	Sportsman, bat and ball	.50
Engineer, gears	.50	Traveler, auto	.50
Forrester, tree	.50		

Pins Award

Gold Quill Award - gold colored quill over blue enamel ink well, 1st issue - safety clasp pin 6.00

2nd issue - same as above, clutch back pin 3.50

Press Club Pin - 2st class emblem over quill on blue enamel, round lettering "PRESS CLUB" 10.00

Organizer Pin - 1st issue - gold colored pin, round, crude type clasp 8.50

2nd issue - gold colored tenderfoot emblem in blue background, gold border has lettering "ORGANIZER BSA", safety clasp pin 5.00

3rd issue - gold colored tenderfoot emblem and lettering "ORGANIZER BSA" on blue background, clutch back pin 2.50

Silver Beaver Award (lapel pin) - 1st issue - gold tenderfoot emblem on blue and white enameled bar, clutch back 8.00

2nd issue - sterling silver beaver, clutch back 5.00

Silver Antelope Award (lapel pin) - 1st issue, gold tenderfoot emblem on yellow and white enameled bar, clutch back 18.00

2nd issue - sterling silver antelope, clutch back 12.00

Silver Buffalo Award (lapel pin) - 1st issue, gold tenderfoot emblem on red and white enameled bar, clutch back 30.00

2nd issue - sterling silver buffalo, clutch back 18.00

Silver World Award (lapel pin) - sterling tenderfoot emblem, lines and stars on blue enamel globe, clutch back 30.00

AWARD
Religious Pins (see Medals)

War Service Pin (WWI) - round button type says "WAR SAVINGS SERVICE - W.S.S." in light brown lettering on dark brown outer circle, center is dark blue with hand and torch of Statue of Liberty in white, straight pin back 12.00

Liberty Loan (all button type)

1st issue - lettering "LIBERTY LOAN" 7.00

2nd issue - lettering "LIBERTY LOAN" 6.00

3rd issue - round red outer border has lettering "THIRD LIBERTY LOAN" on blue, has Liberty Bell 6.00

4th issue - blue with red and white flag 6.00

5th issue - white "V" on blue, ... 5.00

Blue "V" on white 5.00

War Service Pin (WWII) - ribbon bar, red, white, blue, has lettering "WAR LOAN GALLANT" 12.00

One piece button hole lapel pin, lettering "WAR PRODUCTION BOARD BOY SCOUTS WASTE PAPER AWARD", has "1000" over flying eagle 10.00

INSIGNIA
Cub Scout
1st issue - diamond shape, gold wolf head and lettering on blue enamel lettering "CUB SCOUTS BSA", crude type clasp 5.00

2nd issue - diamond shape, gold wolf head and lettering on blue enamel lettering "CUB SCOUTS BSA", safety clasp pin 4.00

3rd issue - diamond shape, gold wolf head and lettering "CUB SCOUTS BSA" on blue enamel clutch back pin 3.00

4th issue - diamond shape, gold wolf head, scout emblem and lettering "CUB SCOUTS" on blue background, double clutch back 1.50

BOY SCOUTS (lapel pins)
Tenderfoot emblem as one piece buttonhole pin with round connector post 2.00

Tenderfoot emblem as one piece buttonhole pin with V connector post 1.00

Tenderfoot emblem with screw back pin 3.00

Tenderfoot emblem with crude type clasp 1.50

Tenderfoot emblem with safety clasp pin 1.25

Tenderfoot emblem with clutch back 1.00

INSIGNIA
Order of the Arrow
Sterling silver arrow lapel pin, safety clasp pin 1.50

Round, red color stylized Indian chief on gold background, safety pin 3.50

Knot Device Pin, small gold color, clutch back pin 1.00

    Cub Scout, diamond shape 1.00

    Boy Scout, tenderfoot emblem 1.00

    Commissioner, round with wreath and 1st class emblem 3.00

    Explorer ('50s), wings-anchor-compass design 1.50

    Explorer ('60s), circle "V" design 1.50

    Explorer ('70s), miniature stylized "E" 1.00

    Sea Explorer (pre '72), Scout emblem on anchor 2.00

    Sea Explorer (70s), "E" on anchor 1.25

Air Scout
    Regular size pin, scout emblem on wings 25.00

    Miniature lapel pin, scout emblem on wings 12.00

Rover Scout, gold color tenderfoot - emblem with circle showing beneath in red, lettering "ROVER SCOUT" also has "BSA" 45.00

Rambler Pin - 1970s - bush design with small tenderfoot emblem at base 10.00

INSIGNIA
Explorers (late 30s - 40s) general pin has tenderfoot emblem over compass ...
18.00

INSIGNIA - General
BOY SCOUT
World Scouting - round fleur-de-lis in silver color, rope outline on purple background, clutch back pin ....

BSA (monogram) - 1st issue has two straight wires to be bent down for fasteners 12.00

    2nd issue has double screw back with star shaped screws 10.00

    3rd issue has double screw back with gear type screw 8.00

Hand Sign - 1st issue - dark metal with screw back 3.50
   2nd issue - bright gold colored metal with clutch back 12.5
Round Button Type - gold stamped tenderfoot emblem on blue background ...
   1.50

Strengthen The Arm of Liberty
   Liberty's head, arm & torch on tenderfoot emblem, lettering "STRENGTH-
   EN THE ARM OF LIBERTY", clutch back 3.50
   Liberty's head, arm & torch on diamond shape, lettering "STRENGTHEN
   THE ARM OF LIBERTY", clutch back 4.00
   One variation of this pin has lettering "FORWARD ON LIBERTY'S TEAM"
   5.00

Onward For God and My Country - round, George Washington kneeling, clutch
   back 2.50
"Wonderful World of Scouting", also has tenderfoot emblem on globe
clutch back 2.00
SEA SCOUT - Insignia - General
   1st class emblem over anchor, large screw back on single post (hat pin) 5.00
   Smaller version of above but with clutch back 3.00
   Smaller version with safety clasp 2.00
LONE SCOUT
Membership Badge - circle over arrowhead, center of circle has initials
   "LSA" and outer border has lettering "LONE SCOUTS OF AMERICA" ....
   15.00

L. S. Service bar 15.00
Silver Badge - circle over arrowhead, center of circle has initials "LSA" and
   outer border says "LONE SCOUTS OF AMERICA", banner above says
   "W.L.S. RADIO TRIBE" 22.00
Totem Pole Lodge Badge - gold totem pole lettering "TOTEM POLE LODGE
   BADGE - LSA" 18.00
Lone Scout Monograms - 1st issue, "LSA" in circle 22.00
   2nd issue - "LSA" (no circle 18.00
LSC Quill - gold color 24.00
   First Degree Badge, bronze, irregular shield shape with standing Indian ...
   15.00
   Second Degree Badge, bronze, triangle over shield, campfire in triangle ...
   18.00
   Third Degree Badge, silver, shield shape with flying eagle 21.00
Lone Scout Booster Button, "LSB" in wreath 22.00
Sagamore Lodge Badge, gold color, Indian on horseback inside wreath, top
   bar says "SAGAMORE LODGE" bottom says "L.S.A." 23.50
Tribe Chief's Pin - irregular shape has chief's head at top, lower portion has
   initials "LSA", middle bar says "TRIBE CHIEF" 35.00

GIRL SCOUT

Trefoil for cap - sew on (has two eyes for thread) bake lite 8.00
G.S. (monogram) - sew on for cap (two eyes for thread), bake lite 6.50
G.S. (monogram) - 'teens, has broad hook type back with pin 10.00
ca. 20s - gold colored trefoil (very thick border) very finely engraved detail ...
   5.00

40's - gold colored trefoil (dull finish) with double loop crude type clasp - war years 4.00

50's - gold colored trefoil, crude type safety pin clasp 3.00

60's up - gold colored trefoil, safety clasp pin 1.00
Round with gold colored trefoil on green enamel, gold border 1.00

60s - miniature, gold colored trefoil with safety clasp bar pin, gold colored, lettering "GIRL SCOUTS USA" in green, crude pin 3.50

1st class pin - green enamel three leaf clover, green outer ring says "BE PREPARED" 15.00

Wing Scout pin - globe on trefoil on wings 12.00

Mariner pin - gold colored trefoil on silver ship's wheel 10.00

Campus Girl Scout Guard - gold colored "CGS" with chain attached to "C" ...
.... 5.00

World Crest pin - round, gold colored three leaf clover (stars on two leaves) gold border, blue enameled fill, crude type clasp 4.00
Round - gold three leaf clover and border, (stars on two leaves), blue enameled fill, wide single hook clasp 1.00

BROWNIE

Outline of dancing elf on trefoil in gold color 1.50

Oval with gold colored hand sign and border, 1st issue painted, royal blue background 3.00
2nd issue, blue enamel fill background 1.50

Dancing gold elf 1.00

Plastic, BROWNIE face pin 1.00

Kneeling BROWNIE with dog on chain 1.00

POSITION PIN
CUB SCOUT

1st issue .... Crude type
2nd issue .... Safety pin clasp
3rd issue .... Safety clasp
4th issue .... Clutch back
5th issue .... Double clutch back

Collar brass for leaders, diamond shape with wolf head, says "CUB SCOUTS", paw print, 3rd issue 2.00
5th issue 1.75

Same except says "CUB SCOUTS", has tenderfoot emblem, 3rd issue 1.50
5th issue 1.25

Den mothers shield pin, shield shape, blue and gold, lettering "DEN MOTHER", has 2 eyelets on each side for sewing to hat 5.00

"Assistant Cub Master," gold lettering and border, green enamel, 1st issue
.... 10.00
2nd issue 9.00
3rd issue 8.00
5th issue 7.50

"Cub Master," silver lettering and border, green enamel, 1st issue 10.00
2nd issue 9.00
3rd issue 8.00
5th issue 7.50

"Pack Committeeman," gold lettering and border, blue enamel 1st issue
...... 10.00

2nd issue 9.00
3rd issue 8.00
5th issue 7.50

BOY SCOUT

Musician, miniature button hole, lapel pin, tenderfoot emblem over lyre 10.00

Assistant Patrol Leader, 1st class emblem over 2 green enamel bars, 1st issue
...... 21.00

2nd issue 18.00

Senior Patrol Leader, 1st class emblem ove 2½ green enamel bars, 1st issue
...... 22.00

2nd issue 21.00

Junior Assistant Scoutmaster, 1st class emblem over 3 green enamel bars, 1st
issue 25.00
2nd issue 21.00
Label, miniature 22.00

Assistant Scoutmaster, 1st class emblem, green enamel fill, Goid lettering,
eagle and border, 1st issue 26.00
2nd issue 22.00

Scoutmaster, 1st class emblem, green enamel fill, silver lettering, eagle and
border, 1st issue 26.00
2nd issue 22.00

COLLAR PINS

Over 260 varieties in assorted collar pins, in wreaths, pins, colors, etc.

Assistant Scoutmaster (1st issue) 1st class emblem on round, green enamel
fill pin,no lettering, emblem and border, crude type pin 25.00

Scout Master (1st issue), 1st class emblem on round, green enamel fill pin, no
lettering, emblem and border, crude type pin 25.00

Layman (1st issue), 1st class emblem on round, blue enamel fill pin, gold
emblem and border, no lettering, crude type clasp 22.00

Assistant Scout Master, Scout Master, and Layman (2nd issue), same except
have lettering "BOY SCOUTS OF AMERICA", 1st issue 25.00
2nd issue 20.00
3rd issue 20.00

Assistant Scout Master, Scout Master, and Layman (3rd issue), have safety
clasp pin back pins, 1st issue 20.00
2nd issue 18.00
3rd issue 18.00

Assistant Scout Master, Scout Master, and Layman (4th issue), same except
has a double clutchback, 1st issue   15.00
2nd issue   15.00
3rd issue 15.00

All other positions, commissioners, chaplain, physician, etc. have had
numerous pins available for each position which makes it nearly impossible to
list all of them in this guide. Generally, they all carry the 1st class emblem
and are found on various backgrounds, from circles to wreaths. They are
found in varied enamel colors: blue, purple red-white-blue, white, and yellow.
Theya re found in both gold and silver. The combination of colors and metal
denote the specific position and generally corresponds with the appropriate

patch (see patch section). Values can range from $25.00 to several hundred dollars per pin. So, it is at this point that we stress: "Know your dealer" or at least have a reputable dealer appraise the piece. It is our hope that these positions can be individually listed in future editions.

EMPLOYEE PIN

1st issue, Bronze tenderfoot emblem with red enamel with red fill 22.50

2nd issue, Tenderfoot emblem on circle, silver color, red enamel fill 10.00

Explorer Scout Hat Pin, Tenderfoot emblem on star on compass circle, gold green 30.00

EXPLORER

Assistant Post Advisor, wings-anchor-campass, gold with blue enamel fill 23.00

Post Advisor, wings-anchor-compass, silver with blue enamel fill 24.00

PROMOTIONAL

There have been hundreds of different varieties manufactured over the years, also many were issued by individual councils and bring lesser amounts. The council issue pins will generally sell .50 to $1.50 depending on type, quality and vintage.

BOY SCOUT

Fold back button, white enamel with black imprint of cub, boy and explorer scout, lettering "I'M SELLING SCOUTING." 1.00

Round pin back button, face of scout with campaign hat, dark blue background 1.50

Round pin back, white tenderfoot emblem with white lettering "OPERATION LIFELINE" on red background .... .75

Round pin back button, white lettering "REACH" on red background ..... .50

Round pin back button, blue lettering "REACH" over blue outlined stylized "E" on white background, blue border .... .50

Round fold back button, tenderfoot emblem on red-white-blue background, white lettering "FRIEND OF SCOUTING - BOY SCOUTS OF AMERICA." 1.50

Round fold back button, tenderfoot emblem on red-white-blue background, white lettering "WE'RE BACKING BOY SCOUTS" 1.25

Vertical odd shape fold back button, walking scout with white lettering "I GAVE" on red background 2.00

Large, flashtype button, yellow dollar mark ($) on green circle, green lettering "RAISE A BILLION - '69 - '76" on white border, changes to bust of scout in center and yellow lettering "SERVE" 6,500,000 in 1976" on green 1.50

Square "F-S" in gold on blue background, gold border, clutch back 1.00

GIRL SCOUT

Large round pin back, red-white-blue design, white lettering "50 YEARS OF SERVICE - ibelong (blue) - LOVE TREE AREA GIRL SCOUT COUNCIL (red)", ... .75

Round crude type back, green trefoil and lettering "RIGHT ON!! - TREFOIL TROOP" on yellow background .... .75

Round pin back, green lettering "FIND THE GIFT IN EVERY CHILD" and green girl scout profile symbol on white background 1.00

Top: Operation Lifeline
Pin 75
2nd row, L to R: Boy Scout
"Reach" pin 50
Explorer "Reach" pin
. 50
Uniformed Scout pin 2.00
Bottom: B.S.A. "Commit-
tee" pin 1.50

Top: Post 433 Drum &
Bugle Corps Booster pin
. . . . 1.00
2nd row, L to R: 1979 Show-
ando "Best Ever" pin .50
1921 Boy Scout Booster
pin 2.50
Bottom: 1957 N.J. pin with
bell and ribbon 5.00

RANK
CUB SCOUT

Bob cat, 1st issue, round, bobcat head, lettering "Bob Cat - Cubs B.S.A.," bronze color, crude type clasp 5.00

2nd issue, bobcat head, lettering "Bob Cat - Cub Scouts B.S.A.," bronze color, crude type clasp 2.00

3rd issue, round bobcat head, lettering Bob Cat - Cub Scouts B.S.A.," bronze color, clutch back pin 1.25

4th issue, diamond shape, bobcat head, lettering "BobCat," scout emblem , clutch back pin .... .50

Wolf, 1st issue, diamond shape, wolf head, paw print, lettering "Cubs B.S.A.," crude type clasp 5.00

2nd issue, diamond shape, wolf head, paw print, lettering "Cub Scouts B.S.A.," crude type clasp 2.00

3rd issue, diamond shape, wolf head, paw print, lettering "Cub Scouts B.S.A." clutch back 1.00

4th issue, wolf head, lettering "Wolf" scout emblem, clutch back .... .50

Bear, 1st issue, diamond shape, bear's head, paw print, lettering "Cubs B.S.A.," crude type clasp 5.00

2nd issue diamond shape, bear's head, paw print, lettering "Cub Scouts B.S.A.," crude type clasp 2.00

3rd issue, diamond shape, bear's head, paw print, lettering "Cub Scouts B.S.A.," clutch back 1.00

4th issue, bear's head, lettering "Bear" scout emblem, clutch back ..... .50

Lion, 1st issue diamond shape, lion's head, paw print, lettering "Cubs B.S.A.," crude type clasp 7.50

2nd issue, diamond shape, lion's head, paw print, lettering "Cub Scouts B.S.A.," crude type clasp 5.00

3rd issue, diamond shape, lion's head, paw print, lettering "Cub Scouts B.S.A.," clutch back 1.25

Weblos, 1970, diamond shape, Weblos emblem, lettering "WEBLOS," scout emblem .... .50

ARROW OF LIGHT

Bar type pin, gold emblem on blue enamel fill, double clutch back 1.00

Miniature bar type, lapel pin, gold color with arrow of light emblem, 1st issue has safety clasp pin 2.50

2nd issue, has clutch back 1.00

BOY SCOUT

1st issue pins from early teens had safety clasp pins, top point of fleu-de-lis was rounded

2nd issue had loose hanging double knots, crude type clasp

3rd issue had later type knots and crude clasp

4th issue had safety pin clasp

6th issue, World War II series, was made of thin metal stamped type

7th issue, ca. late 40's-1950, bar mounted safety clasp pin

8th issue, 1950's, pin shield type pin, this type may have been experimental as it was only used for a short time

9th issue, 1970's, pins no longer had loose hanging knots but knots were part of emblem mold

HAT PINS

1st issue had safety pin clasp

2nd issue, thin stamped (WWII) tenderfoot, 2nd class and 1st class only

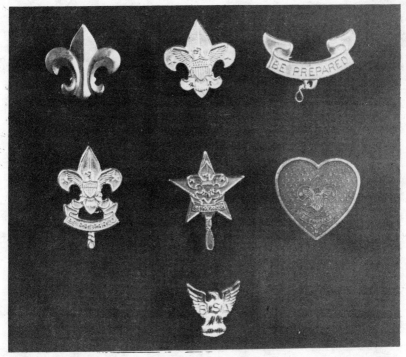

Boy Scout Rank Pins

Top row, L to R: Scout Rank pin 1.50
     Tenderfoot Rank pin 2.00
     2nd Class Rank pin 3.00
     1st Class Rank pin 3.50
     Star Rank pin 4.50
     Life Rank pin 6.00
     Eagle Scout Rank Lapel pin 6.00

There are miniatures and hat pins for all the ranks.

Scout Rank (new rank in 1970's), gold fleu-de-lis, 6th issue .... .75

Tenderfoot, fleu-de-lis with eagle and shield (known generally as scout
    emblem), 1st issue 6.00
2nd issue 6.00
    3rd issue 4.00
    4th issue 3.00
    5th issue 5.00
    6th issue 6.00
    7th issue 2.00
    8th issue 4.00
    9th issue .... .75
2nd Class, bar with lettering "BE PREPARED", has knot suspended below,
    1st issue 11.00
    2nd issue 6.00
    3rd issue 4.00
    5th issue 5.00

6th issue	5.00
7th issue	2.00
8th issue	2.50
9th issue	.50

NOTE: First issue BSA First Class pin 3" variety, crude clasp, rare 50.00

1st Class, scout emblem with stars at eagle's wing tips with bar and lettering "BE PREPARED", knot suspended below, 1st issue	12.00
2nd issue	9.00
3rd issue	6.00
4th issue	5.50
5th issue	8.00
6th issue	11.00
7th issue	4.00
8th issue	7.00
9th issue	.50
Life Badges, emblem on red enameled heart shaped pin, 1st issue	12.00
2nd issue	10.00
3rd issue	10.00
4th issue	5.00
5th issue	not known to exist
6th issue	not known to exist
7th issue	6.00
8th issue	not known to exist
9th issue	1.00

Any rank pins marked "Gold filled" on the back are generally worth about $3.00 more than the price given above for that particular pin.

HAT PINS

Tenderfoot
large, thick metal safety pin clasp	15.00
thin WWII stamped metal, crude type clasp	15.00

2nd Class
Large, thick metal safety pin clasp	20.00
Thin WWII stamped metal, crude type clasp	15.00

1st Class
Large, thick metal, safety pin clasp	15.00
Thin, WWI stamped metal, crude type clasp	15.00

Eagle pins are generally classed as hat pins.

Oval, sterling silver 1st class emblem over red-white-blue enamel, silver border, lettering says "EAGLE SCOUT - BOY SCOUTS OF AMERICA"	75.00
2nd pin, same as above but with B.S.A. on eagle	60.00
Error Pin, where colors were reversed (blue on left, white, red on right)	100.00
Ribbon Bar Pin, red, white, blue crude pin, plain ribbon, Standard Military Size	40.00
Same but with miniature on ribbon bar	40.00
Same only very narrow bar	30.00

EXPLORERS

40's miniature RANGER, powder horn (same as medal)	50.00
50's same as medals (silver award), Type 1	30.00
Type 2	25.00

AIR SCOUT
Ace miniature pin (sterling silver) see medal 50.00

SEA SCOUT
Miniature (sterling silver) Quartermaster medal 20.00
Ribbon bar pin, navy blue ribbon bar (standard size) crude pin 50.00
GIRL SCOUT
Golden eaglette, odd shield shape, gold colored, has eagle in form of shield
..... 100.00-200.00

1st Class pin, green enameled three leaf clover in red enamel circle with bow
at bottom 10.00

TENURE - Service Stars, Girl scouts, Gold colored six pointed stars, 1st issue,
(screwback with flower type screw) 1.75
2nd issue (screwback with gear type screw) 1.25
3rd issue (clutch back) .... .75
4th issue, same as 3rd issue with colored plastic discs denoting program, red
for senior girl scouts, white for cadets, yellow for Junior girl scouts, green
for Brownies .... .25

Membership numeral guard pins (or chains) go from 5 to 50 in roman numeral
(by 5 increments) and in arabic numbers go 5 to 65 (by 5 increments).
Roman Numeral 1.00-2.50
Arabic Numbers 75-2.00

Boy Scouts - Service Stars
Gold colored

1st issue, screwback with gear type disc, had felt background as follows:
yellow felt - cub scout 1.00-1.25
green felt - boy scout 1.00-1.25
red felt - 5 year 2.00
purple felt - 10 year 3.50
blue felt, adult leader 1.25-2.50
Ones with screwbacks, besides being a plain star were numbered from 1 to 30
in one year increments and 5 year increments thereafter.

Same pin with clutch back plain star, yellow plastic disc is cub
Green plastic disc for Boy Scout
Red plastic disc for Explorer
Blue plastic disc for Adult Leader
These also exist numbered from 1 to 10 by 1 year increments and from 70 by 5
year increments.

BOY SCOUT VETERAN PINS
5 year is diamond shape with 1st class emblem safety clasp pin 10.00
10 year, round with 1st class emblem on blue enamel with roman numeral X
..... 9.00
15 year, round 1st class emblem over roman numeral 15 on blue enamel
...... 10.00
20 year, same as above but roman numeral 20 .... 10.00
25 year, round sterling silver has tenderfoot emblem, pin says "TWENTY
FIVE YEAR VETERAN", safety clasp pin 15.00
30 year, round 1st class emblem over roman numeral 30, blue enamel . 12.00
35 year, round 1st class emblem has arabic 35 at bottom 10.00
40 years, same as above except has arabic number 40 .... 8.00
45 year, same as above except has arabic number 45 .... 8.00

2nd issue, in 5 year increments, starting at 5 through 65, irregular round shape, tenderfoot emblem on gold, arabic numerals at bottom against gold background, border is blue enamel, clutch back, except for 25 year pin . 5.00

2nd issue, 25 year pin, sterling silver 12.00

3rd issue, round tenderfoot emblem on gold color background, arabic numeral at bottom on blue enamel rear of border also blue enamel, start with 10 year to 70 in 5 year increments, clutch back, except for 25 year pin 2.00

3rd issue, 25 year pin, sterling silver 5.00

MISCELLANOUS

1953, round pin, gold color, covered wagon says 'NATIONAL JAMBOREE IRVINE RANCH, CALIFORNIA, 1953", no enamel , clutch 15.00

1957, round, kneeling Washington says "NATIONAL JAMBOREE VALLEY FORGE", clutch 7.00

1957, round pin back says "4th BOY SCOUTS JAMBOREE VALLEY FORGE PENNSYLVANIA 1957" in blue on white background, has bell on bottom and purple ribbon , clutch 6.00

1957, says "B.S.A. also ONWARD FOR GOD AND MY COUNTRY", no enamel 6.00

1960, round, gold color, says "NATIONAL JAMBOREE-COLORADO SPRINGS", plain enamel 6.00

1964, round, gold color, kneeling Washington says "NATIONAL JAMBOREE VALLEY FORGE-BOY SCOUTS OF AMERICA", also "1964" 6.00

1967, rectangular, WORLD JAMBOREE, Gold color, has fleur-de-lis, mountain range and says "WORLD JAMBOREE 1967", also in enamel pin, Plain
...... 4.50

Enamel , clutch 6.00

1969, round, gold color, sasy "NATIONAL JAMBOREE-IDAHO," has deer and landscape, also in enamel pin, plain 4.00

Enamel 5.00

1973, square, gold color, tree design with scout emblem upper right corner, also in enamel pin, Plain, 2.00

Enamel 3.00

1977, rectangle, gold color, "National Scout Jamboree-1977", red, white blue background, compass in center white portion, scout emblem in upper left red portion (1977 in blue) also in enamel pin 1.50

Enamel 2.50

Oval shape-green enamel, IDAHO on gold background, white border, lettering says "GIRL SCOUTS - SENIOR ROUNDUP" 5.00

Odd shape, white enamel filled daisy on green enamel, gold colored banner with "JULIETTE LOW BIRTHPLACE" in green 2.50

50th Anniversary Pin, round, trefoil in green, "50" in center, on white background, green border with lettering "GIRL SCOUTS OF THE U.S.A. 1912-1962" 2.50

NAME BADGE PINS

2nd issue, Bars with small cub to side, double clutch back, various titles .. 3.50

Schiff Scout reservation name badge holder, green tulip on cream color card inserts with plastic card holder with pin 4.00

1971 National Order AC Name Badge, button type with clear acetate window for name white celluloid reads "National Conference O.A. Committee"
...... 4.00

ORDER OF THE ARROW PINS

1973 NOAC Pin, White plastic with red printed Indian Head (for National Committee) 10.00

Top row, L to R: 35 year Veteran pin, 1st issue 10.00
    35 year Veteran pin, 2nd issue 5.00
    35 year Veteran pin, 3rd issue 2.00
2nd row, L to R: Cub Wolf pin with BSA and pawprint ... 5.00
    Cub Bear pin with Scout Emblem .... .50
    Cub Lion pin with BSA and pawprint 7.50
3rd row, L to R: Cub Leaders pin, gold with blue enamel . 1.00
    Cub Summertime Pack Award pin .... .50
    Miniature Commissioners pin, 1930's 18.00
    Commissioners Knot Service pin 1.00
4th row, L to R: 1973 N. J. brass pin 4.00
    1973 N. J. enameled pin 6.00
    Explorer "E" miniature pin, 1970's 1.00
    Scout handsign pin 2.00
Bottom row, L to R: O.A. Vigil Honor lapel pin 3.50
O.A. Silver Arrow pin for lapel 1.00

MEDALS

Contest - (standard issue)
1st place .... gold color
2nd place .... silver color
3rd place .... bronze color
All are octagonal with ribbon
Cub Scout ribbon is blue and yellow, Boy Scout ribbon is red and white, 1st
    place 3.00
    2nd place 2.50
    3rd place 2.00
1st issue of Boy Scout medal had 1st Class emblem (40's and 50's), 1st place
    .... 8.00
    2nd place 7.00
    3rd place 6.00
2nd issue of Boy Scout medal had tenderfoot emblem (late 60's), 1st place
    .... 3.50
    2nd place 3.00
    3rd place 2.50
Explorer (50's) had wings-anchor-compass emblem, 1st place 10.00
    2nd place 9.00
    3rd place 8.00
Cubs also have round medals in gold color, silver color and bronze for Pine
    Wood Derby, Space Derby and Regatta, medals are smaller and ribbons
    more narrow than standard issue 2.00
Explorers - (60's) Explorer Olympics, 1st place, gold color 7.00

Explorers - (60's) Explorer Olympics, medal has wreath with figure in center
    with raised arms, 1st place, gold color 7.00
    2nd place, silver color 6.00
    3rd place, bronze 5.00
Teens - 1929, all medals are suspended from folded ribbon, one end of ribbon is
    fringed, gold color, silver color and bronze. There were 4 field event
    medals:
    Sprints (runner in crouched starting position) 15.00
    Cross-country (runner upright) 15.00
    Tug-o-war 15.00
    Swimming 15.00
Others from the teens - '29 included two for rally prizes:
    Irregular round shape with wreath 20.00
    Octagonal with wreath 18.00
Signal Award - irregular round shape with wreath, has crossed semaphore
    flags and torch 20.00
First Aid Award - has seated Liberty with eagle and flags, has cross in right
    lower side 20.00

1929-CA. '39

Medals are round and suspended from three striped ribbon, all are found in
    gold color, silver color and bronze and were awarded for signaling, cooking,
    bugling, knife and axe, knot typing, camping, wall scaling, firemaking,
    handicraft, tent pitching, tower building, archery, canoeing, bridge building
    ..... 12.00-20.00

Three medals were issued in an irregular round shape in gold color, silver color and bronze suspended from red, white and blue ribbon:

Track, runner in crouched starter position, 1st place 12.00
    2nd place 10.00
    3rd place 10.00
Cross Country, runner and half wreath, 1st place 12.00
    2nd place 10.00
    3rd place 8.00
Cross country, runner and half wreath, 1st place 10.00
    2nd place 8.00
    3rd place 6.00

DISTINGUISHED AWARDS

SILVER FAWN - sterling silver on neck ribbon .... discontinued 85.00

SILVER BEAVER - up to '80 was sterling silver on a ribbon of light blue, white, light blue. In 1980 they began producing them in Rhodium rather than silver. Value of silver 40.00-50.00
    Rhodium 25.00

SILVER ANTELOPE - sterling silver on ribbon of yellow, orange, white, yellow, orange 200.00

SILVER BUFFALO - sterling silver on ribbon of red, white, red old var. 300.00

SILVER WORLD - round replica of globe with sterling silver on blue enamel, red and white striped ribbon .... old variety 450.00

New variety, 1970-83, less 25 per cent

GRAY RUNNING WOLF - Sterling silver wolf suspended from ribbon (extremely rare since only 1 per year is awarded to an American Indian) 300.00

<table>
<tr><td align="center">SILVER BEAVER
Medallion is silver and is suspended from a lt. blue, white, lt. blue neck ribbon, silver varieties 60.00-70.00
Rhodium .... 40.00</td><td align="center">BSA DISTINGUISHED AWARDS
SILVER ANTELOPE
Medallion is silver and is suspended from a yellow, white, yellow neck ribbon .... 300.00</td></tr>
</table>

SILVER BUFFALO
Medallion is silver and is suspended from red, white, red neck ribbon
.... 500.00

SILVER WORLD
Medallion is silver with blue enamel and is suspended from red & white striped neck ribbon 800.00

ORDER OF THE ARROW DISTINGUISHED SERVICE AWARD - silver arrowhead (arrow through) suspended from white ribbon with red arrows
...... 75.00

SILVER-A-HEAD, green ribbon 45.00

COUNCIL ISSUE DISTINGUISHED AWARDS
William T. Hornaday Award - medal depicts land, forest, mountain and water for conservation. Supspended on green neck ribbon (extremely rare)
...... 125.00

Liberty Bell - oval with Liberty Bell on plain light blue ribbon, from Philadelphia Council, ca. 1950's 25.00

Long Rifle + Tennessee long rifle on ribbon from Middle Tennessee Council
..... 20.00

TRAIL MEDALS
Historic trail medals number in the hundreds. Keep in mind that extinct trail medals bring slightly more, as do other variations 5.00-12.00

TRAINING
Den Mothers Training Award - tenderfoot emblem on diamond shape, ribbon is white with one green stripe 3.00

Den Leader Coach Training Award - tenderfoot emblem on diamond shape, white ribbon with two green stripes 3.00

Note: the following are often found with miniature pins affixed to denote the program for which earned.

Scouters Training Award - 1st issue - tenderfoot emblem on "A", solid green ribbon 10.00

2nd issue - tenderfoot emblem on "A", green ribbon with one thin white stripe 4.50

Scouters Key Award - 1st class emblem on key, green ribbon, white stripes
...... 15.00

2nd issue, tenderfoot emblem on key, green ribbon with wide white stripe
...... 5.00

WAR SERVICE
WWI - Liberty Loan Medals (1st-5th) silver color, red ribbon (includes "Victory" medal), add 5.00 for each bar attached 50.00
War Savings Service Ace, oval on red, white, blue ribbon, also found with large palms affixed 50.00
Victory Liberty Loan Medal, round silver colored medal with hole punched in top and red ribbon 50.00
WWII - Eisenhower Waste Paper Campaign, small bronze likeness of IKE suspended from small red, white, blue, ribbon, 1st issue 20.00
2nd issue, same suspended from red & white striped ribbon band 12.00
MacArthur Victory Garden - suspended from red ribbon 20.00
suspended from green ribbon 16.00

HIKING TRAIL MEDALS
Top row, L to R: Wa-Ha-La Trail medal 5.00
Pan Beard Trail medal 6.00
President's Trail medal 6.00
Red Caboose Trail medal 6.00
Center row, L to R: Old Bison Trail medal 6.00
Ozark-Shawnee Trail medal (restricted) 15.00
Black Hawk Trail medal (3rd issue) 6.00
Chief Shablona Trail medal 6.00
Bottom row, L to R: Anthony Wayne Trail medal 6.00
Capitol View Trail medal 6.00
Silver Moccasin Trail medal 6.00
Pioneer Trail medal 6.00

B.S.A. TRAINING MEDALS
L to R: Scouters Training Award, 1st issue 10.00
Scouters Training Award, 2nd issue 4.50
Scoutmaster Key Award, 2nd issue 5.00
Den Leaders Training Award 3.00
Den Leader Coach's Training Award 3.00

LIFE SAVING
Highest award, Honor Medal, gold with blue and red on solid red ribbon, 1st
Maltese cross medallion suspended from folded red ribbon 350.00
  2nd , round, gold with blue and red on solid red ribbon 200.00
2nd highest award, Medal of Merit - tenderfoot emblem and feather, blue
enamel fill, ribbon is yellow, blue, yellow 110.00
3rd highest award, issued in 1980 tenderfoot emblem and feather but red
enamel fill on gold, ribbon is red, white, red 85.00

RELIGIOUS (Have Pins to Match)
Armenian Church of America:
ARARAT MEDAL - Cross suspended from solid dark blue ribbon attached to
bar with letters "ARARAT" 15.00
Baptist:
GOD AND COUNTRY MEDAL - shield shape with circle in center (inside
circle is open bible and cross), bar across top of shield with lettering
"BAPTIST", shield is suspended from solid ribbon attached to bar with
lettering "GOD AND COUNTRY" 10.00
Buddhist:
METTA MEDAL - spoked wheel design (similar to ships wheel) attached to
bar with lettering "METTA" (no ribbon) 10.00
SANGHA MEDAL - spoked wheel designed suspended from five striped
ribbon attached to bar with lettering "SANGHA" 15.00
Church of Jesus Christ of Latter-Day Saints (Mormon)
DUTY TO GOD MEDAL - a steer skull with circular insignia suspended from
green, yellow, green striped ribbon attached to bar with lettering "DUTY
TO GOD" 18.00

WAR SERVICE MEDALS

Top row, L to R: WWI Liberty Loan medal with 4 bars
    attached 50.00
    Victory Liberty Loan medal 50.00
    WWI War Savings Service Ace medal 50.00
2nd row, L to R: WWI War Savings Service "WSS" pin back
    button 8.00
    Third Liberty Loan pin back button 6.00
    Fourth Liberty Lan pin back button 6.00
    Fifth (Victory) Liberty Loan pin back button 5.00
3rd row, L to R: Eisenhower Masterpaper Campaign medal
    (2nd issue) 15.00
    Eisenhower Masterpaper Campaign medal (1st issue)
    ...... 25.00
    MacArthur Victory Garden medal (green ribbon) ... 25.00
Bottom row, L to R: WWII War Loan Gallant Ribbon Bar
    ...... 12.00
    War Production Board, 1,000 LB. Wastepaper label button
    ...... 10.00

CURRENT ISSUE: LIFE SAVING MERIT
left: MEDAL OF MERIT (2nd highest) medallion is gold colored, outer ring has blue enamel fill, ribbon is yellow, blue, yellow 110.00

center: HONOR MEDAL (highest), medallion is gold colored with red, white, blue center, ribbon is solid red 135.00

right: LIFESAVING MEDAL (3rd highest), medallion is gold colored, outer ring has red enamel fill, ribbon is red, white, red 85.00
Older issues merit more money.

FAITH IN GOD - oval medallion depicting family and church and rope border suspended from bar with lettering "Faith In God" 12.00

ON MY HONOR - Fleur-de-lis medallion with boy blowing horn suspended from green, yellow ribbon attached to bar with wording "On My Honor" 15.00

Reorganized Church of Jesus Christ of Latter-Day Saints
LIGHT OF THE WORLD - medallion is Stylized Globe with cross at top depicting a girl, a lion, a fawn, suspended from a blue, yellow, blue ribbon attached to a bar with lettering "World Community" 15.00

Eastern Orthodox Church:
ALPHA OMEGA MEDAL - cross suspended from light blue ribbon with 7 narrow white stripes, attached to bar with lettering "ALPHA OMEGA" 12.00

CHI RHO - red and white enameled fill cross suspended from bar with lettering "Chi Rho" 10.00

Episcopal:
GOD AND COUNTRY MEDAL - Shield shape with cross on it and blue field with stars in upper left quadrant suspended from solid red ribbon attached to bar with lettering "GOD AND COUNTRY" 10.00

GOD AND FAMILY - same with gold bar at top of medal which says "GOD AND FAMILY", medal is suspended directly from "God and Country" bar, no ribbon 8.00

Islamic:
IN THE NAME OF GOD MEDAL - irregular shaped octagon suspended from solid green ribbon attached to bar with lettering "In The Name of God the Beneficient, the Merciful" 20.00

Jewish:
ALEPH MEDAL - diamond shape suspended from bar with lettering' "ALEPH" 10.00
NER TAMID MEDAL - irregular shaped medallion suspended from blue, white ribbon attached to bar with lettering "Eternal Light" 10.00

Lutheran:
PRO DEO ET PATRIA MEDAL - shield shape with cross suspended from solid blue attached to bar with lettering "PRO DEO ET PATRIA" 10.00
PRO DEO ET PATRI - GOD AND FAMILY - shield shape with cross, lettering on top of shield says "GOD AND FAMILY" - medal suspended from bar only with lettering "PRO DEO ET PATRIA" 8.00

Polish National Catholic:
BOG I OJCZYZNA - Red cross on white shield suspended from solid blue ribbon with bar with lettering "GOD AND COUNTRY" affixed to the ribbon is an emblem depicting an open bible, cross, sheaf and scrolls 20.00

Protestant:
GOD AND COUNTRY MEDAL - Shield shape with cross, "GOD AND FAMILY" at top of shield, suspended from bar with lettering "GOD AND COUNTRY" 9.00
Shield shape with cross, says "GOD AND CHURCH" at top of shield, suspended from solid blue ribbon attached to bar with lettering "GOD AND COUNTRY" 8.00
Shield shape with cross, says "GOD AND LIFE" at top of shield, attached to bar with lettering "GOD AND COUNTRY" 8.00

Roman Catholic:
AD ALTARE DEI - cross suspended from multi-striped ribbon attached to bar with lettering "AD ALTARE DEI" 8.00
PARVULT DEI - diamond shape suspended from bar with lettering "PARVULI DEI" 7.00
PIUS XII - triangular shape suspended from two yellow, white ribbons attached to bar with lettering "PLUS XII" 10.00

Salvation Army:
SILVER CREST - 1st issue, red, yellow, blue ribbon bar with small medallion in center 11.00
2nd issue, small medallion suspended from red, yellow, blue ribbon bar 8.00
GOD AND COUNTRY - blue enameled fill medallion with lettering "The Salvation Army" suspended from solid blue ribbon attached to bar with lettering "God and Country" 10.00
GOD AND LIFE - same with medallion attached directly to bar, no ribbon 10.00

Unitarian Universalist:
RELIGION IN LIFE - replica of globe with eternal flame, suspended from solid blue ribbon, attached to bar with lettering "RELIGION IN LIFE" 12.00

Eastern Rite Catholic:
LIGHT IS LIFE - Maltese cross medallion suspended from blue ribbon attached to bar with lettering "Light Is Life" 11.00

SCOUTING RELIGIOUS MEDALS
Upper left: God and Country (Protestant) medal, 1st design
...... 10.00
Upper center: God and Country lapel pin, safety clasp in
...... 3.50
Lower center: Ad Altare Dei (Catholic) medal 8.00
Upper right: God and Country (Episcopal) medal 10.00

RANK

Eagle - feathers all sides except 4th issue, all suspended from red, white, blue ribbons, 1st issue, "scrawny" eagle in silver, has pot metal appearance 110.00

2nd issue, silver eagle finely designed, double knot suspended from bar 85.00

3rd issue, silver eagle not engraved as well as 2nd issue, single knot wire, wings curved and no "BSA" on eagle 45.00

4th issue, silver eagle has flat reverse side with no "BSA" on eagle, single knot wire 40.00

5th issue, silver eagle is finely engraved with "BSA", single wire knot . 35.00

6th issue, eagle not as finely engraved at 5th issue, has single wire knot, "BSA" on eagle 25.00

7th issue, same as 6th issue but in Rhodium, not silver, believed to have 1st been issued in 1980 .... 20.00

EXPLORER SILVER AWARD MEDAL, 2nd issue 140.00

SEA SCOUT EXPLORER

Quartermaster award, 1st issue, ships wheel (silver) suspended from solid
    navy ribbon 50.00
    2nd issue, ships wheel (nickel) suspended from solid navy ribbon 40.00

Ribbon bar pin for above, ca. 1930's, solid blue 30.00

AIR SCOUT-EXPLORER

Ace model, silver compass with eagle and plane 625.00

Explorer Medals:

40's - RANGER AWARD - sunburst over compass, powder horn in center,
    suspended on ribbon 400.00

50's - SILVER AWARD - (1st type) wings, anchor, compass suspended on red
    and yellow ribbon (extremely rare with ribbon in good condition) 350.00
    SILVER AWARD - (2nd type), silver compass with flying eagle suspended
    from white ribbon with narrow red and narrow blue stripe 140.00

50's - GOLD AWARD - wings, anchor, compass suspended from ribbon, medal
    is gold in color, extremely rare 400.00

GIRL SCOUTS

Thanks Badge Medal - (for adults) gold filled with red, white, blue design
    (trefoil with triangle in center - all in circle) 8.00

Life Savings Award:

Bronze Cross - has girl scout emblem in center suspended from red ribbon,
    attached to bar with lettering "FOR VALOR" 50.00

Gold Trefoil - has embedded diamond in trefoil suspended from red ribbon
    attached to plain gold bar 50.00

WORLD JAMBOREE (U.S. Contingent) MEDALS

1920 .... 1200.00
1924 .... 1200.00
1929 .... 250.00
1933 .... 800.00

RINGS, PINS, CUFF BUTTONS

Scout Jewelry Set, sterling silver scarf pin, cuff links and tie clasp, each
    article die stamped with tenderfoot badge 10.00
    Same as above but has 2nd class emblem die stamped 15.00
    Same as above but has 1st class emblem die stamped 15.00

Sterling Silver Ring has 1st class emblem and rope design on outside edge
    ...... 20.00

Sterling Silver Ring, bears 1st class emblem 8.50

Gold Filled Ring, bears 1st class emblem 15.00

Solid Gold Ring, bears 1st class emblem 20.00

Sterling Lapel Pins, bears 1st class emblem 2.50

WATCH FOBS
Scout

Tenderfoot 20.00
Tenderfoot Patrol Leader 30.00
Tenderfoot 20.00
Tenderfoot Patrol Leader 20.00
Second Class 22.00
Second Class Patrol Leader 42.00
First Class 29.00
First Class Patrol Leader 44.00
First Class Scouts' Fob, gold plated, rose finish without enamel 50.00

WATCH FOBS
Leader
The following are rolled gold, rose finish, enamel, heavy silk ribbon.
Assistant Scoutmaster 25.00
Scoutmaster, green ribbon 25.00
Assistant Deputy Scout Commissioner, light blue ribbon 30.00
Deputy Scout Commissioner, dark blue ribbon 30.00
Scout Commissioner, dark blue ribbon, has wreath on fob 65.00
Troop Committees and Local Councils, white ribbon with wreath on fob
...... 25.00

TIE BARS
Tie Bars were issued in basically 2 sizes called "regular bar" and "short bar" types. Unless designated as "short bar", all are assumed to be "regular bar" size.
Merit Badge Counselor 1.00
100 Club 1.25
Century Club 1.25
Major Member 1.25
Philmont Scout Ranch short bar 3.00
Schiff Scout Reservation 5.00
Tenderfoot 1.00
1st Class 1.25
1st Class, large emblem, short bar 3.50
Sea Explorer, E on anchor 1.50
Tenderfoot emblem, gold, chain type 2.00
1st Class emblem, gold, chain type 3.00
Explorer, 1950's emblem (wings, anchor, compass), chain type 3.50
Explorer, 1960's emblem (circle V), chain type 2.00
Explorer, 1960's emblem (circle V), bar type 1.50
1967 World Jamboree 6.00
1971 World Jamboree 5.50
1973 National Jamboree 6.00
1975 World Jamboree 4.00
1977 National Jamboree 3.50
1981 National Jamboree 2.50

PATCHES

We have tried here to give a fair representation of the various patches issued by Scouting over the years. No work of this kind could possibly list every patch issued as that would include well over a million patches. So, keep in mind that there are often many variations of the patch and each variation can vary in value. In the case of council insignia, some councils have issued many different patches over the years and some have not. The older issues will generally be worth more, as well as those that were issued in limited quantity. Remember, all values given are for "MINT" condition items. Used patches will be worth less.

ACHIEVEMENT

BSA 20 Night Camper, rectangle, embroidered twill 2.00

1st year 100 per cent Camper, round, embroidered twill 1.00

National President Unit Award, rectangle, embroidered twill, white on light
    blue, set of 4, each .... .75
    No Star, One Star, Two Star, Three Star Honor Unit '78, '79, '80, set 3.00

Paul Bunyan Axman Award:
    Axe shape, embroidered red axe on white twill, black cut edge 4.00
    Axe shape, embroidered black axe with red handle on white 3.00
    Silk woven red axe on black (strip type), rectangle 6.00
    Same on white silk 6.00
    (Axe shape) embroidered black axe and handle on white twill, red cut edge
    .... 1.00
    (Rectangle shape, embroidered black axe, red handle on white twill says
    "Paul Bunyan Axeman Award" 1.00

Mile Swim, round, embroidered twill 1.00

Historic Trails, light brown leather 4.00
    Dark brown leather 2.00
    Embroidered twill, rectangle 1.00

50 Miler Award, Muleskin 6.00
    Light brown leather 5.00
    Dark brown leather 2.00
    Embroidered twill, rectangle 1.00

Interpreter Strips, rectangle, embroidered twill, 1st series 1.50-3.00
    2nd series 50-1.00

Pope Paul the 6th Unit Recognition (embroidered) 1.50

Scout Life Guard, 3" square, life ring on crossed oars over tender foot emblem
    on blue twill, red rope border, cut edge says "Scout Lifeguard BSA", square
    ...... 2.00
    3" diamond, life ring over crossed oars over tender foot emblem on blue
    twill, red rope border, cut edge, says "Scout Lifeguard BSA" 1.00

Local Standard Senior Scout Unit, rectangle, embroidered 6.00

Regional Standard Senior Scout Unit, rectangle, embroidered 10.00

National Standard Senior Scout Unit, rectangle, embroidered 8.00

Local Standard Explorer Unit, rectangle, embroidered 3.00

Regional Standard Explorer Unit rectangle, embroidered 3.00

National Standard Explorer Unit, rectangle, embroidered 4.00

Local Standard Flagship Unit, rectangle, embroidered 7.00

Regional Standard Flagship Unit, rectangle, embroidered 10.00
National Standard Flagship Unit, rectangle, embroidered 12.00
Long Cruise, square, fully embroidered on both white and navy, each 3.00
    Red Arc for long cruise 1.00
    White Arc for long cruise 1.00
World Conservation, round, embroidered twill 1.50

MERIT BADGES

Merit Badges, 1st, embroidered on square tan material 5.00-8.00
    NOTE: Wide and narrow, tan crimped, wide, $2.00 more
    2nd, embroidered on crimped edge tan 3.00-6.00
    3rd, embroidered on crimped edge khaki 1.25-3.50
    4th, embroidered on khaki twill, rolled edge 75-2.00
    5th, fully embroidered, rolled edge, cloth back 50-1.00
    6th, fully embroidered, rolled edge, plastic back .... .50
Air Scout, tan crimped edges on tan background 15.00
    Tan crimped edges fully embroidered on blue background 10.00
    Fully embroidered on powder blue crimped edge 15.00
    Fully embroidered on khaki crimped edge 10.00

RATING STRIPS

Explorer 4.00-8.00
Air Scout 10.00-25.00
Explorer Senior Scout Segments 8.00-15.00
Handicapped Scout Segments, each 1.00

ANNIVERSARY

50th Anniversary Set (6) 125.00
North Carolina 50th variety, rare 50.00
Cub Scout Jubilee Patches, round, embroidered twill 5.00
    Round, woven 5.00
Jubilee Camporee, round, embroidered twill 4.00
Jubilee Field Day, round, embroidered twill 6.00
Schiff Scout Reservation (Jubilee) round, embroidered twill 60.00
Philmount Scout Ranch (Jubilee) round, embroidered twill both rectangular
    ...... 40.00
50th Anniversary Achievement Award, (2), rectangular, embroidered felt
    ...... 3.50
    Rectangular, woven silk 7.00
1960 National Jamboree, round, embroidered twill 10.00
    Embroidered back patch, round, embroidered twill 18.00
    Leather back patch, round 22.00
Cub Scout 50th Anniversary (1980) diamond, embroidered twill 1.00
OA, 50th Anniversary Achievement award strip, white twill, 1 cut edge .. 10.00
    60th Anniversary, odd shape, embroidered twill 5.00
Girl Scout, 50th Anniversary patch 10.00
International Year of the Child, square, embroidered twill 2.00

Girl Scout, 50th Anniversary patch, International Year of the Child, square,
    embroidered twill 5.00
American Revolution, Bi-Centennial, rectangle, embroidered twill 2.00
100th Anniversary, birth of Juliette Low, ship style, green with daisy in center,
    1860 on left, 1960 on right, embroidered twill 2.50

PAUL BUNYAN AXEMAN AWARD PATCH
Top: red on black, woven silk 6.00
2nd from top: red on white, woven silk 6.00
3rd from top: embroidered patch, black axehead & handle,
    red cut edge border 1.00
bottom: embroidered patch with rolled edge 1.00

INTERPRETER STRIPS

Top to bottom: I speak Italian strip, 1st series 1.50
Italian strip, 2nd series .... .50
Spanish strip, 2nd series .... .50
Japanese strip, 2nd series 1.00
German strip, 2nd series .... .50
Polish strip, 2nd series .... .75
French strip, 2nd series .... .50
Yiddish strip, 2nd series .... .75

Boy Scout Bi-Centennial Gift, rectangle, embroidered twill 2.00
  Be prepared for life, rectangle, embroidered twill 2.00
  Heritage 76, rectangle, embroidered twill 2.00
  Festival U.S.A., rectangle, embroidered twill 2.00
  Horizons 76, rectangle, embroidered twill 2.00
  Bi-Centennial, set of above 5 .... 12.00
Scouting Spirit 76, shield, embroidered twill 1.50
Growing with America 76, round, embroidered twill 1.50

BACKPACKING AND HIKING
10 Miler, Du Page Council 800 Miler Award, Main back patch, "1st 50 miles"
  the early patch is rectangle, embroidered twill with plain 1st class emblem
...... 5.00
  "1st 50 miles" fully embroidered rectangle, 1st class emblem has shield
...... 5.00
  Eight additional mileage segments, rectangle, each 1.00
Evanston, Illinois Century Club, One Main patch, diamond, embroidered twill
...... 2.50
  Cycling, 1,000 miles, 4 segments of 250, each 1.25
  Hiking, up to 2,500 miles, 25 segments, each 1.00
  Canoeing, 1,000 miles, 10 segments, each 1.25
There are other long distance awards, all valued at from anywhere from
..... 1.00-10.00

CAMP
There are numerous patches for each Scout camp, all issued originally by the
  local council, old types, felt embroidered, each   1.00-3.00
  Embroidered, each 50-1.50

CAMPOREE
Council issue 50-1.00
National issues bring slightly higher.

CANOEING
Local issue 75-1.00

COMMUNITY STRIPS
  Community strips, all embroidered twill, arc, red on khaki, 30's to 50's (Boy
  Scout) 2.00
  Yellow on blue, 30's to 60's (Cub Scout) 2.00
  White on blue, 30's to 60's (Cub Scout) 2.50
  White on blue, 30's to 58 (Sea Scout)................................. 2.50
  Blue on white, 30's to 58 (Sea Scout) 2.50
  Royal blue on light blue, 50-58 (Air Scout) 4.00
  Brown on green, 48-60's (Explorer) 2.50
  White on red, 60-70's (all program) 50-1.00

Top row, L to R: B.S.A. Instructor patch 1.25
   Mile Swim patch 1.00
Middle: Aquatic Instructor patch 1.00
Bottom row, L to R: Scout Life Guard patch 2.00
   Scout Life Guard patch 1.00

EXPLORER INTERPRETA STRIPS
Top row, L to R: Aviation 4.00
   Weather 4.00
2nd row, L to R: Communications 3.00
   Physical Fitness 3.50
3rd row, L to R: Mechanics 3.50
   Seamanship 4.00
4th row, L to R: Emergency Skills 5.00
   Navigation 4.00
Bottom row, L to R: Craft Skills 3.00
   vocational Exploration 3.50

B.S.A. BI-CENTENNIAL PATCHES, each 2.00
Set of 5 .... 12.00

Top row, L to R: 1965 Senior Girl Scout Roundup patch . 10.00
Juliette Gordon Low Scout, center patch 2.00
Center: Juliette Low birthplace pin 3.00
Bottom: Girl Scout, 100th Anniversary of birth of Juliette
Low strip patch 2.50

94

COUNCIL PATCHES

Abraham Lincoln Council, oval, red letters, man walking, white twill, brown
rolled edge 2.50
   oval, red letters, man walking, blue twill, brown rolled edge 2.00
Adobe Walls Area Council, round, red letters, Scout and Indian, white twill,
black rolled edge 5.00
   Round, red letters, Scout and Indian, white twill, black rolled edge 2.50
   Round, red letters, Scout and Indian, white twill, red rolled edge 2.00
Akron Area Council, round with tab, white silkscreened Indian and letters,
blue felt 20.00
   Round with tab, white silkscreened Indian and letters, green felt 10.00
Alabama-Florida Council, diamond, red letters, Indian headdress, white twill,
blue cut edge 2.50
Alameda.Council, dome, yellow letters, constoga wagon, white twill, blue cut
edge 5.00
   Dome, white letters outlined in black, green twill, black cut edge 3.00
   Square, blue and red letters, white twill, light blue rolled edge 2.00
Alamo Area Council, round, hat and fleu de lis, white and brown field, brown
rolled edge 2.00
   Round, Alamo and needle, yellow field, brown rolled edge, brown letters
   ...... 2.00
Alaska Council, round, blue and red letters, white twill, gold cut edge ... 15.00
Allegheny Highlands Council, odd shape, blue letters, first anniversary, white
twill, red rolled edge 2.75
   Round, green letters, yellow twill, green rolled edge 2.00
Aloha Council, round, gold letters, American Samoa, red twill, gold rolled
edge 4.00
   Round, gold letters, Guam, red twill, gold rolled edge 3.50
   Round, gold letters, Hawaii, red twill, gold rolled edge 3.00
   Round, gold letters, Kwajalein, red twill, gold rolled edge 4.50
   Round, gold letters, Marshall Islands, red twill, gold rolled edge 4.50
   Round, gold letters, Micronesia, red twill, gold rolled edge 5.00
   Round, gold letters, Midway, red twill, gold rolled edge 4.50
   Round, gold letters, Wake Island, red twill, gold rolled edge 4.50
Anthony Wayne Area Council, Round, blue letters, scale, orange twill, red
rolled edge 2.00
Anthracite Council, round, black letters, gold fleur de lis, white twill, red
rolled edge 10.00
Appalachian Council, dome, red and blue letters, turquoise twill, white rolled
edge 2.75
   Round, red letters, conestoga wagon, white twill, black rolled edge 2.00
Arbuckle Area Council, dome, red letters, navy blue twill, turquoise cut edge
   ...... 2.50
Arrowhead Council, round, blue letters, Indian and teepee, green twill, brown
cut edge 3.50
   Round, blue letters, Indian and teepee, white twill, red rolled edge 2.75
   Round, red letters, Lincoln and arrowhead, green twill, green cut edge . 2.50
Arrowhead Area Council, round with two hanging feathers, black letters,
white twill, red cut edge 5.00
   Round, red and blue letters, 50th anniversary, gold field, blue rolled
edge 3.00

Diamond, black letters, fleur de lis, white twill, red cut edge 2.50
Atlanta Area Council, round, green letters, man and burro, white twill, green
    cut edge 3.50
    Round, white letters, black twill, black rolled edge 2.00
Audubon Council hat, red letters, cardinal and pallet, green twill, yellow cut
    edge 4.00
    Hat, red letters, cardinal and pallet, gray twill, yellow cut edge 3.00
    Hat, red letters, cardinal and pallet, white twill, yellow cut edge 2.25
Badger Council, round, black letters, badger, orange twill, brown rolled edge
    ...... 10.00
Bay Area Council, hat, green letters, camping scene, gray twill, red cut edge
    ...... 2.75
    Round, red letters, palm and dolphin, blue twill, red rolled edge 2.00
Bay Lakes Council, rectangle, white letters, pale green twill, gold rolled edge
    ...... 5.00
Bayonne Council, round, black letters, red twill, gray rolled edge 2.25
Black Beaver Council, round, black letters, Indian and state, turquoise twill,
    black rolled edge 2.50
    Round, black letters, Indian and Oklahoma, blue twill, black rolled edge
    ...... 2.00
Black Hills Area Council, round, blue and gray letters, Rushmore, navy blue
    twill, yellow rolled edge 2.50
    Round, blue and gray letters, Mount Rushmore, red twill, brown rolled edge
    ...... 2.00
Blackhawk Area Council, round, yellow letters, Indian head, black felt, red
    cut edge 3.50
    Round, yellow letters, Indian head, black twill, red cut edge 2.75
    Oval, yellow letters, 50th anniversary, orange twill, yellow rolled edge . 2.50
Blue Grass Council, octagon, red and black letters, white twill, green cut edge
    ...... 3.50
    Hat, green letters, navy blue twill, red cut edge 2.50
Blue Mountain Council, round, white letters and rams head, navy blue twill,
    white cut edge 2.50
Boston Council, square, red letters, Paul Revere statue, blue-gray woven 2.00
Boulder Dam Area Council, round, red letters and dam, white twill, red cut
    edge 8.00
    Round, green letters and dam, gray twill, green cut edge 5.00
    Rectangle, blue letters, white twill, gold rolled edge 3.25
    Rectangle, orange letters, yellow twill, brown cut edge 3.00
    Rectangle, orange letters, yellow twill, brown rolled edge 2.50
    Round, red letters, orange twill, yellow rolled edge 2.00
Buckeye Council, round, black letters, 50th anniversary, 1977, blue twill, red
    rolled edge 2.50
Bucks County Council, twill 2.00
Buckskin Council, round, gold letters, 50th anniversary, blue twill, gold rolled
    edge 2.50
Bucktail Council, round, blue letters, buck, white twill, red cut edge 2.50
Buffalo Area Council, round, blue letters and buffalo, white twill, red cut edge
    ...... 10.00
    Round, green letters, buffalo, tan twill, red rolled edge 8.00
Buffalo Bill Council, hat, red letters, yellow twill, black cut edge 10.00

Buffalo Trail Council, round, red letters, black buffalo, orange twill, red cut edge 2.50

Burlington County Council, dome, black and red letters, gray woven, red rolled edge 2.00

Buttes Area Council ...... rectangle, red letters, white twill, red cut edge 8.00
Rectangle, red letters on bonnet, blue-gray woven, red inner border 5.00
Round, yellow letters, 50th anniversary, navy blue twill, blue rolled edge
.... 3.00
Round, red letters, light blue twill, gold rolled edge 2.00

Cache Valley Council, odd shape, brown beaver and letters, white felt, brown border 7.50
Arrowhead, red letters, blue twill, light brown cut edge 3.00

California Inland Empire Council, round, black letters, multicolor field, orange rolled edge 3.50

Calumet Council, round, white letters, polar bear, navy blue twill, blue rolled edge 4.00
Rectangle, gold and red letters, dark blue twill, green rolled edge 3.50
Oval, black letters, calumet, white twill, gold rolled edge 2.00

Cambridge Council, round, black letters, Indian head, red twill, red rolled edge 7.50

Camden County Council, round, Indian head, orange twill, red cut edge .. 3.00

Cape Fear Area Council, dome, red letters and tent, green trees, white twill, brown cut edge 4.50
Diamond, green letters, white twill, brown cut edge 3.00

Capitol Area Council, round, purple letters, orange twill, purple cut edge . 3.50
Round, white letters, Texas and capitol, orange twill, black rolled edge 2.00

Cascade Area Council, round, green letters, white twill, yellow cut edge .. 5.00
Round, red letters, white twill, black rolled edge 2.50
Round, yellow letters, blue twill, yellow rolled edge 2.00

Catalina Council, round, brown letters, tan twill, brown cut edge 4.00
Round, red letters, orange twill, red-brown rolled edge 3.50
Round, 50th anniversary, multicolor field, orange rolled edge 3.00

Cedar Valley Area Council, diamond, black and gold letters, white twill, red cut edge 10.00

Central Florida Council, round, orange and saturn, multicolor, gold rolled edge 3.50
Round, yellow letters, launch scene, multiocolor, yellow rolled edge ... 2.75

Central Minnesota Council, dome, black letters, white twill, red silkscreened edge 7.50
Dome, black letters, Paul Bunyan, white twill, red cut edge 3.50

Central Missouri Council, chevron, tan silkscreened letters and design, green felt 18.00

Central Ohio Council, hat, red letters, red, blue and gold design, white twill, red cut edge 3.00
Round, black letters, Ohio behind fleur de lis, blue twill, red rolled edge
.... 2.50

Chamorro Council, diamond, brown letters, blue twill, yellow cut edge .. 25.00
Round, green letters, white twill, gold rolled edge 15.00

Chattahoochee Council, round, black letters, red twill, black rolled edge . 2.00

Chehaw Council, round, red letters, dancing Indian, tan twill, red cut edge
...... 2.00

Chicago Area Council, blue twill, skyline scene, pocket patch 2.00
Blue twill, skyline scene, jacket patch 4.00
Buckingham Fountain scene, pocket patch 2.00
Buckingham Fountain scene, jacket patch 4.25

Chief Cornstalk Council, round, green letters, design green and gold, white
twill, red rolled edge 2.00

Chief Logan Council, dome, black letters and design, red twill, black cut edge
...... 3.50
Round, Chief Logan, brass field, blue rolled edge 2.00

Chief Seattle, round, green letters, blue twill, red cut edge 5.00
Round, green letters, blue twill, red rolled edge 2.00

Chief Shabbona Council, dome, yellow letters, red twill, black cut edge ... 7.50

Chippewa Valley .... oval, red letters, Indian dancing, white field, blue rolled
edge 2.50

Choccolocco Council, round, green letters, white twill, red rolled edge 4.00
Odd shape, red, gold letters, white twill, green and gold cut edge 2.50

Circle Ten Council, round, red letters, powder horn, light brown twill, brown
cut edge 4.00

Coastal Carolina Council, square, red letters, outline of state, blue-gray woven
...... 5.00
Round, red letters, outline of state, white twill, blue rolled edge 2.25

Chochise Council, round, black and red letters, head of Cochise, white twill,
red rolled edge, ... 10.00

Columbia Pacific Council, round, orange letters, light blue twill, gold rolled
edge 2.50
Round, orange letters, fleur de lis, light blue twill, gold rolled edge 2.00

Columbiana Council, round, red letters, paddle wheeler, white twill, blue cut
edge 3.75
Round, black letters, 50th anniversary, red twill, red rolled edge 2.50

Commanche Trail Council, hat, red letters, Indian dancing, white twill, blue
cut edge 12.00

Concho Valley Council, round, blue letters, Indian dancing, yellow twill, red
rolled edge 2.00

Corn Belt Council, round, white letters, polar bear, navy blue twill, blue cut
edge
Edge 3.00

Cornhusker Council, hat red letters, camping scene, white twill, red cut edge
...... 3.00
Round, red letters, head of corn, white twill, gold rolled edge 3.50
Round, red letters, head of corn, white twill, green rolled edge 2.50
50th aniversary 3.00
Bi-Centennial 3.50

Coronado Area Council, hat, red letters, helmet, white twill, red cut
edge 2.50

Covered Wagon Council, round, red letters, conestoga wagon, dark blue twill,
white cut edge 3.00

Crater Lake Council, rectangle, yellow letters, white twill, blue cut edge . 3.00
  Round, gold letters, light blue twill, gold rolled edge 2.00
Crescent Bay Area Council, round, white letters, coastal scene, red twill, gold
  cut edge 8.00
  Round, white letters, coastal scene, red twill, gold rolled edge 5.00
Cumberland Council, hat, brown letters, camp scene, blue twill, brown cut
  edge 20.009
Dan Beard Council, round, white letters, powder horn, green twill, white cut
  edge 18.00
  Round, white letters, powder horn, light green twill, white cut edge ... 12.00
  Round, yellow letters, camp fire, blue twill, red rolled edge 8.00
  Round, yellow letters, camp fire, blue twill, red rolled edge 5.00
  Round, black letters, camp fire on blue field, white twill, red rolled edge
                                                                 ...... 2.50
Daniel Boone Council, round, blue letters, Daniel Boone's head, white twill,
  red cut edge 5.00
  Round, white letters, Daniel Boone's head, dark gray twill, orange cut edge
                                                                 ...... 3.00
Daniel Webster Council, dome, red letters, frontiersman, orange twill, black
  cut edge 6.00
  Round, red letters, frontiersman, orange twill, black cut edge 3.50
  Round, red letters, frontiersman, orange twill, black rolled edge 2.00
Del-Mar-Va Council, round, blue letters, red disk, white teepee, orange twill,
  white cut edge 5.00
  Round, blue letters, red disk, white teepee, orange twill, white rolled edge
                                                                 ...... 3.00
  Round, red letters and council outline, white twill, red rolled edge 2.00
Desert Trails Council, round, brown letters, desert scene, white twill, brown
  rolled edge 2.50
  Hat, brown letters, desert scene, white twill, brown cut edge 2.00
Detroit Area Council, rectangle, white letters, fleur de lis, green twill, gold
  rolled edge 2.50
  Round, blue letters, gold center, white twill, gold rolled edge 2.00
  Round, black letters, green center, white twill, green rolled edge 2.00
  Round, black letters, blue center, white twill, blue rolled edge 2.00
  Round, black letters, red center, white twill, red rolled edge 2.00
Dupage Area Council, round, red letters, canoe on river, multicolor field, red
  cut edge 2.25
  Round, red letters, canoe on river, multicolor field, red rolled edge 2.00
Eagle Rock Council, round, white letters, eagle descending, blue twill, yellow
  rolled edge 4.00
East Valley Area Council, round, red and black letters, scout sign, white twill,
  black rolled edge 2.00
Egyptian Council, round, yellow letters, head of Egyptian, dark blue twill,
  yellow cut edge 5.00
  Round, brass letters, scarab beetle, dark blue twill, blue cut edge 3.50
Evergreen Area Council, round, green and red letters, pine tree, white twill,
  red cut edge 3.00
  Round, green and red letters, pine tree, white twill, red rolled edge 2.00
Far East Council, round, blue letters, tori and Fujiyama, white twill, red cut
  edge 7.50
  Round, blue letters, tori and Fujiyama, white field, red cut edge 5.00

Round, red and white letters, eagle, dark blue twill, blue rolled edge ... 3.50
Round, red letters, map of council, white twill, blue rolled edge 3.50
Finger Lakes Council, round, blue letters, white twill, red cut edge 3.00
Firelands Area Council, round, brown letters, log cabin, green twill, brown cut
   edge 5.00
Round, brown letters, log cabin, green twill, brown rolled edge 3.00
Round, red letters, log cabin, green twill, yellow rolled edge 2.25
Flint River Council, odd shape, red letters, orange twill, green rolled edge
   ...... 2.50
Fort Simcoe Council, round, white letters, mountain cabin, dark blue twill,
   white cut edge 3.00
Round, white letters, pine tree, dark blue twill, white rolled edge 2.00
Fort Steuben Area Council, round, green letters and fort, orange twill, green
   cut edge 3.00
Forty Niner Council, square, red letters, prospector and burro, white woven
   ...... 3.50
Round, red letters, pick, shovel and gold pan, tan twill, brown cut edge . 2.00
Four Lakes Council, rectangle, white letters, tan twill, gold rolled edge .. 2.00
Four Rivers, hat, red letters, council area in green, white twill, red cut edge
   ...... 3.50
French Creek Council, round, green letters, tan twill, yellow rolled edge . 2.00
Gateway Area Council, dome, brown letters and gateway, white twill, brown
   cut edge 5.50
Dome, red letters, brown gateway, white twill, brown cut edge 3.50
General Greene Council, round, yellow letters, General Greene, black twill,
   white rolled edge 2.50
Round, yellow letters, General Greene, white twill, white rolled edge ... 2.00
Genesee Council, round, black letters, mountain valley, green twill, blue cut
   edge 5.00
George H. Lanier Council, diamond, green letters, white twill, green cut edge
   ...... 2.00
George Washington Council, round, red letters, totem pole, white twill, red
   rolled edge 3.00
Georgia-Carolina Council, round, brown letters, outline of council, white twill,
   blue rolled edge 2.00
Golden Empire Council, round, red letters, state and capitol, dark blue twill,
   gold cut edge 10.00
Round, red letters, state and capitol, green twill, gold cut edge 6.50
Round, black letters, state and capitol, red twill, gold cut edge 4.50
Round, red letters, state and capitol, dark blue twill, gold rolled edge .. 3.00
Round, red letters, state and capitol, green twill, gold rolled edge 2.25
Round, black letters, state and capitol, red twill, gold rolled edge 2.00
Grand Canyon Council, odd shape, red letters, gray twill, red cut edge ... 5.00
Grand Valley Council, odd shape, red letters, green twill, red cut edge .. 22.00
Dome, white letters, dog sled and igloo, red twill, green cut edge 18.00
Dome, white letters, dog sled on ice, light blue twill, red cut edge 15.00
Rectangle, red and black letters, white twill, red cut edge 12.00
Round, white letters, polar bear, dark blue twill, blue cut edge 10.00
Grayback Council, round, orange letters, blue twill, orange rolled edge .. 8.00
Great Rivers Council, round yellow letters, green design, red twill, green cut
   edge 3.00

Great Salt Lake Council, dome, white letters, mountain lake scene, blue twill, green cut edge 4.00

Dome, brown letters, mountain scene, blue woven, green rolled edge ... 2.00

Round, red letters, mountain lake scene, multicolor, black rolled edge . 3.00

Great Salt Plains Council, round, brown silkscreened letters and design, orange felt 4.00

Round with 5 hanging feathers, red letters, turquoise twill, brown cut edge 3.00

Great Smoky Mountain Council, dome, yellow letters, Indian head, blue twill, red cut edge 8.00

Greater New York Council, square, red and white letters, white twill, blue rolled edge 2.00

Square, red and white letters, white twill, blue rolled edge 4.00

Greater Niagara Frontier Council, round, red letters, white twill, blue rolled edge 3.50

Green Mountain Council, round, silver letters, covered bridge and state, green twill, silver rolled edge 2.00

Greensboro Council, dome, red letters, General Greene on horse, white twill, red cut edge 15.00

Gulf Ridge Council, odd shape, black letters, blue twill, yellow rolled edge 2.75

Gulf Stream Council, dome, red letters, alligator on beach, white twill, red rolled edge 2.25

Harrison Trails Council, round, red letters, outline of council, blue twill, gold cut edge 10.00

Hawk Mountain Council, round, black letters, hawk head, fleur de lis, yellow twill, black rolled edge 2.00

Hawkeye Area Council, round, red letters, hawk and fleur de lis, bright blue twill, red rolled edge 2.25

Round, red letters, hawk and fleur de lis, gray-blue twill, red rolled edge 2.25

Round, red letters, hawk in scout hat and n-c, blue twill, black rolled edge 2.00

Headwaters Area Council, dome, black letters, yellow twill, black rolled edge 2.50

Hendrick Hudson Council, dome, white letters, ship on sea, red twill, blue cut edge 7.50

Hiawatha Council, odd shaped, red letters, calumet and scout emblem, yellow field, red rolled edge 3.00

Round red letters, calumet and scout emblem, yellow field, red rolled edge 2.25

Hudson-Delaware Council, round, red, blue and gold letters, profiles, white twill, gold rolled edge 3.00

Round, red letters, 50th anniversary, blue twill, yellow rolled edge 2.50

Odd shape, red letters, yellow twill, blue rolled edge 2.25

Hudson-Hamilton Council, round, yellow and green letters, red twill, black rolled edge 2.25

Idaho Panhandle Council, round, red letters, yellow twill, green cut edge . 4.50

Hat, red letters, yellow twill, red cut edge 2.75

Hat, blue letters, yellow twill, blue cut edge 2.50

Hat, red letters, white twill, red cut edge 2.00

Imperial Yuma Area Council, round, khaki silkscreened letters and design, white felt 18.00
Dome, white letters, red twill, white cut edge 10.00
Rectangle, brown letters, light tan twill, brown cut edge 7.50
Indian Nations Council, rectangle, white letters, tepee and headdress, blue twill, red rolled edge 2.00
Indian Trails, round, red letters, tipi and bear paws, yellow twill, black cut edge 2.50
Inland Empire Council, round, red letters, camp fire and sky, white, brown rolled edge 6.50
Hat, white letters, cub scout designs, dark blue twill, gold cut edge 4.00
Hat, gold letters, 1967-1969 Jamboree, blue twill, gold cut edge 3.50
Istrouma Area Council, round, brown letters, orange twill, red rolled edge 2.50
Jim Bridger Council, round, gold letters, green twill, black rolled edge ... 2.75
Round, blue letters, orange twill, green rolled edge 2.25
Kansas City Area Council, round, gold letters, navy blue twill, red cut edge 8.00
Kedeka Area Council, round, white letters, Indian head, green twill, red cut edge 12.00
Kenosha Council, round, blue letters, Indian head with bonnet, white twill, red cut edge 8.00
Kern County Council, hat, white letters, vertical stitch blue, green twill, red cut edge 7.50
Hat, white letters, horizontal stitch blue, green twill, red cut edge 5.00
Keystone Area Council, odd shape, yellow letters, Indian head, green twill, red cut edge 6.0
Odd shape, red letters, Indian head, white twill, blue cut edge 4.50
Odd shape, red letters, Indian head, white twill, blue cut edge 4.50
Odd shape, yellow letters, tomahawk-calumet, white twill, red cut edge 3.00
Square, blue letters, scout hand sign, red twill, blue rolled edge 2.50
Square, gold letters, white twill, red, white, blue rolled edge 2.25
Kikthawenund Area Council, rectangle, red, white letters, multicolor field, metallic gold rolled edge 7.50
Kilauea Council, round, gold letters, volcano and Hawaiian, blue twill, gold rolled edge 10.00
Kit Carson Council, odd shape, red letters, yellow twill, black, blue, brown cut edge 3.00
Lake Bonneville Council, round, gold letters, multicolor, gold rolled edge 2.50
Lake Superior Council, triangle, red letters, white twill, gold rolled edge . 3.00
Round, red letters, blue twill, white rolled edge 2.25
Land O Lakes Council, round, red letters, Wisconsin, dark blue twill, yellow rolled edge 2.50
Round, white letters, polar bear, navy blue twill, gray cut edge 2.50
Lebanon County Council, twill 50.00
Lewis Clark Council, round, green letters, white twill, red rolled edge 2.50
Lewiston Trail Council, round, black letters, white twill, black cut edge .. 3.25
Rectangle, black letters, conestoga wagon, oxen, red twill, black cut edge 2.50

Licking County Council, round, gold letters, 50th anniversary, blue twill, gold rolled edge 2.50

Llano Estacado Council, round, black letters, buffalo, yucca and helmet, blue twill, red rolled edge 2.25

Long Beach Area Council, dome, red letters, tent and oil derricks, white twill, red cut edge 6.00
    Dome, red letters, tent and camp fire, yellow twill, red cut edge 3.50
    Odd shape with tab, red letters, white twill, gold rolled edge 2.50
    Rectangle, red letters, camping scene, orange twill, red rolled edge 2.25
    Round, black letters, Queen Mary and globe, white twill, red rolled edge
    ...... 2.00

Los Angeles Area Council, round, red letters, bear head, black twill, gold cut edge 4.00
    Round, red letters, bear head, black twill, gold rolled edge 2.50
    Round, brown letters, coastal scene, blue field, gold rolled edge 2.00

Louis Agassiz Fuertes Council, dome, yellow letters, dark blue twill, white rolled edge 3.00
    Round, black letters, white twill, yellow rolled edge 2.25

Mahoning Valley Council, round, white letters, candle, dark blue twill, yellow cut edge 3.50

Marin Council, hat, red letters, bridge scene, multicolor field, red cut edge
    ...... 2.50
    Odd shape, white letters, bridge scene, multicolor field, white rolled edge
    ...... 2.50
    Odd shape, white letters, bridge, multicolor field, gold rolled edge 2.25
    Round, twill 1.75

Maui County Council, round, yellow letters, Hawaiian head, green twill, brown rolled edge 5.00

McKinley Area Council, round felt, with tab, various segments are known to exist 30.00

Mid America Council, square, white letters, blue field, yellow rolled edge 2.50
    Round, black letters, Indian head, eagle, multicolor field, blue rolled edge
    ...... 2.25

Mid-Iowa Council, rectangle, blue letters, polar bear, blue twill, white rolled edge 2.25

Middlesex Council, round, red letters, oak leaf and scout logo, white twill, green rolled edge 12.00

Midnight Sun Council, round, blue letters, white twill, red rolled edge 5.00
    Quarter circle, red letters, white twill, red rolled edge 7.50
    Dome, white letters, Eskimo, blue twill, blue rolled edge 3.00

Minnesota Valley Area Council, dome, red letters, viking ship, white twill, light blue rolled edge 9.00

Minuteman Council, dome, blue letters, minuteman, red twill, gray rolled edge 2.25

Mission Council, rectangle, red letters, letters in script, blue twill, red rolled edge 4.00
    Rectange, red letters black letters, blue twill, red rolled edge 3.50
    Rectangle, red letters, no clouds, blue twill, red rolled edge 2.75
    Rectangle, red letters, no clouds, blue field, red rolled edge 2.50
    Round, white letters, polar bear, dark blue twill, blue rolled edge 2.25

Missouri Valley Council, round, black letters, coyote, bow and arrow, red twill, white rolled edge 8.00

Mo-Kan Council, odd shape, 50th anniversary, white twill, yellow rolled edge
...... 2.50

Modoc Area Council, round, letters and Indian head, black twill, yellow cut edge 2.00
Round, black letters, Indian head, yellow twill, black cut edge 1.50

Monongahella Valley Council, odd shape, gold letters, 50th anniversary, red twill, blue rolled edge 7.50

Montana Council, black letters, bull's skull, blue field, black rolled edge .. 2.25

Moraine Trails Council, round, yellow and black letters, white twill, blue rolled edge 2.25

Mound Builders Council, round, green silkscreened letters and design, white felt 3.50

Mount Baker Council, round, gold letters, totem pole, red twill, gold rolled edge 2.50
Round, gold letters, totem pole, red twill, gold rolled edge 2.25

Mount Diablo Council, hat, orange letters, blue twill, black cut edge 4.50
Dome, orange letters, blue twill, black rolled edge 2.75
Dome, orange letters, blue twill, red rolled edge 2.25

Mount Rainier Council, round, yellow letters, green twill, red rolled edge . 2.50
Round, blue letters, yellow twill, green rolled edge 2.25

Mountaineer Area Council, round, blue and goldd letters, white twill, red rolled edge 2.25

Muskingum Valley Council, round, black letters, yellow twill, red and purple cut edge 4.50
Round, orange letters, blue twill, purple rolled edge 2.75
Round, black letters, orange twill, purple rolled edge 2.25

Nassau County Council, round, blue letters, Long Island, scout logo, white twill, red rolled edge 3.50

National Trails Council, diamond, blue letters, white twill, gold cut edge 12.00

Nemacolin Trails Council, round, red letters, signal tower, white twill, red rolled edge 8.00

Nevada Area Council, rectangle, gold letters and state, dark blue field, gold rolled edge 2.25
Rectangle, gold letters, state is silver, dark blue field, gold rolled edge . 2.00

Niagara Frontier Council, round, blue letters, Indian and waterfall, white twill, blue cut edge 7.50

North Bay, round, black letters, witch and Massachusetts, blue twill, red rolled edge 2.75
Round, red letters, lake scene, white twill, red rolled edge 2.25

North Central Montana, round, yellow letters, Indian head, black twill, red cut edge 15.00
Round, yellow letters, Indian head, black twill, red rolled edge 10.00

North Central Washington Council, round, blue letters, mountain scene, white twill, purple cut edge 2.75

North Florida Council, oval, white letters, Baden-Powell, Gray-green twill, yellow rolled edge 2.75

North Orange Council, rectangle, gold letters, multicolor field, gold rolled edge 2.25

North Shore Area Council, round, yellow letters, green twill, black cut edge
...... 10.00
Round, blue letters, orange twill, red rolled edge 7.50

Northeast Georgia Council, rectangle, black letters, yellow twill, green rolled edge 2.25

Northeast Ohio Council, dome, white letters, cargo ship on lake, white twill, red rolled edge 2.25

Northern Indiana Council, round, white letters, polar bear, dark blue, white rolled edge

Northern Orange County Council, round, white letters, blue twill, red rolled edge 4.00

Nottawa Trails Council, round, white letters, polar bear, blue twill, blue rolled edge 4.00

Oakland Area Council, round, blue and green letters, orange twill, red cut edge 3.50

Occoneechee Council, triangle, red letters and tepee, white twill, green cut edge 7.50

    Square, blue letters, outline of North Carolina, tan woven 5.00

Old Baldy Council, round, green letters, blue twill, orange rolled edge ... 11.00

    Round, red letters, light tan, red rolled edge 8.00

    Round, white letters, orange twill, white rolled edge 6.00

    Round, green letters, blue twill, orange cut edge 5.00

    Round, green letters, yellow twill, orange cut edge 4.50

    Round, green letters, red twill, orange cut edge 4.00

    Round, red letters, scouts hiking, white woven, red rolled edge 2.75

    Round, red letters, scout hiking, white twill, gold rolled edge 2.50

    Diamond, brown letters, white twill, red cut edge 2.25

Old Colony Council, round, red letters, blue twill, red rolled edge 2.25

Old Hickory Council, round, blue letters, white twill, orange rolled edge .. 2.50

    Odd shape, red letters, white twill, brown cut edge 2.50

Old Kentucky Home Council, round, white letters, Kentucky and globe, pale green twill, white rolled edge 2.25

Olympic Area Council, round, white letters, green twill, white cut edge .. 18.00

    Round, white letters, green twill, white rolled edge 10.00

    Round, white letters, white twill, blue rolled edge 8.00

Onandaga Council, round, black letters, Indian head, light brown twill, black cut edge 16.00

    Round, red letters, longhouse and campfire, yellow twill, red rolled edge 11.00

Orange Empire Area Council, rectangle, brown letters, yellow twill, brown cut edge 8.00

    Rectangle, brown letters, yellow twill, brown rolled edge 8.00

Ore-Ida Council, round, brown letters, backpacker, blue twill, green rolled edge 2.25

    Hat, red letters, green twill, red cut edge 2.00

Oregon Trail Council, round, red and yellow letters, green twill, yellow cut edge 3.00

    Hat, white letters, covered wagon, green twill, yellow cut edge 2.00

Otetiana Council, dome, red, yellow and blue letters, white twill, yellow cut edge 8.00

Ouachita Valley Council, round, red letters and Indian head, white twill, red cut edge 2.75

Overland Trails Council, hat, blue letters, white twill, red cut edge 2.00

Paul Bunyan Council, round, red letters, Paul Bunyan head, white twill, brown cut edge 5.00
   Round, red letters, Paul Bunyan head, white twill, red cut edge 4.00
   Round, red letters, Paul Bunyan head, white twill, red rolled edge 2.50
   Dome, black letters, 20th anniversary, white twill, red rolled edge 2.50

Penn Mountains Council, hat, black letters, white twill, red cut edge 2.50

Pennsylvania Council, 50th anniversary 3.00

Pequot Council, round, black letters, Indian head, yellow twill, black rolled edge 10.00

Pheasant Council, diamond, red letters, white twill, red cut edge 7.50

Philadelphia Council, square, black and blue letters, white twill, pale yellow rolled edge 2.25

Piedmont Council, twill cut edge 4.00
Twill, 4.00

Round red letters, pine tree and letters, green felt, yellow cut edge 3.00

Pinellas Area Council, round, white letters, white twill, light blue rolled edge 6.00

Pioneer Trails Council, hat, red letters, blue twill, brown cut edge 6.50
   Hat, red letters, blue twill, white cut edge 5.00
   Hat, red letters, orange twill, white cut edge 3.00
   Dome, red letters, yellow twill, light brown rolled edge 2.75
   Round, red and gold letters, blue twill, gold rolled edge 2.25
   Round, red letters, 50th anniversary, blue twill, gold rolled edge 2.50

Pokagon Trails Council, round, white silkscreened design, embroidered circles, green felt 10.00
   Round, red letters, Indian head, green twill, black cut edge 7.50
   Round, red letters, Indian head, white twill, black cut edge 5.00

Pony Express Council, hat, yellow letters, red twill, green cut edge 2.25
   Hat, yellow letters, red woven, green cut edge 4.00

Portage Trails, round, red letters, green twill, red cut edge 8.00
   Round, red and green letters, white twill, green rolled edge 5.00
   Round, white letters, polar bear, navy blue twill, gray rolled edge 3.50

Portland Area Council, round, orange letters, blue twill, gold rolled edge . 9.00

Pottawattomie Council, round, gold letters, black twill, black rolled edge 3.00
   Round, red letters, navy blue twill, black rolled edge 2.2

Prairie Council, odd shape, green letters, shape of covered wagon, white felt 7.50
   Round, brown letters, orange twill, brown cut edge 5.00
   Round, black letters, white field, black cut edge 3.50

Prairie Gold Area Council, hat, brown and blue letters, white twill, blue cut edge 2.50

Quapaw Council, round, brown letters, Arkansas, light brown field, brown cut edge 3.00

Quivira Council, rectangle, black letters, light blue, red rolled edge 2.25

Rainbow Council, round, red letters, orange twill, green cut edge 5.50
   Round, white letters, polar bear, navy blue twill, light blue cut edge 4.00
   Odd shape, black letters, blue twill, black cut edge 5.00

Red River Valley Council, round, red and black letters, white twill, red rolled edge 15.00

Redwood Area Council, round, brown letters, sawdust burner, yellow twill, green rolled edge 2.75

Round, brown letters, rod, reel and fish, light tan twill, green rolled edge
...... 2.25

Rio Grande Council, diamond, black letters, white twill, black cut edge .. 3.50

Rip Van Winkle Council, dome, red letters, green twill, white cut edge 3.50
Dome, green letters, white twill, brown rolled edge 2.25

Riverside County Council, round, black letters, yellow man, clack outline, white twill, black cut edge 7.50
Round black letters, black man, yellow outline, white twill, black cut edge
...... 5.00
Rectangle, metallic gold letters, anniversary, navy blue twill, metallic gold rolled edge 6.50

Robert E. Lee Council, square, red letters, blue-gray woven 2.50

Robert Treat Council, round, white letters, light blue twill, white rolled edge
...... 5.00

Rockland County Council, round, blue letters, orange twill, blue cut edge . 5.00
Round, yellow letters, red twill, blue cut edge 3.00

Rocky Mountain Council, hat, brown letters, pale blue twill, red cut edge . 2.50

Roosevelt Council, round, yellow letters, blue twill, yellow cut edge 13.00
Round, yellow letters, vertical stitch in sun, blue twill, yellow cut edge 10.00
Round, gold letters, horizontal stitch in sun, blue twill, gold cut edge ... 7.50

Sabine Area Council, rectangle, red letters, blue twill, red rolled edge 7.50

Sac-Fox Council, diamond, green letters, orange twill, red cut edge 8.00
Round, green letters, white twill, black rolled edge 5.00

Sachem Council, round, white letters, blue twill, green cut edge 15.00
Round, blue letters, white twill, red cut edge 10.00

St. Lawrence Council, rectangle, green and red letters, white twill, green rolled edge 2.50

St. Louis Council, hat, red letters, horse head, yellow twill, blue cut edge . 2.25

Samoset Council, round, white letters, polar bear, navy blue twill, gray cut edge 2.50

San Diego County Council, rectangle, red letters, blue twill, yellow cut edge
...... 5.00
Rectangle, red letters, blue twill, yellow cut edge 3.00
Rectangle, red letters, white twill, gold rolled edge 2.50
Rectangle, red letters, blue twill, gold rolled edge 2.25

San Fernando Valley Council, round, brown letters, yellow twill, red cut edge
...... 11.00
Round, red letters, beaver, white twill, green cut edge 7.50
Round, red letters, pine tree, white twill, green cut edge 5.00
Dome, red letters, dark green trees, blue twill, purple cut edge 3.50
Dome, red letters, dark green trees, white twill, purple cut edge 3.00
Dome, red letters, dark green trees, yellow twill, purple cut edge 2.75
Dome, red letters, light green trees, yellow twill, purple cut edge 2.50
Round, white letters, vertical stitch brown only, blue twill, white rolled edge
...... 2.25
Round, white letters, vertical, horizontal brown, blue twill, white rolled edge 2.00

San Francisco Council, round, yellow letters, blue twill, yellow cut edge .. 6.00
Round, yellow letters, blue twill, yellow rolled edge 4.00

San Francisco Bay Area Council, rectangle, orange letters, multicolor, gold rolled edge 2.75

Round, blue letters, blue twill, orange rolled edge 2.25
San Gabriel Valley Council, round, red letters, white twill, black cut edge 4.50
Round, red letters, white twill, black rolled edge 3.50
Round, metallic gold letters and design, black field, metallic gold rolled
edge 3.00
Round, dark blue letters, white twill, white rolled edge 2.25
San Mateo County Council, round yellow letters, white twill, yellow cut edge
...... 4.50
round, yellow letters, multicolor woven, yellow rolled edge 3.00
round, white letters, blue twill, yellow rolled edge 2.25
Round, white letters, blue twill, light yellow rolled edge 2.00
Santa Fe Trail Council, round, red letters, vertical stitch blue, white twill, red
cut edge 5.00
Round, red letters, horizontal stitch blue, white twill, wide red cut edge 3.00
Round, red letters, white twill, gold rolled edge 2.25
Santa Lucia Area Council, round, red letters, white twill, blue cut edge ... 5.00
Round, red letters, staff, white twill, blue cut edge 4.00
Round, red letters, totem pole, white twill, blue rolled edge 4.50
Dome, brown letters, blue twill, blue rolled edge 2.25
Scenic Trails Council, odd shape, white letters, green twill, red cut edge .. 3.50
Schenectady Councy Council, round purple letters, brown twill, brown cut
edge 2.75
Seneca Council, round, red letters, Indian head, light tan twill, black cut edge
...... 10.00
Round, yellow letters, orange twill, light blue rolled edge 6.00
Sequoia Council, round, yellow and purple letters, turquoise twill, yellow
rolled edge 3.00
Round, green letters, gold scout emblem, white twill, brown rolled edge 2.50
Round, green letters, white scout emblem, white twill, brown rolled edge
...... 2.00
Shawnee Council, round, black letters, 50th anniversary, yellow twill, red
rolled edge 2.50
Shenandoah Area Council, round, red letters, white twill, green rolled edge
and design 2.50
Silverado Area Council, round, blue and gold letters, blue twill, gray rolled
edge 2.25
Sioux Council, round, red letters, white twill, brown rolled edge 2.50
Siwanoy Council, round, orange letters and design, black felt, orange
silkscreened border 12.00
Snake River Area Council, round, green letters, white twill, gold rolled edge
...... 2.25
Sanoma-Mendocino Area Council, round, white letters, red twill, red rolled
edge 2.25
South Florida Council, oval, purple letters, yellow twill, black rolled edge 2.25
South Plains Council, triangle, green letters, light tan twill, brown cut edge
...... 3.75
Southeast Alaska Area Council, rectangle, blue letters, white woven, blue and
yellow border 6.00
Round, gold letters, navy blue twill, gold rolled edge 3.50
Round, gold letters, navy blue twill, gold rolled edge 3.00

Southern New Jersey Council, round, red letters, white twill, black rolled edge 2.25

Southern Sierra Council, odd shape, black letters, white twill, black cut edge 3.50

Southwest Florida Council, rectangle, yellow letters, khaki twill, khaki rolled edge 3.00
  Round, black letters, navy blue twill, yellow rolled edge 2.25

Southwest Iowa Council, hat, red letters, blue twill, gold cut edge 2.00

Southwest Michigan Council, round, red letters, white twill, red rolled edge 2.50

Squanto Council, rectangle, 1969 50th anniversary patch, orange twill, red rolled edge and red tab 10.00

Stanford Area Council, round, red letters, blue twill, dark blue cut edge .. 3.00

Starved Rock Area Council, diamond, red letters, white twill, black cut edge 8.00

Steuben Area Council, round, red letters, white twill, blue cut edge 3.00
  Round, red letters, white twill, blue rolled edge 2.25

Suffolk County Council, round, blue letters, Indian head, orange twill, red rolled edge 2.50
  Round, dark blue letters, blue twill, dark blue rolled edge 4.00

Sunnyland Council, 50th anniversary 3.00

Tahoe Area Council, round, white letters, orange twill, white cut edge ... 11.00
  Rectangle, red letters, white twill, brown rolled edge 8.00
  Oval, red letters, white twill, yellow rolled edge 6.00

Tall Corn Area Council, round, red letters, white twill, green rolled edge . 8.00
  Round, red letters, white twill, green rolled edge 9.00

Tall Pine Council, round, red letters, metallic silver field, yellow rolled edge 3.00
  Odd shape, red letters, white twill, red rolled edge 2.25

Tendoy Area Council, hat, red letters, yellow twill, red cut edge 2.00
  Round, red letters, multicolor, black rolled edge 2.25

Teton Peaks Council, round, black letters, blue twill, gold rolled edge 2.25

Thatcher Woods Area Council, rectangle, gold letters, light blue twill, blue rolled edge 5.00

Theodore Roosevelt Council, round, gold letters, blue twill, gold rolled edge 2.50
  Round, white letters, 50th anniversary, yellow twill, tan rolled edge 2.50

Three Rivers Council, rectangle, white letters, polar bear, dark blue twill, gray cut edge 5.00
  Round, white letters, polar bear, dark blue twill, gray rolled edge 2.25

Tidewater Council, diamond, white letters and design, green twill, white cut edge 3.50
  Odd shape, red letters, blue twill, red cut edge 2.75

Timber Trails Council, round, red letters, black twill, gold cut edge 4.50
  Round, red letters, black twill, gold rolled edge 3.75

Tioughnioga Council, hat, yellow letters, Cortland, New York, black twill, red cut edge 11.00
  Hat, yellow letters, council name only, black twill, red cut edge 8.00

Transatlantic Council, round, white letters, blue twill, black rolled edge .. 3.50

Tri Trails Council, round, brown letters, white twill, red rolled edge 2.25

Tumwater Area Council, odd shape, blue letters, yellow twill, brown rolled edge 3.00

Twin City Council, covered wagon, light tan twill, metallic gold and brown cut edge 10.00

Twin Harbors Council, round, white letters, blue twill, blue rolled edge ... 3.25
Round, blue letters, white twill, red rolled edge 2.50

U.S. Grant Council, round, red letters, silkscreened letters and design, white felt 12.00
Shield, red and black letters, black twill, red cut edge 8.00
Round, white letters, polar bear, navy blue twill, white rolled edge 5.00

Union Council, hat, green letters, Indian head, orange twill, green cut edge
...... 5.00

Utah National Parks Council, round, red letters, white twill, black cut edge
...... 4.50
Round, red letters, 50th anniversary, dark blue field, metallic gold rolled edge 2.50

Uwharrie Council, round, green letters, white felt, white cut edge 4.50
Odd shape, red letters, yellow twill, red rolled edge 2.50

Valley Council, round, red letters, white twill, red rolled edge 8.00

Valley Forge Council, odd shape, gold letters, Washington kneeling, multi-color, gold rolled edge 3.50
Odd shape, gold letters, winter cabin scene, multicolor, gold rolled edge
...... 2.25

Valley Trails Council, round, gold letters, red twill, gold cut edge 7.50

Ventura County Council, round, white letters, council number on condor, multicolor, red rolled edge 3.00
Round, white letters, no council number, multicolor, red rolled edge ... 2.50

Verdugo Hills Council, dome, black letters, orange twill, red cut edge 7.50
Dome, gray letters and design, green twill, gray cut edge 4.00
Round, yellow and brown letters, yellow twill, brown rolled edge 2.25

Vigilante Council, round, gold letters and design, red twill, gold cut edge 12.00

Viking Council, round, black letters, white twill, black rolled edge 2.25

Virgin Islands, odd shape, navy blue letters, blue twill, light blue rolled edge
...... 5.00
Round, blue letters, white twill, red rolled edge 3.50
Diamond, red letters, white twill, blue cut edge 2.75

Wabash Valley Council, round, green letters, white twill, green cut edge . 4.00

Watchung Area Council, round, red letters, white twill, blue rolled edge .. 2.25

West Branch Council, dome, red letters and bridge, white twill, brown cut edge 8.00
Dome, red letters and bridge, white twill, gold rolled edge 5.00

West Suburban Council, odd shape, white letters, red twill, gold and white cut edge 4.50

Western Alaska Council, round, blue and red letters, white twill, gold cut edge
...... 7.00
Odd shape, black letters, round with arc, white twill, gold cut edge 7.00
Square, red letters, blue twill, red rolled edge 7.00
Square, gold letters, blue twill, brown rolled edge 4.00
Square, white letters, one mountain, blue twill, gold rolled edge 3.75
Square, red letters, two mountains, blue twill, gold rolled edge 2.75
Square, red letters, fish jumping, blue twill, red rolled edge 2.75

Western Colorado Council, round, green letters, yellow twill, brown cut edge 3.00

Western Montana Council, round, red silkscreened letters and design, green felt 15.00

Hat, red letters, light tan twill, red cut edge 8.00

Whitewater Valley Council, round, red and black letters, white twill, green rolled edge 3.25

Will Rogers Council, square, yellow letters, blue field, red cut edge 3.50

Winnebago Council, hat, black letters, white twill, red cut edge 2.75

Wyoming Valley Council, hat, black letters, white twill, red cut edge 6.00

Yellowstone Valley Council, round, purple and brown letters, yellow twill, brown cut edge 18.00

Odd shape, gold letters, white twill, gold rolled edge 12.00

Yocona Council, hat, black and white letters, blue twill, metallic gold cut edge 10.00

Yohagania Council, round, blue letters, white twill, gold rolled edge 8.00

Yonkers Council, dome, yellow and blue letters, white twill, blue cut edge 3.50

Yosemite Area Council, dome, red letters, gray twill, red cut edge 8.00

Dome, yellow letters, white twill, blue cut edge 6.00

Square, red letters, green twill, brown cut edge 4.00

Square, black letters, gray woven, black and white border 2.75

Dome, red letters, yellow twill, black rolled edge 2.25

Yucca Council, dome, red letters, blue twill, tan cut edge 3.50

COUNCIL

Council, shoulder patches (see appendix A in Chapter 10 for list of councils)

Red on khaki (KRS) Boy Scout 3.50

Yellow on blue (BYS) Cub Scout 4.00

Brown on green (BYS) Explorer 5.00

White on blue (BWS) Sea Scout 4.00-15.00

Blue on white (WBS) Sea Scout 4.00-15.00

Red on white (½ strip) 5.00-15.00

Red on white (shoulder patch) 2.00-20.00

Multi-colored (CSP), ... 2.00-250.00

There are 1 or 2 extremely rare issues known to exist which have sold for nearly $1,000.00 each.

District patches 1.00-2.00

HISTORICAL SITE OR EVENT

U.S. Grant Pilgrimage 1.50-10.00

Lincoln Pilgrimage 1.00-7.50

W.D. Boyce Pilgrimage 1.50-10.00

Tours of other sites 1.00-6.00

MISCELLANEOUS EVENTS

Friendship Camporees, standard state shaped patch 2.50

Special jacket patches (round, etc.) 4.00

COUNCIL PATCHES (CP)

Top row, L to R: New York City (souvenir patch) 1.75
    San Francisco Bay Area Council 2.75
2nd row, l to R: U.S. Grant Council (merged) 5.00
    Squanto Council (merged) 5.00
    Black Hawk Area Council (anniversary) 2.50
3rd row, L to R: Chief Seattle Council 2.50
    Will Rogers Council hat patch 1.50
Bottom row, L to R: 1960 Central Ohio Council 2.00
    Rip Van Winkle Council 2.25
    1955 Central Ohio Council 4.00

COUNCIL SHOULDER PATCHES
Top: Blue Water Council, ½ strip, R & W 8.00
Middle: Abraham Lincoln Council, RWS 2.00
Bottom: North Florida Council CSP 1.75

PHILMONT SCOUT RANCH
Philturn patch, first issue, 2 varieties 125.00
35th Anniversary, light blue twill, black rolled edge, 73-74 .... 6.00
50th Anniversary, yellow twill, yellow rolled edge, 1960 .... 45.00
Bicentennial, solid embroidered multi-color, white rolled edge, 1976 ..... 10.00
Burro Race, 1st Place, round white twill, red rolled edge, 1973 .... 15.00
Camper, arrowhead brown twill, brown cut edge (other variations), 1961
...... 15.00

CAMPOREE PATCHES (Council Issue)
These particular ones depict Norman Rockewells' picture
"The Scoutmasters", each 1.00

Camper, round multi-color on white twill, black rolled edge, 1972 .... 2.00
Camp Uracca, round yellow twill, red rolled edge, 70-72 .... 12.00
Commissary, arrowhead, brown twill, says "Commissary Staff", 65-66 . 30.00
Director, round khaki twill, brown tent with yellow lettering & cut edge, 40's
...... 65.00
Fieldsports Tournament, turqouise twill, black cut edge, 50's 52.00
50-Miler Award, mule skin with stamped design, 40's-50's 10.00
Indian Writings Staff, round blue twill, '73 .... 30.00
Kit Carson Men, round blue twill, white lettering, black rolled edge, '68 .. 42.00
Kit Carson Museum, blue twill, '72 .... 3.00
Kit Carson Trek, round blue twill, black rolled edge, '74 .... 12.00
Mountain Man, round yellow twill, red rolled edge, 70-74 .... 40.00
Mountain Man and Woman, round yellow twill, red rolled edge, '74 ...... 52.00
Nature Award-Indian Head, leather, black printed design, also a brand
variety, 52-59 .... 25.00
Orienteering, square red twill, silver design, black rolled edge, '73 ...... 20.00
Ranger, round backpatch, yellow twill 35.00
Ranger 1969, round backpatch, yellow twill 35.00
Ranger 1970, round backpatch, yellow twill 30.00
Ranger 1971, round backpatch, yellow twill 30.00
Ranger 1972, round backpatch, yellow twill 30.00
Rayado Program, gray twill, black lettering and rolled edge, '76 .... 42.00
Scouter, round blue twill, black lettering and rolled edge, '69 .... 22.00
Seton Library & Museum, blue twill, brown rolled edge, '69 .... 3.00
Staff, arrowhead, brown twill, '61 .... 22.00
Round multi-color on orange twill, black cut edge, 50-60 .... 13.00
Round blue twill, yellow rolled edge 7.50
Round jacket patch, multi-color on white twill, black rolled edge, '72 ..... 4.50
Round leather with embossed design, '72 .... 5.00
Hat patch, white twill arrowhead 5.00
Arrowhead jacket patch, brown twill, '71 (unofficial) 12.00

Arrowhead jacket patch, brown twill, '73 (unofficial) 12.00
Staff backpatch, USA shape, blue twill, yellow cut edge, '53-'55 .... 150.00
Staff trainee, green lettering on tan twill, '40s 85.00
Felt bull-men, black felt 5.00
Felt bull-women, white felt (obsolete) 10.00
Segment-Camper, black dutch oven on red twill, red cut edge, 50-60 ..... 8.00
Segment-Conservationalist, brown beaver lodge on yellow twill, red cut edge,
   50-60 .... 8.00
Segment-Horseman, yellow spur on black twill, red cut edge, 50-60 ...... 8.00
Segment-Mountainman, black musket on yellow twill, black cut edge, 50-60
                                                                       50.00
Segment-Naturalist, brown mesa, green pine tree on blue twill, red cut edge,
   50-60 .... 8.00
Segment-Staff, "Staff" in red lettering on orange twill, black cut edge, 50-60
                                                                   ..... 26.00
Segment-Sportsman, red cap on black twill, red cut edge, 50-60 .... 8.00
Segment-Woodsman, brown log cabin on blue twill, red cut edge, 50-60 .. 8.00
Shield shape, red twill, National Explorer Elected Leader Training Course,
   white cut edge, mid 50's 42.00
Shield shape, red twill, National Senior Crew Leader Training Course, white
   cut edge, 53-55 .... 65.00
Shield shape, red twill, National Junior Leader Training Camp, white cut edge
   early 60's 30.00
Shield shape, red twill, National Junior Leader Instructor Training Camp,
   white rolled edge, 63-72 .... 24.00
Shield shape, red twill, National Troop Leader Development, white rolled
   edge, 73-74 .... 22.00
Shield shape, red twill, National Conservation Training Camp, white rolled
   edge, has blue loop, '72 .... 22.00
Shield shape, red twill, National Explorer Elected Leader Training Course,
   white rolled edge, 57-58 .... 45.00
Shield Shape, red twill, National Conservation Training Camp, white rolled
   edge, no loop, 64-68 .... 28.00
Shield shape, red twill, Conservation Instructor Training Camp, white rolled
   edge, 69-72 .... 33.00
25th Anniversary, round orange twill, white rolled edge, '75 .... 5.00
Handicraft participant, brown leather with stamped design (also white) 12.00
Staff, round yellow twill, red, white, black design, white rolled edge, 70-71
                                                                   ..... 21.00
Round, orange twill, red, white, black design, white rolled edge, '73 ...... 4.00
Round, orange twill, red, white design, red rolled edge, small, 71-73 ...... 6.50
Round, yellow twill, red, white design, red rolled edge, 70-71 .... 3.00
Round, yellow twill, 69-70 .... 3.50
CTC, arrowhead, brown twill, embroidered CTC, 62-74 .... 60.00
Indian Leaders' Seminar, round blue twill, rolled edge, '74 .... 40.00
Lifeline USA, triangle, blue twill, blue rolled edge, '74 .... 20.00
National Catholic Training, round, yellow twill, black rolled edge 25.00
Junior Leader Training, USA shape red felt, white cut edge 100.00
OA Indian Seminiar, round, blue twill, rolled edge, '74 .... 25.00
Round, yellow twill, red, white, black design, red rolled edge, '74 .... 2.50

SCHIFF SCOUT RESERVATION ITEMS

Top row, L to R: Schiff Shield patch 5.00
   Schiff B.S.A. 50th anniversary patch 50.00
2nd row, L to R: Schiff Scout Reservation plastic n-c slide
   (Neal) 5.00
   Schiff Scout Reservation patch, 1st issue 25.00
   Schiff NJLITC plastic n-c slide (neal) 6.00
3rd row, L to R: Hiker of Schiff Trails plastic n-c slide (Neal)
   Schiff Professional Training Course 7503 patch 6.50
   Schiff Shield, metal n-c slide 5.00
   Schiff NJLITC plastic n-c slide 5.00

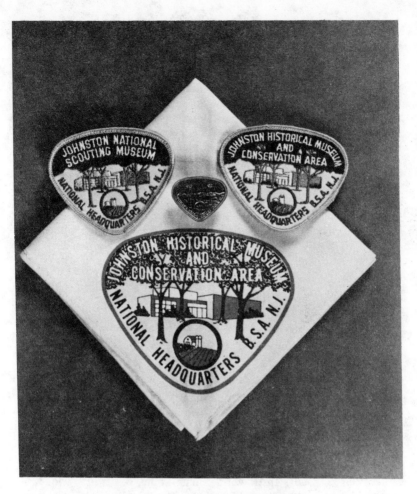

JOHNSTON SCOUT MUSEUM ITEMS
Top row, L to R: Johnston National Scouting Museum patch
...... 10.00
   Johnston Historical Museum and Conservation Area metal
   n-c slide 5.00
   Johnston Historical Museum and Conservation Area
   pocket patch 7.50
Bottom: Johnston Historical Museum and Conservation Area
   n-c 6.00

PHILTURN ROCKY MOUNTAIN SCOUTCAMP

Round, orange twill, red letters, black cut edge, black 70.00

Blue twill, black letters, yellow cut edge, black 75.00

Khaki twill, khaki mountains, blue sky & lake, red letters, black cut edge,
black 80.00

Round, orange twill, red letters, black cut edge, black 70.00

Round, blue twill, black letters, yellow cut edge, black 75.00

Round, khaki twill, khaki mountains, blue sky & lake, red letters, black cut
edge, black 80.00

Round, orange twill, orange mountains, blue sky & lake, red letters, black cut
edge, red 50.00

Round, orange twill, orange mountains, blue sky & lake, red letters, black cut
edge, black 45.00

Round, blue twill, light brown mountains, blue sky & lake, red letters, lt.
brown cut edge, black 50.00

Philmont segment, this is white twill arc segment with green "Philmont" and
green border with a cut edge 2.50

SCHIFF SCOUT RESERVATION
(Now Closed)

50th Anniversary, round, yellow twill, yellow rolled edge, '60 .... 50.00

Conservation Training Camp, round, yellow twill 32.00

National Explorer Elected Leader Training Camp, shield shape, red twill,
white cut edge 52.00

National Troop Leader Development, shield shape, red twill, white rolled edge
...... 18.00

National Ecology Workshop, shield shape, red twill, white rolled edge ... 40.00

National Explorer Elected Leader Training Camp, shield shape, red twill,
white rolled edge 42.00

National Junior Leader Training Camp, shield shape, red twill, white rolled
edge 26.00

National Junior Leader Instructor Training Camp, shield shape, red twill,
white rolled edge 22.00

National Junior Leader Instructor Training Camp, red twill shield, white
rolled edge 26.00

National Conservation Instructor Training Camp, red twill shield, white rolled
edge 41.00

Square khaki, green emblem, bronze lettering 25.00

Round khaki, green emblem, bronze lettering 20.00

Fully embroidered shield, yellow badge over red, yellow rolled edge, white &
blue shield issued '56 .... 5.00

N.E.I. Course patch, various, each 5.00

JOHNSTON SCOUT MUSEUM
Now Relocated to Kentucky

Rounded triangle, yellow twill, orange rolled edge, lettering at top reads
'Johnston National Scouting Museum' 6.00

Rounded triangle, orange rolled edge, lettering at top reads 'Johnston
Historical Museum and Conservation Area.' 4.50

PHILMONT PATCHES

Top row: Philmont 35th anniversary patch 6.00

2nd row, L to R: Philmont Seton Museum patch 3.00
 Philmont arc segment 2.50
 Kit Carson Museum patch 3.00

3rd row: Philmont arrowhead hat patch 5.00
 Philmont Bicentennial patch 10.00
 Philmont Training Center patch, small, orange twill, red
 rolled edge 6.50

4th ro, L to R: Philmont Training Center patch, yellow twill,
 red border 3.50
 Philmont Scout Ranch patch with 5 segments starting at
 top moving clockwise 18.00
 Camper, Woodsman, Conservationist, Naturalist and
 Sportsman, each 12.00
 Philmont Scout Ranch pocket patch, white twill 2.00

Bottom row, L to R; Philmont Training Center patch, orange
 twill, white rolled edge (25th anniversary) 5.00
 Philmont Volunteer Training Center patch 2.50
 Philmont Training Center patch, orange twill, red rolled
 edge 3.50

PHILMONT ITEMS

Top row, L to R: Philmont Volunteer Training Center metal,
n-c slide 2.50

1949 U.S. Grant Council Philmont contingent jacket patch,
black on white felt 20.00

Philmont arrowhead emblem tie bar, short bar type .. 2.00

2nd row, L to R: Philmont arrowhead metal n-c slide 5.00

Philmont 1966 Buffalo Head Plaster n-c slide 5.00

3rd row, L to R: Philmont Scout Ranch leather patch 5.00

Philmont Bull patch, white 12.00

Bottom row, L to R: Philmont Tooth of Time plaster n-c slide
(brown on white) 2.75

Philmont Brand plaster n-c slide 3.00

Philmont Tooth of Time plaster n-c slide (white on brown)
...... 6.00

Philmont Scout Ranch arrowhead patch 15.00

SOMMERS WILDERNESS CANOE BASE
Region 10 Canoe Base

Historic Trails, round turquoise twill, white lettering, red rolled edge & tab, '76 .... 18.00

Northern Expedition, round turquoise twill, white bear & lettering, white rolled edge, cotton tab 15.00

Northern Expedition, round jacket patch, turquoise twill, white bear & lettering, white rolled edge, cotton tab 21.00

Okpik, round dark blue twill, white snow owl with black outline, red lettering, white rolled edge, white cotton tab on back, 72-75 .... 18.00

Okpik, round dark blue twill, white snow owl, black outline, red lettering, white rolled edge, blue cotton tab on back, '76 .... 18.00

Okpik, round jacket patch, black twill, white snow owl, black outline, red letters, white rolled edge 28.00

Staff, blue twill rectangle, black loon, red letters "Staff", red rolled edge 18.00

Staff, blue twill rectangle, red rolled edge & letters "Staff", black letters "Les Voyageurs", standing trapper with paddle 15.00

Round blue felt, red lettering & robe 60.00

Round dark blue twill, white lettering, red cut edge 41.00

Round blue twill, white lettering "Region Ten B.S.A. Wilderness Canoe Trails" red cut edge, embroidered loop 45.00

Round blue twill, says "Region Ten B.S.A. Wilderness Canoe Trials" face finely detailed, red cut edge 36.00

Round blue twill, white lettering "Charles L. Sommers Wilderness Canoe Trails" red cut edge 28.00

Round blue twill, white lettering "Charles L. Sommers Wilderness Canoe Base" red cut edge 30.00

Round blue twill, white lettering "Charles L. Sommers Wilderness Canoe Base B.S.A." red rolled edge & red cotton loop 8.00

Round blue twill, white lettering "Charles L. Sommers Wilderness Canoe Base B.S.A." red rolled edge, no tab 8.00

Round blue twill, white lettering "Charles L. Sommers Canoe Base B.S.A." white rolled edge, white cotton tab '76 .... 6.00

Round jacket patch, blue twill, white lettering, red rolled edge 6.00

NORTHERN WISCONSIN NATIONAL CANOE BASE
Region 7 Canoe Base

25th Anniversary, red twill, red canoe, yellow lettering "25th Anniversary Explorer Canoe Base B.S.A.", silver mylar cut edge and center 16.00

30th Anniversary, white twill, yellow lettering "30th" and "7", blue paddles andd lettering "Anniversary", red canoe and lettering "Canoe", green "BSA" and tree, yellow rolled edge 12.00

Staff, red twill shield, gray lettering and canoe, yellow paddles and cut edge 18.00

Red twill rectangle, white canoe, red rolled edge 12.00

Red twill, white lettering "Canoe Base B.S.A.", gold mylar "7" and paddles, silver mylar canoe, yellow rolled edge 9.00

Red twill, white lettering "Explorer Canoe Base B.S.A", silver mylar canoe, gold mylar "7" and paddles, yellow rolled edge 8.00

Segment-Leader, red twill, white lettering, yellow cut edge 10.00

Segment-Staff, red twill, white lettering, yellow cut edge 10.00

Segment-Voyageur, red twill, white lettering, yellow cut edge 8.00

Round orange twill, green emblem with lettering "Region Seven Scout Landing" green cut edge 42.00

Round red twill, white lettering "Region Seven B.S.A. Explorer Canoe Base" white canoe, yellow cut edge, yellow embroidered loop 12.00

Round red twill, white lettering, yellow cut edge, no loop 12.00

Round red twill, white lettering "Region Seven B.S.A. Explorer Canoe Base" yellow paddles and loop, yellow rolled edge 9.00

Round red twill, white lettering "Region Seven B.S.A. Canoe Base" yellow paddles, yellow rolled edge, white loop at top 6.00

Round red twill, white lettering "Region Seven B.S.A. Canoe Base", yellow paddles and rolled edge 6.00

Round red twill, white lettering "Northern Wisconsin Nat'l Canoe Base", orange paddles, yellow rolled edge 4.00

MAINE NATIONAL HIGH ADVENTURE BASE
Region 1 Canoe Trails

Round white felt, red lettering and paddle tips, yellow paddles, green tree, black outline 50.00

Round white felt, hiker and trees, green outline, '48 .... 45.00

Maine Matagamon BSA 1971, yellow twill, shape of Maine, red lettering, "1971" in black, black cut edge, '71 .... 24.00

Maine Matagamon BSA, yellow twill, shape of Maine, red lettering, embroidered water, black cut edge, '72 .... 22.00

Matagamon BSA, yellow twill, shape of Maine, solid embroidered water, red lettering, black cut edge, '73 .... 16.00

Matagamon, yellow twill shape of Maine, red lettering, loop on back, black cut edge, '74 .... 16.00

Maine National High Adventure Area, yellow twill jacket patch, black lettering, red rolled edge, '74 .... 11.00

Maine Matagamon, yellow twill hat patch, diamond, black cut edge, '71 . 8.00

Maine Matagamon, yellow twill rectangle, black letters and rolled edge, '72 ...... 11.00

Maine BSA, yellow twill rectnagle, black lettering and rolled edge, 73-74 10.00
Same only with "MAINE B.S.A." in black rectangle 8.00

Seboomook BSA 1973, yellow twill shape of Maine, black "1973" and cut edge, red lettering, '73 .... 21.00

Seboomook BSA, yellow twill shape of Maine, red lettering, black cut edge, loop on back, '74 .... 16.00

Syslodobsis Expedition 1975, round yellow twill, black design, red rolled edge, '75 .... 12.00

Round souvenir patch, red twill, white letters, black moose and rolled edge, '76 .... 9.00

Round bicentennial, white twill, Liberty Bell, red rolled edge, '76 .... 7.50

Staff, Base Director, yellow twill rectangle, black letters, rolled edge, '74 ...... 25.00

Staff, Base Staff, yellow twill rectangle, black letters, rolled edge, '74 ... 20.00

Staff, Chief Guide, yellow twill rectangle, black letters, rolled edge, '74 . $18.00

Staff, Coordinator, yellow twill rectangle, black letters, rolled edge, '74 . 15.00
Staff, Crew Leader, yellow twill rectangle, black letters, rolled edge, '75 10.00
Staff, Guide, yellow twill rectangle, black letters, rolled edge, '74 ...... 12.00
Staff, Manage M&T, yellow twill rectangle, black letters, rolled edge, '74
...... 22.50

LAND BETWEEN THE LAKES BASE
(Closed in 1980)
Round jacket patch, green twill, orange lettering, blue rolled edge, '75 .. 15.00
Round pocket patch, green twill, orange lettering, blue rolled edge, '75 .. 10.00
Round pocket patch, green twill, orange lettering with "TVA", blue rolled
edge, '76 .... 12.00

NATIONAL CAMPING SCHOOL (N.C.S.)
Assistant Director, tan square cut twill, Tepee in circle with yellow star horns
above, lettering "Assistant Director" 40.00
Director, tan square cut twill, Tepee in circle with yellow star horns above,
lettering "Director" 50.00
Chief Director, tan square art twill, Tepee in circle with yellow star horns
above, lettering "Chief Director" 63.00
Assistant Director, Khaki square cut twill, Tepee in circle with yellow star
horns above, lettering "Assistant Director" 22.00
Director, Khaki square cut twill, Tepee in circle with yellow star horns above,
lettering "Director" 29.00
Chief Director, Khaki square cut twill, Tepee in circle with yellow stag horns
above, lettering "Chief Director" 40.00
National Camping School patch, Khaki twill rectangle, Tepee in circle with
lettering "National Camping School" stag horns above with "B.S.A."
yellow cut edge 5.00
Same as above but with red lettering "Staff" over the tepee 15.00
Same as above except no "Staff" and lettering reads "National Camping
Award" 44.00
National Camping School Handicraft School, Khaki twill rectangle, tepee in
circle with lettering "National Camping School" totem pole above (believed
to be a short term experimental item), rare 60.00
National Camping School, khaki twill rectangle, tepee in circle with lettering
"National Camping School" stag horns above with "B.S.A." yellow rolled
edge 3.00
Same as above with addition of red "Staff" over tepee 10.00
Jacket Patch, same design as pocket patch only much larger yellow rolled
edge 12.00

NAMES OF BOY SCOUT PATROLS

1st series, black on red felt, 73
Alligator
American Bison
Antelope
Badger
Bat
Bear
Beaver
Black Bear
Blazing Arrow
Bobcat
Bobwhite
Buffalo
Bull
Cat
Cobra
Condor
Covered Wagon
Crow
Cuckoo
Curlew
Dan Beard
Duck
Eagle
Elephant
Flying, or Airplane
Flying Eagle
Fox
Frontiersman
Hawk
Hippo
Horse
Hound
Hyena
Indian
Jackal
Kangaroo
Lark
Lion
Longhorn
Mongoose
Moose
Other
Owl
Panther
Paul Bunyan
Peacock
Pedro
Peewit
Pelican
Penguin
Pine Tree
Porcupine
Raccoon

Ram
Rattlesnake
Raven
Rhino
Roadrunner
Rocket
Seagull
Seal
Squirrel
Stag
Stork
Swallow
Tiger
Whipporwill
Wild Boar
Wood Pigeon
Wolf
Wolverine
Woodpecker
Blank (plain)

2nd series, black on red twill, 52
Alligator
American Bison
Antelope
Badger
Bat
Bear
Beaver
Black Bear
Bobcat
Bobwhite
Buffalo
Cat
Cobra
Covered Wagon
Crow
Cuckoo
Dan Beard
Duck
Eagle
Flaming Arrow
Flying Eagle
Fox
Frontiersman
Hawk
Horse
Indian
Lion
Longhorn
Moose
Otter
Owl
Panther

Paul Bunyan
Pedro
Pelican
Pine Tree
Porcupine
Raccoon
Ram
Rattlesnake
Raven
Road Runner
Rocket
Seagull
Squirrel
Stag
Tiger
Whipporwill
Wolf
Wolverine
Woodpecker
Blank (plain)

3rd series, multicolored, 36
Alligator
Antelope (2 variations)
Badger
Bat
Bear
Beaver
Bison
Bobcat
Bobwhite
Cobra
Eagle
Flaming Arrow
Flying Eagle
Fox
Frog
Frontiersman
Hawk
Indian
Liberty
Moose
Owl
Panther
Pedro
Pheasant
Pine Tree
Raccoon
Ram
Rattlesnake
Raven
Road Runner
Stag
Tiger

Viking
Wolf
Blank, (plain)

GIRL SCOUT TROOP CREST NAMES
Bluebell
Bluebird
Bluebonnet
Brown Pansy
Buttercup
Cardinal (Bird)
Cardinal (Flower)
Carnation
Clover
Clover Leaf
Corn Flower (discontinued)
Crocus
Daffodil
Daisy
Dogwood
Forget-Me-Not
Fuchsia (discontinued)
Goldenrod
Holly
Iris
Jonquil
Lily of the Valley
Meadow Lark
Morning Glory
Mountain Laurel
Narcissus
Nasturtium (discontinued)
Oak
Pine Cone
Pine Tree
Poppy
Purple Pansy
Purple Violet
Red Rose
Robin
Scarlet Pimpernil
Star of Bethlehem
Wild Rose
Blank (plain)

B.S.A. NATIONAL CAMPING SCHOOL ITEMS

Top row, L to R: N.C.S. Director Patch, khaki twill 29.00

    N.C.S. Jacket Patch 12.00

    N.C.S. Pocket patch, cut edge 5.00

Middle: N.C.S. Neckerchief, emblem is silk screened cream

    n-c 6.50

Bottom row, L to R: N.C.S. Handicraft School pocket patch,

    cut edge 60.00

    N.C.S. pocket patch, rolled edge 3.00

    N.C.S. Staff pocket patch, rolled edge 10.00

POSITION (Office)
Boy Scouts

Assistant Patrol Leader

Teens, one green felt bar on tan twill, square cut 10.00

20's, one embroidered green bar on tan twill, square cut 3.00

1946, one embroidered green bar on khaki, cut edge 2.00

Early 60's, one embroidered green bar on khaki, cut edge with border, heavy twill 1.00

Late 60's, one embroidered green bar on khaki, cut edge with border, cotton, polyester .... .75

1970, one embroidered green bar on khaki, rolled edge with border, cotton, polyester. NOTE: Most of this series is quite rare 1.50

1973, one embroidered green bar on 3" round green twill, yellow rolled edge .... .50

Patrol Leader, all same description and dates as assistant patrol leader, but instead of one bar, the patrol leader has two bars. Values for this position are about the same as for the assistant patrol leader ....

Asisstant Senior Patrol Leader, has all same description and dates as assistant patrol leader but has 2 bars and 1st class emblem. Vaues prior to 1960 are slightly higher tan for Patrol Leader, after 1960, the same ....

Senior Patrol Leader, has all same description and dates as assistant patrol leader but has 2½ bars with 1st class emblem. Value prior to 1960 are slightly higher than for Assistant Senior Patrol Leader, after 1960, the same.

Bugler, bugle on patch instead of bars, rest of description is same ....

Cabin Boy, yellow anchor on navy background on tan twill, yellow oval (ca. '35-'45), rare 20.00

Chaplain Aid, 1973 white twill, blue rolled edge, round 1.50

1977 green twill, yellow rolled edge, round .... .50

Den Chief, 1973 .... .50

Historian, 1975 .... .50

Librarian, 1946 .... .50

Musician, yellow lyre, scout emblem on black background, green rolled edge 10.00

3" round green twill, red rolled edge, music note over staff .... .50

Quartermaster, values the same as bugler ....

Scribe, values the same as bugler ....

Leadership Corp, 1973 odd shape red twill, yellow lettering, yellow rolled edge 1.00

Junior Assistant Scout Master

Teens, 3 plain green felt bars on tan 28.00

20's, 3 green embroidered bars on tan, 1st class emblem over bars 18.00

1937, 2½" round green twill, no wording, brown rings and 1st class emblem, cut edge 10.00

1943, 2½" round green twill, no wording, brown ring, yellow 1st class emblem 6.50

1956, 2½" round green twill, lettering "Boy Scouts of America", brown ring, yellow 1st class emblem, cut edge 4.00

1967, 2¼" round green twill, lettering "Boy Scouts of America", brown rolled edge 1.50

1970, 2½" round green twill, lettering "Boy Scouts of America", yellow rolled edge 1.00

1973, 3" round green twill, white lettering "Jr. Assistant Scout Master", tenderfoot emblem, white rolled edge .... .75

PATROL LEADER PATCHES

Top to bottom: 1973 series, round .... .50
Early 1960 series, cut edge 1.00
1946 series, square cut khaki 2.00

B.S.A. BOY LEADER PATCHES

Top row, L to R: Musician patch, 1st series 10.00
   Musician patch, early 1960's cut edge 1.00
   Musician patch, late 1960's, cut edge .... .75
Middle row: Quartermaster patch, 1973 series .... .50
   Musician patch, 1973 series .... .50
Bottom row: Quartermaster patch, 1946 series 2.00
   Quartermaster patch, early 1960's series 1.00
   Quartermaster patch, late 1960's series .... .75

ASSISTANT SCOUTMASTER

1910, red embroidered outline of 1st class emblem on khaki, red background, light brown eagle 42.00

1920, yellow embroidered outline of 1st class emblem on khaki, light green background, yellow eagle 22.50

1938, yellow embroidered outline of 1st class emblem on green twill, yellow background and eagle 5.00

1967, fully embroidered 1st class emblem with yellow outline on twill, green background with yellow eagle, cut edge 1.50

1970, green 1st class emblem on green cloth, yellow lettering, rolled edge . 1.00

1973, yellow 1st class emblem on green cloth, yellow border and lettering, rolled edge .... .75

2nd, mylar rolled edge (for training) 1.50

SCOUTMASTER

1910, dark green outline of 1st class emblem on khaki, dark green background, brown eagle, 3 varieties, green, lime, dark green 48.00

1920, white outline of 1st class emblem on khaki, light green background, white eagle, 3 varieties, green, lime, dark green 10.00

1938, white outline of 1st class emblem with white background on green twill, white eagle 6.00

1967, fully embroidered 1st class emblem with white outline on twill, white eagle, cut edge 1.50

1970, green 1st class emblem on green cloth, white lettering, rolled edge .. 1.00

1973, yellow 1st class emblem on green cloth, white border and lettering, rolled edge .... .75

2nd, Mylar rolled edge (for training) 1.50

PRIMARY LEADER

1975, yellow 1st class emblem on green cloth, yellow border and letters, rolled edge 12.00

CHAPLAIN

1931, yellow outline of 1st class emblem with yellow background on khaki, yellow eagle 26.00

1956, fully embroidered yellow 1st class emblem on yellow background, yellow eagle, cut edge 12.00

1967, fully embroidered yellow 1st class emblem on yellow background, yellow eagle, rolled edge 7.00

1968, fully embroidered yellow 1st class emblem on yellow background, brown eagle, oval shaped, rolled edge 7.50

1973, embroidered yellow 1st class emblem on white cloth, blue border and letters, rolled edge 1.50

PHYSICAN

1931, yellow outline of 1st class emblem with yellow background on khaki, yellow eagle 26.00

1956, fully embroidered yellow 1st class emblem on yellow background, yellow eagle and yellow caduceus, cut edge 12.00

1958, same as 1956 except caduceus is red 15.00

1967, fully embroidered yellow 1st class emblem on yellow background, yellow eagle, rolled edge 6.00

1970, yellow embroidered 1st class emblem, yellow lettering, says "Physician" rolled edge 6.00

1973, yellow embroidered 1st class emblem on white cloth with blue border and lettering, rolled edge 1.50

INSTITUTIONAL REPRESENTATIVE
1973, yellow 1st class emblem on blue cloth, yellow border and letterings, rolled edge 1.50

1975, same for SCOUTING COORDINATOR (position name changed) 1.00

TROOP COMMITTEE (Committeeman)
1920 (see layman description for 1929. Title of position changed in 1929) ....

1970, blue embroidered 1st class emblem on blue cloth, yellow lettering, rolled edge 1.50

1973, yellow embroidered 1st class emblem on green cloth, bronze border and lettering, rolled edge 1.00

TROOP COMMITTEE CHAIRMAN
1973, white embroidered 1st class emblem on green cloth, white border and lettering, rolled edge 1.00

LAYMAN (old title for committeeman, etc. to designate lay volunteers serving as various levels)
1929, yellow outline of 1st class emblem with blue background on khaki, yellow eagle 25.00

1932, fully embroidered yellow 1st class emblem with yellow background on khaki, yellow eagle 18.00

1938, round, fully embroidered 1st class emblem with yellow background on khaki, yellow eagle 12.00

1943, yellow, fully embroidered 1st class emblem with yellow background on blue twill, yellow eagle 10.00

1956, yellow embroidered 1st class emblem on blue background, yellow eagle, cut edge 4.00

1967, same only with rolled edge 2.00

NEIGHBORHOOD COMMISSIONER (was formerly titled Asst. Deputy Scout Commissioner)
1932, yellow outline of 1st class emblem with blue background on khaki, yellow eagle and yellow wreath 22.00

1956, yellow embroidered 1st class emblem with blue background, yellow eagle and yellow wreath, cut edge 6.00

1967, yellow embroidered 1st class emblem with blue background, yellow eagle and wreath, rolled edge 2.50

1970, yellow badge on blue cloth, yellow lettering, rolled edge 1.25

UNIT COMMISSIONER
1975, yellow badge on blue cloth, yellow border and lettering, rolled edge 26.00
  Yellow badge on red cloth, yellow border and lettering, rolled edge 1.00
  Yellow badge on red cloth, yellow lettering, silver mylar rolled edge ... 1.50

UNIT COMMISSIONER
1973, yellow badge on red cloth, white border and lettering, rolled edge ... 3.00

JUNIOR ASSISTANT SCOUTMASTER PATCHES

Top row, L to R: 1937 series 10.00

　1967 series 1.50

Middle row, L to R: 1943 series 6.50

　1970 series 1.00

Bottom row, L to R: 1956 series 4.00

　1973 series .... .75

SCOUTMASTER PATCHES

Top: 1920 series 10.00
2nd row, L to R: 1938 series 6.00
    1970 series 1.00
Center: 1967 series 1.50
Bottom row, l to R: 1973 series .... .75
    1975 series (trained) 1.50

TROOP COMMISSIONER
1975, yellow badge on blue cloth, yellow border and lettering, rolled edge 20.00
    Yellow badge on red cloth, yellow border and lettering, rolled edge 1.00
    Yellow badge on red cloth, yellow lettering, silver mylar rolled edge ... 1.50

PACK COMMISSIONER
1975, yellow badge on blue cloth, yellow border and lettering, rolled edge 18.00
    Yellow badge on red cloth, yellow border and lettering, rolled edge 1.00
    Yellow badge on red cloth, yellow lettering, silver mylar rolled edge ... 1.50

SCOUT ROUNDTABLE STAFF
1970, yellow badge on red cloth, green center and yellow lettering, rolled edge
    ...... 1.50

ASSISTANT ROUNDTABLE COMMISSIONER
1970, yellow badge on blue cloth, yellow lettering, rolled edge 1.50

ROUNDTABLE COMMISSIONER
1970, yellow badge on blue cloth, yellow lettering, rolled edge 1.50

SCOUT ROUNDTABLE COMMISSIONER
1973, yellow badge on red background, green center, yellow border, yellow
    lettering, rolled edge 1.00

SPONSOR COORDINATOR
1973, yellow badge on blue cloth, yellow border and lettering, rolled edge . 1.00

PARAPROFESSIONAL
1970, yellow badge on red cloth, yellow lettering, rolled edge 4.50

EMPLOYEE
1926, bronze outline of 1st class emblem with red background on khaki, bronze
    eagle 50.00
1956, yellow embroidered 1st class emblem with red background on khaki,
    yellow eagle, cut edge 10.00
1967, yellow embroidered scout emblem with yellow background, yellow
    eagle, rolled edge 6.00
1970, yellow badge on red cloth, white lettering, rolled edge 4.00
1975, yellow badge on red cloth, yellow border and lettering, rolled edge .. 2.00

ASSISTANT RANGER
1956, yellow embroidered 1st class emblem with yellow background, yellow
    eagle, cut edge 15.00
1967, yellow embroidered 1st class emblem with yellow background, yellow
    eagle, rolled edge 8.00
1970, yellow badge on red cloth, white lettering, rolled edge ·............. 3.50
1975, yellow badge on red cloth, yellow border and lettering, rolled edge .. 2.50

RANGER
1947, yellow outline of 1st class emblem with red background on khaki, yellow
    eagle 20.00
1956, yellow embroidered 1st class emblem on yellow background, yellow
    eagle, cut edge 12.00

1967, yellow embroidered 1st class emblem on yellow background, yellow eagle, rolled edge 3.50

1970, yellow badge on red cloth, white lettering, rolled edge 3.50

1975, yellow badge on red cloth, yellow border and lettering, rolled edge .. 2.50

ASSISTANT DISTRICT COMMISSIONER
1956, white embroidered 1st class emblem on blue background, yellow eagle and wreath, cut edge 8.00

1967, same, only with rolled edge 4.00

1970, yellow badge on blue cloth, yellow lettering, rolled edge 2.50

1973, yellow badge on red cloth, yellow border and lettering, rolled edge .. 1.25

DISTRICT COMMISSIONER (was formerly titled Deputy Scout Commissioner.)
1926, white outline of 1st class emblem with blue background, yellow wreath and white eagle, on square cut, tan 35.00

1943, same only now on khaki 12.00

1956, white embroidered 1st class emblem on blue background, white eagle, yellow wreath, cut edge 7.00

1967, white embroidered 1st class emblem on blue background, white eagle, yellow wreath, rolled edge 4.25

1970, yellow tenderfoot badge on blue twill, yellow lettering, rolled edge .. 3.00

1973, yellow tenderfoot emblem on red twill, white lettering and border, rolled edge 1.25-

DISTRICT EXECUTIVE STAFF
1973, yellow tenderfoot emblem on maroon twill, yellow border and lettering, rolled edge 5.00

ASSISTANT DISTRICT EXECUTIVE STAFF (formerly Asst. Field Scout Executive.)
1926, yellow outline of 1st class emblem with red background on square tan, yellow eagle and wreath 30.00

1943, same only now on khaki 18.00

1956, same but now a standard cut edge patch, no outside excess cloth ... 11.00

DISTRICT EXECUTIVE (was formerly titled Field Scout Executive.)
1926, white outline of 1st class emblem with red background on square tan, yellow eagle and wreath 30.00

1943, same only now on khaki 18.00

1956, same but now a standard cut edge patch, no outside excess cloth ... 11.00

1967, white embroidered 1st class emblem on red background, yellow eagle and wreath, rolled edge 6.00

1973, yellow tenderfoot emblem on maroon twill, white border and lettering, rolled edge 5.00

DISTRICT COMMITTEE
1970, blue tenderfoot emblem on blue twill, yellow lettering, rolled edge .. 3.00

1973, yellow tenderfoot emblem on blue twill, bronze border and lettering, rolled edge 1.00

DISTRICT CHAIRMAN
1973, yellow tenderfoot emblem on blue twill, white border and lettering, rolled edge 1.25

CHAPTER ADVISOR
1973, round, yellow tenderfoot emblem on blue cloth with yellow lettering and border, rolled edge 1.50

ASSISTANT COUNCIL COMMISSIONER
1968, white embroidered 1st class emblem on blue background, white wreath, yellow eagle, rolled edge 4.50

1970, yellow tenderfoot emblem on blue twill, yellow lettering, rolled edge 4.00

1973, yellow tenderfoot emblem on red twill, yellow border and lettering .. 2.00

1973, yellow tenderfoot emblem on red twill, yellow border and lettering, rolled edge 2.00

COUNCIL COMMISSIONER (formerly titled Scout Commissioner)
1926, white embroidered 1st class emblem on blue background, white eagle and wreath, on square cut twill 45.00

1943, same only now on khaki twill 22.00

1956, white embroidered 1st class emblem on blue background, white eagle and white wreath, cut edge 12.00

1967, white embroidered 1st class emblem on blue background, white eagle and white wreath, rolled edge 5.00

1970, yellow tenderfoot emblem on blue twill, yellow lettering, rolled edge
...... 6.00

1973, yellow tenderfoot emblem on red twill, white border and lettering, rolled edge 1.50

COUNCIL EXECUTIVE STAFF
1973, yellow tenderfoot emblem on maroon twill, yellow border and lettering, rolled edge 6.50

COUNCIL EXECUTIVE (formerly Scout Executive)
1926, embroidered white 1st class emblem, eagle and wreath on square cut tan, red background 30.00

1943, same only now on khaki 20.00

1956, same only now a standard cut edge patch, no outside excess material
...... 15.00

1967, same as 1956 only now has rolled edge 10.00

1970, white scout emblem and lettering on red cloth, white rolled edge ... 8.00

1973, yellow tenderfoot emblem on maroon background, white border and lettering, rolled edge 5.00

COUNCIL COMMITTEE (formerly Local Councilman)
1920, white 1st class emblem with dark brown eagle, on tan square cut twill, no wreath 60.00
NOTE: position abolished in 1928 and reverted to "Layman" title until 1970.

1970, blue tenderfoot emblem on blue twill, yellow lettering, rolled edge .. 4.50

1973, yellow tenderfoot emblem on blue twill, bronze border and lettering, rolled edge 2.00

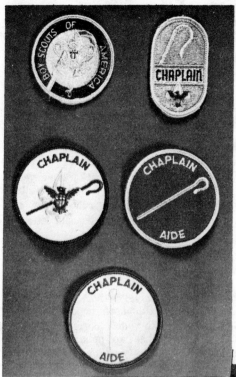

BSA CHAPLAIN & CHAPLAIN AIDE PATCHES
Top row, L to R:
Chaplain, 1967
Top row, L to R:
Chaplain, 1967
series 10.00
Chaplain, 1968
series 7.50
Middle row, L to
R: Chaplain,
1973 series .. 1.50
Chaplain Aide,
1975 series ... .50
Bottom: Chaplain
Aide, 1973 series
.... 1.50

BSA PHYSICIAN PATCHES
Top row, L to R:
1956 series . 20.00
1970 series .. 7.50
Bottom row, L to
R: 1967 series ...
10.00
1973 series .. 1.50

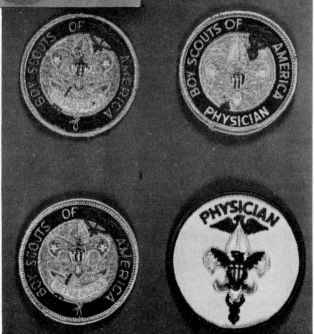

COUNCIL EXECUTIVE BOARD
1973, yellow tenderfoot emblem on blue twill, white border and lettering, rolled edge 2.50

COUNCIL VICE PRESIDENT
1973, yellow tenderfoot emblem on blue twill, yellow border and lettering, rolled edge 2.50

COUNCIL PRESIDENT
1956, yellow embroidered 1st class emblem with yellow background, yellow wreath and eagle, blue center, cut edge has hands pointing out 28.00

1967, yellow embroidered 1st class emblem with yellow background, yellow wreath and eagle, blue center, rolled edge, has hands pointing out 22.00

1968, yellow embroidered 1st class emblem with yellow background, yellow wreath, brown eagle, blue center, rolled edge, has hands pointing out . 15.00

1970, white tenderfoot emblem on blue twill, white lettering, rolled edge . 7.00

1973, yellow tenderfoot emblem on blue twill, white border and lettering, rolled edge 5.00

COUNCIL PAST PRESIDENT
1956, yellow embroidered 1st class emblem with yellow background, yellow wreath and eagle, blue center, cut edge, has hand pointing down 30.00

1967, yellow embroidered 1st class emblem with yellow background, yellow wreath and eagle, blue center, rolled edge, has hand pointing down ... 26.00

1968, yellow embroidered 1st class emblem with yellow background, yellow wreath, brown eagle, blue center, rolled edge, has hand pointing down 18.00

1970, white tenderfoot emblem on blue twill, white letters, rolled edge ... 8.00

1973, yellow tenderfoot emblem on blue twill, white border and lettering, rolled edge 5.00

LODGE ADVISOR
1973, round, yellow tenderfoot emblem on blue cloth with white lettering and border, rolled edge 2.00

AREA COMMITTEE
1973, yellow tenderfoot emblem on dark green twill, bronze border and lettering, rolled edge 8.00

AREA PRESIDENT
1973, yellow tenderfoot emblem on dark green twill, white border and lettering, rolled edge 12.00

SECTION ADVISOR
1973, round yellow tenderfoot emblem on dark green cloth, white lettering and border, rolled edge 6.50

REGIONAL SCOUT EXECUTIVE
1923, yellow outline of 1st class emblem with yellow background on khaki, yellow wreath and eagle, red, white, blue center 50.00

1940, DISCONTINUED

REGIONAL COMMITTEE
1973, yellow embroidered tenderfoot emblem on wine twill, bronze border and lettering, rolled edge 10.00

REGIONAL PRESIDENT
1973, yellow embroidered tenderfoot emblem on wine twill, white border and lettering, rolled edge 15.00

NATIONAL COMMITTEE (formerly National Council and National Councilman)
1910, purple 1st class emblem with dark brown eagle on square cut tan, no wreath 100.00-120.00

NOTE: This position was discontinued in 1930 and reverted to Layman until 1973.

1973, round, yellow tenderfoot emblem on purple cloth with tan letters and border, rolled edge 15.00

1980, round, same design as 1973 series only now background is fully embroidered 10.00

NATIONAL STAFF
1932, white outline of 1st class emblem with yellow background on tan, yellow wreath and eagle, red, white, blue center 60.00

1940, white outline of 1st class emblem with white background on khaki, yellow wreath and eagle, red, white, blue center 40.00

1956, white embroidered 1st class emblem with white background, yellow wreath and eagle, red, white, blue center, cut edge 12.00

1967, white embroidered 1st class emblem with yellow background, yellow wreath and eagle, red, white, blue center, rolled edge 10.00

1970, yellow tenderfoot emblem on red twill, yellow lettering, white and blue center, rolled edge 10.00

NATIONAL EXECUTIVE STAFF (name changed from National Staff)
1973, yellow tenderfoot emblem on maroon twill, yellow border and lettering, red, white, blue center, rolled edge 10.00

SPECIAL NATIONAL FIELD SCOUT COMMISSIONER
1920, white outline of 1st class emblem with purple background on square cut tan, yellow wreath and eagle, red, white, blue center 145.00

1923, white outline of 1st class emblem with white background on square cut tan, yellow wreath, white eagle, dark blue center 110.00

1940, white outline of 1st class emblem with light blue background on khaki, yellow wreath, white eagle, red, white, blue center 95.00

1956, white embroidered 1st class emblem with white background, yellow wreath, white eagle, purple center, cut edge 75.00

1961, white embroidered 1st class emblem with white background, yellow wreath, brown eagle, purple center, cut edge 65.00

1967, white embroidered 1st class emblem with white background, yellow wreath, white eagle, purple center, rolled edge 35.00

1970, replaced by National Partner Representative.

NATIONAL PARTNER REPRESENTATIVE (replaced Special National Field Scout Commissioner)
1970, yellow tenderfoot emblem on purple twill, white lettering is "National Partner Representative" around top border, rolled edge 20.00

1973, yellow tenderfoot emblem on purple twill, white border and lettering is "National" around top and "Partner Representative" around bottom, rolled edge 10.00

NATIONAL SCOUT COMMISSIONER

1915, yellow outline of 1st class emblem with yellow background on square cut tan, yellow wreath, white eagle, white powderhorn 200.00

1923, yellow outline of 1st class emblem on square cut tan, yellow wreath, white eagle, white powderhorn 160.00

1937, white outline of 1st class emblem with white background on square cut tan, white wreath and eagle, white powderhorn 150.00

1940, yellow outline of 1st class emblem with yellow background on khaki, yellow wreath and eagle, yellow powderhorn 125.00

1956, white embroidered 1st class emblem with white background, white wreath and eagle, white powderhorn, cut edge 110.00

1958, white embroidered 1st class emblem with white background, white wreath, brown eagle, cut edge 85.00

1959, DISCONTINUED

ASSISTANT NATIONAL FIELD SCOUT EXECUTIVE

1920, yellow outline of 1st class emblem with purple background on square cut tan, yellow wreath, yellow eagle 125.00

1920, white outline of 1st class emblem with purple background on square cut tan, yellow wreath and eagle 125.00

DEPUTY CHIEF SCOUT EXECUTIVE

1920, white outline of 1st class emblem with purple background on square cut tan, yellow wreath, white eagle 220.00

1923, white outline of 1st class emblem with white background on square cut tan, yellow wreath, white eagle, red, white, blue center 180.00

1943, same only now on khaki 150.00

1956, white embroidered 1st class emblem on white background, yellow wreath, white eagle, red, white, blue center, cut edge 135.00

CHIEF SCOUT EXECUTIVE

1920, white outline of 1st class emblem with purple background on square cut tan, white wreath and eagle 250.00

1923, white outline of 1st class emblem with white background on square cut tan, white wreath, white eagle, red, white, blue center 200.00

1943, same only now on khaki 120.00

1956, white embroidered 1st class emblem with white background, white wreath and eagle, red, white, blue scroll, cut edge 110.00

1959, white embroidered 1st class emblem with white background, white wreath and eagle, red, white, blue twill scroll, cut edge 110.00

1967, white embroidered 1st class emblem with white background, white wreath and eagle, red, white, blue center, rolled edge 90.00

1970, white tenderfoot emblem on red twill, white lettering, white, blue center, rolled edge 60.00

1973, white tenderfoot emblem on maroon twill, white border and lettering, red, white, blue center, rolled edge 45.00

CHIEF SCOUT

1943, white outline of 1st class emblem with white background on khaki, white wreath, brown eagle 210.00

1956, white embroidered 1st class emblem with white background, white wreath, brown eagle, cut edge 125.00

NATIONAL EXECUTIVE BOARD

1929, white outline of 1st class emblem with purple background on khaki, yellow eagle 110.00

1956, white embroidered 1st class emblem on purple background, yellow eagle, cut edge 60.00

1967, white embroidered 1st class emblem on purple background, yellow eagle, yellow rolled edge 45.00

1968, yellow embroidered 1st class emblem on purple background, yellow eagle, purple rolled edge 28.00

1970, white tenderfoot emblem on purple twill, white lettering, rolled edge 15.00

1973, yellow tenderfoot emblem on purple twill, tan border and lettering, rolled edge 10.00

1980 round, same as 1973 series only now background is fully embroidered 12.00

NATIONAL VICE PRESIDENT

1970, white tenderfoot emblem on purple twill, white lettering, rolled edge 15.00

1973, yellow tenderfoot emblem on purple twill, yellow border and lettering, rolled edge 15.00

1980, round, same design as 1973 series only now background is fully embroidered 12.00

NATIONAL PRESIDENT

1931 round badge with "Boy Scouts of America" around top border, 1st class emblem at bottom over stylized fleur de lis with 2 hands pointing out, on square cut tan 275.00

1932, white wreath and 1st class emblem on yellow arrowhead over axe and gavel with 2 yellow hands pointing out, on square tan 180.00

1943, same only now on square cut khaki 110.00

1958, white embroidered 1st class emblem on white background, white wreath and eagle, white stars, cut edge 90.00

1959, white embroidered 1st class emblem on white background, white wreath, brown eagle, white stars, cut edge 85.00

1968, white embroidered 1st class emblem on white background, white wreath, brown eagle, white stars, rolled edge 60.00

1970, white tenderfoot emblem on purple twill, white lettering, rolled edge 40.00

1973, yellow tenderfoot emblem on purple twill, white border and lettering, rolled edge 26.00

NATIONAL PAST PRESIDENT

1931, round badge with "Boy Scouts of America" around top border, 1st class emblem at bottom over stylized fleur di-lis with hand pointing down, on square cut tan 250.00

Top row, L to R: National Partner Representative, 1973
series 10.00
National Committee, 1980 series 10.00
National Executive Board, 1980 series 12.00
2nd row, L to R: National Vice President, 1980 series ... 12.00
National President, 1973 series 26.00
National Staff, 1970 series 10.00
3rd row, L to R:
National Executive Staff, 1973 series 10.00
Chief Scout Executive, 1973 series 45.00
Bottom: International Commissioner, 1967 .... 100.00

B.S.A. ADULT LEADER PATCHES

Top row, l to R: District Commissioner, 1956 series 9.50
   Unit Commissioner, 1973 series 3.00
Middle row, L to R: Council Commissioner, 1967 series .. 5.00
   Troop Commissioner, 1975 (trained) 1.50
Bottom row, L to R: ..... Neighborhood Commissioner, 1970
   series 1.25
   Pack Commissioner, 1975 (trained) 1.50

1932, white wreath and 1st class emblem on yellow arrowhead over axe and gavel with yellow hand pointing down, on square cut tan 110.00

1943, same only now on square cut khaki 85.00

1958, white embroidered 1st class emblem with white background, white wreath and eagle, white star, cut edge 60.00

1959, white embroidered 1st class emblem with white background, white wreath, brown eagle, white star, cut edge 42.00

1968, white embroidered 1st class emblem with white background, white wreath, brown eagle, white star, rolled edge 38.00

1970, white tenderfoot emblem on purple twill, white lettering, rolled edge 22.00

1973, yellow tenderfoot emblem on purple twill, white border and lettering, yellow rolled edge 18.00

INTERNATIONAL COMMISSIONER

1931 yellow outline of 1st class emblem with yellow background on square cut tan, brown eagle, green center, blue lettering, hands clasping at each cardinal compass point 410.00

1943, same only now on square cut khaki 320.00

1956, yellow embroidered 1st class emblem with yellow background, brown eagle, blue, white, red, yellow rays, green center, cut edge 300.00

1958, white embroidered 1st class emblem with white background, white wreath, brown eagle, khaki embroidered edge 210.00

1967, white embroidered 1st class emblem with white background, white 100.00

wreath and eagle, white, red, blue, center, rolled edge 1.00

LADY SCOUTER

1968, 1st, blue outline of tenderfoot emblem on small cream square 2.00

1968, 2nd, yellow outline of tenderfoot emblem on small navy square 2.00

1970, 3rd, blue tenderfoot emblem on small white square 1.00

WOMEN'S RESERVE

Waving flag shape, "WOMEN'S RESERVE" in script in black on khaki, black cut edge (Rare) 22.00

3" round, white twill, blue lettering "WOMEN'S RESERVE" and blue rolled edge 1.50

CUB SCOUTS

ASSISTANT DENNER

'30's, 1 yellow embroidered bar on square cut blue material 3.50

Early '60's, 1 yellow embroidered bar on heavy blue twill, cut edge with border 1.25

Late '60's, 1 yellow bar on blue cotton, polyester, cut edge with border 1.00

'70's, 1 plain yellow bar on blue cotton, polyester, rolled edge 1.50

1973, not patch, went to shoulder cord.

DENNER

'30's, 1 yellow embroidered bar on square cut blue material 3.50

Early '60's, 1 yellow embroidered bar on heavy blue twill, cut edge with border 1.25

Late '60's, 1 yellow bar on blue cotton polyester, cut edge with border 1.00
'70's, 1 plain yellow bar on blue cotton polyester, rolled edge 1.50
1973, no patch, went to shoulder cord.

ASSISTANT DEN MOTHER-LEADER
Assistant, strip, blue on yellow orange twill, says "Assistant", cut edge went
  below appropriate patch 2.00
1973, 3" round blue twill "Assistant Den Mother" 1.50
1975, 3" round "Assistant Den Leader", went below appropriate patch ... 1.00
1973, 3" round, same only fully embroidered and with gold mylar thread
  (trained) 1.50

DEN MOTHER-LEADER
1930, yellow emblem on royal blue, shield shape 8.50
1956, yellow emblem on navy, shield shape 4.00
1968, oval on khaki, says "CUB SCOUT DEN LEADER" 2.00
1973, 3" round blue twill 8.50
1975, 3" round blue twill, Den Leader 4.00
1973, 3" round, same only fully embroidered and with silver mylar thread
  (trained) 1.50

WEBELOS LEADERS

ASSISTANT WEBELOS DEN LEADER
1973, 3" round blue twill 1.00
1975, 3" round fully embroidered, gold mylar lettering and border 1.50
1975, 3" round fully embroidered, gold mylar lettering and border (trained)
  ...... 1.50

WEBELOS DEN LEADER
1967, diamond shape blue twill, yellow border, yellow emblem and lettering
  (no wording) 1.25
1973, 3" round blue twill 1.00
1975, 3" round blue fully embroidered, gold mylar lettering and border,
  rolled edge (trained) 1.50

DEN LEADER COACH
1967, blue diamond twill, white emblem and lettering, rolled edge (no
  wording) 1.25
1973, 3" round blue twill 1.00
1975, 3" fully embroidered with mylar 1.50

ASSISTANT CUB MASTER
1930's, green felt diamond, yellow design and border 10.00
1956, diamond shape, green twill, yellow design and border, cut edge 5.00
1967, diamond shape, green twill, yellow design and border, no wording, rolled
  edge 2.00

1970, same only now patch says "Assistant Cubmaster" 1.25
1973, 3" round, blue twill 1.00
1975, 3" round, fully embroidered blue with gold mylar 1.50

INSIGNIA PATCHES

CUB SCOUTING

1½" diamond, yellow on blue, "CUB SCOUTS" with paw print (same exist with "CUB SCOUTS", "BSA" and with "CUB SCOUTS" and tenderfoot

1½" diamond, yellow on blue, "CUB SCOUTS" with paw print 2.50
   Same with "CUB SCOUT BSA" 1.50
   Same with "CUB SCOUTS" and tenderfoot emblem 1.00

1" diamond, yellow on blue, "CUB SCOUTS BSA" paw print 2.50
   Same with "CUB SCOUTS BSA" 1.50
   Same with "CUB SCOUTS" and tenderfoot emblem 1.00

1½" diamond, yellow on blue, "CUBS BSA" and paw print 3.00

1½" diamond, stylized "W" in blue on yellow flame on dark blue twill, yellow cut edge 1.00

1958, 1½" blue "W" on orange twill, narrow, blue cut edge 1.50

1962, 1½" blue "W" on orange twill, wide blue cut edge 1.00

BOY SCOUTING

1¼" diamond, tenderfoot emblem on tan twill, "BSA" above 1.25

1½" diamond, tenderfoot emblem on khaki twill, "BSA" above 1.00

1½" diamond, tenderfoot emblem on greyish-green, "BSA" above 1.50

1½" diamond, tenderfoot emblem on gabardine, "BSA" above 1.50

1½" diamond, tenderfoot emblem on dark green, "BSA" above 1.25

1½" diamond, plain yellow tenderfoot emblem on khaki, no "BSA" 1.00

1½" diamond, plain yellow tenderfoot emblem on red twill, no "BSA" 1.25

1½" diamond, yellow tenderfoot emblem on red twill 1.25

2½" oval, tenderfoot emblem on red twill, "BSA" above emblem, rolled edge
   ...... 2.00

2½" oval, tenderfoot emblem on green twill, "BSA" above emblem, rolled edge 3.50

CUBMASTER

1930, Green felt diamond, white design and border 10.00

1956, diamond shape, green twill, white design and border, cut edge 5.00

1967, diamond shape, green twill, white design and border, rolled edge, no lettering 2.00

1970, same only now patch says "Cubmaster" 1.25

1973, 3" round blue twill, white lettering and white rolled edge 1.00

1975, same only fully embroidered and with silver mylar thread (trained) 1.50

PACK COMMITTEE

1930, blue felt diamond with bronze design and border 10.00

1956, diamond shape, blue twill, bronze design and border, cut edge 6.00

1967, diamond shape, blue twill, bronze design and border, rolled edge, no lettering 2.00

1970, same only now patch says "Committeeman" 1.25

1973, 3" round, blue twill, yellow lettering and border, rolled edge 1.00

PACK COMMITTEE CHAIRMAN

1973, 3" round, blue twill, white lettering and border, rolled edge 1.225

ASSISTANT PACK COMMISSIONER
1975, 3" round, yellow tenderfoot emblem and wreath on blue twill, yellow lettering and border, rolled edge 20.00

1975, 3" round yellow tenderfoot emblem and wreath on red twill yellow lettering and border, rolled edge 1.25

1975, 3" round, same as above only with silver mylar border 1.25

ASSISTANT DISTRICT CUB COMMISSIONER
1975, 3" round, yellow tenderfoot emblem and wreath on blue twill, yellow lettering and border, rolled edge 20.00

1975, same only on red twill 1.25

DISTRICT CUB COMMISSIONER
1975, 3" round, yellow tenderfoot emblem and wreath on blue twill, yellow lettering, silver mylar, rolled edge 15.00

1975, same only on red twill and wording reads "District Cub Scout Commissioner" 1.25

CUB SCOUT ROUNDTABLE COMMISSIONER
1975, yellow tenderfoot emblem and wreath on red twill, yellow lettering and border, rolled edge 1.25

EXPLORERS
1950's 1st Assistant Crew Leader, white wings, anchor, compass emblem over one yellow bar, on blue twill, rectangle 10.00

Crew Leader, white wings, anchor, compass emblem over two bars on blue twill, rectangle 14.00

1st Secretary, white wings, anchor, compass emblem over yellow crossed quills on blue twill, rectangle 18.00

Deputy Senior Crew Leader, white wings, anchor, compass emblem over three yellow bars on blue twill, rectangle 16.00

Senior Crew Leader, round yellow wings, anchor, compass emblem on blue twill, inner and outer rings are yellow cut edge 16.00

Assistant Post Advisor, round, white wings, anchor, compass emblem on blue twill, inner ring is white, outer ring is yellow 18.00

Post Advisor, round, white wings, anchor, compass emblem on blue twill, inner and outer rings are white 16.00

2nd
Assistant Crew Leader, rectangle, white wings, anchor compass emblem over one yellow bar, a square cut green twill 14.00

Crew Leader, rectangle, white wings, anchor, compass emblem over two yellow bars, on square cut green twill 13.00

Secretary, rectangle, white wings, anchor, compass emblem over yellow crossed quills on square cut green twill 14.00

Deputy Senior Crew Advisor, rectangle, white wings, anchor, compass emblem over three yellow bars in square cut green twill 14.00

Senior Crew Leader, round, yellow wings, anchor, compass emblem on green twill, inner and outer rings are yellow cut edge 8.00

Assistant Post Advisor, round, white wings, anchor, compass emblem on green twill, inner ring is white, outer ring is yellow, cut edge 9.00

Post Advisory, round, white wings, anchor, compass emblem on green twill, inner and outer rings are white cut edge 10.00

3rd

Assistant Crew Leader, rectangle, white wings, anchor, compass emblem over yellow bar on green twill with green border, cut edge 6.00

Crew Leader, rectangle, white wings, anchor, compass emblem over two gold bars on green twill with green border, cut edge 6.00

Secretary, rectangle, white wings, anchor, compass emblem over crossed yellow quills on green twill with green border, cut edge 7.50

Deputy Senior Crew Leader, rectangle, white wings, anchor, compass emblem over three yellow bars, on green twill with green border, cut edge
...... 7.50

Senior Crew Leader, unchanged from 2nd series ....

Assistant Post Advisor, unchanged from 2nd series ....

Post Advisor, unchanged from 2nd series ....

1960's, all are green twill strip patches with green border, cut edge and red lettering

Advisor	1.00	Quartermaster	1.00
Associate Advisor	1.00	Representative	1.00
Cabinet Officer	1.00	Secretary	1.00
Post Committee	1.00	Treasurer	1.00
President	1.00	Vice President	1.00

AIR SCOUTS

Assistant Flight Pilot, wing shaped, embroidered yellow, one blue bar in
...... 18.00

Flight Pilot, wing shaped, embroidered yellow, two blue bars in center, cut edge 15.00

Squadron Secretary, wing shaped, embroidered yellow, two blue crossed quills in center, cut edge 16.00

Assistant Squadron Pilot, wing shaped, embroidered yellow, two and a half blue bars in center 20.00

Squadron Pilot, wing shaped, embroidered grey, two and a half blue bars in center 16.00

Assistant Squadron Leader, yellow wing shaped over blue circle, embroidered, yellow tenderfoot emblem in center 16.00

Squadron Leader, grey wing shaped over blue circle, embroidered, grey tenderfoot emblem in center, cut edge 16.00

AIR EXPLORER

Note: Badges remained unchanged from the Air Scout program except for the following:

Deputy Senior Crew Leader, (Assistant Squadron Pilot), wing shaped, yellow embroidered, three blue bars in center, cut edge 15.00

Senior Crew Leader (Squadron Pilot), embroidered, grey wing shaped over blue circle, three blue bars in center, cut edge 15.00

SEA SCOUTS

Note: All badges come in white on blue and in blue on white. The value is about the same for each color scheme.

Coxswain, one felt chevron below embroidered Sea Scout emblem 21.00

Boatswain Mate, two felt chevrons below embroidered Sea Scout emblem
...... 20.00

Boatswain, three felt chevrons below embroidered Sea Scout emblem ... 20.00

B.S.A. CUBMASTER PATCHES

Top: 1956 series, cut edge 5.00

Middle row, L to R: 1967 series 2.00

1970 series ....; 1.25

Bottom: 1973 series 1.00

1950's EXPLORER INSIGNIA, 3rd SERIES

Top row, L to R: Assistant Crew Leader 6.00
   Crew Leader 6.00
2nd row, L to R: Post Secretary 7.50
   Deputy Senior Crew Leader 7.50
3rd row, L to R: Senior Crew Leader 8.00
   Assistant Post Advisor 9.00
   Post Advisor 10.00

SEA EXPLORER

1950's Assistant Crew Leader, Sea Scout emblem on one chevron 1.50

Crew Leader, Sea Scout emblem on two chevrons 1.75

Boatswain's Mate, Sea Scout emblem on two chevrons with a third chevron below 2.00

Boatswain, Sea Scout emblem on two chevrons with a 3rd chevron and a star below 2.50

Bugler, a bugle 2.50

Purser, Sea Scout emblem on two crossed keys 2.50

Specialist, Sea Scout emblem with wording "SPECIALIST" below 2.50

Storekeeper, open book on two crossed oars 2.50

Yeoman, Sea Scout emblem on two crossed quills 2.00

Junior Assistant Mate, (the quartermaster rank patch was used for this position) 4.00

Mate, Sea Scout emblem with one star below 2.50

Skipper, Sea Scout emblem with one star and bar below 3.00

Ship Committee, Sea Scout emblem on an oval with one star below 3.00

Ship Chairman, Sea Scout emblem in a diamond with one star below 3.25

Council Staff, Sea Scout emblem with two stars below 3.50

Council Committee, Sea Scout emblem in an oval with two stars below ... 3.75

Council Chairman, Sea Scout emblem in a diamond with two stars below . 4.00

Regional-National Staff, Sea Scout emblem with four stars below 4.50

Regional-National Committee, Sea Scout emblem on an oval with four stars below 4.75

Regional+National Chairman, Sea Scout emblem in a diamond with four stars below 5.00

1960's
In the late 1960's the following strip insignia were added:

Cabinet Officer, white lettering on blue felt 1.00

Cabinet Officer, blue lettering on white twill with white border, cut edge . 1.00

Representative, white lettering on blue felt 1.00

Representative, blue lettering on white twill with white border, cut edge . 1.00

Treasurer, white lettering on blue felt 1.00

Treasurer, blue lettering on white twill with white border, cut edge 1.00

EXPLORERS

1950, 2¼" round, explorer emblem on navy, embroidery is all white, yellow outline of tenderfoot emblem 5.00

Same, but green 4.50

Same, but red 3.50

1950, 1½" diamond, explorer emblem on red twill 3.00

1960, 1½" x 2" rectangle, emblem on dark green, cut edge with border ... 1.50

1960, 2½" x 3¼", explorer emblem on dark green twill, folded edges 1.50

1960, 2½" x 3¼", explorer emblem on green twill, cut edge with border 1.25

1960, 2½" x 3¼" explorer emblem on green twill (very thin material), folded edges 1.00

1960, 2½" x 3¼", explorer emblem on red twill with folded edges 1.75

Same, only with cut edge with border 2.00

1970, 3½" round, explorer emblem in yellow on orange, fully embroidered white wreath, orange cut edge (exist also on Red, Light Blue, Navy Blue) each 1.50

1970, shield shape, fully embroidered metallic silver emblem with two gold metallic sheaths of wheat on navy blue with metallic silver rolled edge 5.00

1970, 4" round, with multi-color shield, small metallic gold explore "E" in center, says "NATIONAL ASSOCIATION OF LAW ENFORCEMENT EXPLORERS" on blue twill, metallic gold, rolled edge 4.00

1970, 3" round, emblem over caduceus, two yellow wheat sheaths, says "MEDICAL EXPLORER" on blue twill, yellow rolled edge 1.00

1970, 3" square, blue emblem inside scales of Justice over stylized design, says "LAW EXPLORER" on white twill, yellow rolled edge 1.00

AIR SCOUT-EXPLORER

1940, 4" embroidered grey wings with Tenderfoot emblem (top of wings came very close to emblem) 10.00

1940, 2½" embroidered grey wings with Tenderfoot badge 6.00

1943, embroidered grey wings, Tenderfoot emblem over 2½" round blue twill, blue cut edge 20.00

1950, 4" embroidered grey wings with Tenderfoot emblem 6.50

1970's, 3" round stylized wing, says "AVIATION EXPLORING", yellow rolled edge 1.00

70's, 3" round stylized blue "E" over yellow stylized wing, says "AOPA AVIATION EXPLORING" 2.00

Explorer Leader strips, 1960s, each 1.00

AIR SCOUT - EXPLORER PATCHES

Top row: Air Scout tenderfoot candidate patch 20.00

2nd row: Air Explorer Senior Crew Leader patch 15.00

3rd row: Air Scout Assistant Flight Pilot patch 15.00
   Air Scout Squadron Secretary patch 16.00

4th row: Air Scout Assistant Squadron Pilot patch 20.00
   Air Explorer Navigation rating strip 12.00

SEA SCOUT ITEMS

Top: Sea Scout Universal Emblem patch, 1940's 5.00

Bottom row, L to R: Coxswain, on white 21.00
   Coxswain, on blue 21.00

SEA SCOUT-EXPLORER

All badges in 2 color schemes, white on blue, blue on white, generally valued the same.

30's, 2½" diamond Sea Scout emblem on navy felt, cut edge 8.00

40's and 50's, 2½" oval sea scout emblem on navy felt, cut edge 5.00

1960, 2½" x 3¼", explorer emblem on navy felt 3.50
Same, except on navy garbardine 1.50

2" round yellow tenderfoot emblem over sideways blue "V" on white twill, red rolled edge 2.50

1960's, 2½" round embroidered sea explorer emblem, navy on white twill, rolled edge (exists white on navy twill) 2.00

1970's, large felt square, stylized "E" in yellow outline with explorer emblem in "E", blue rolled edge 2.50

2" round, white "E" over anchor, white wreath, white rolled edge, all on blue twill 1.50

2" square, yellow "E" over anchor on white twill, white rolled edge 1.50

2" square, yellow "E" with explorer emblem on white twill, blue rolled edge (also with white rolled edge) 1.50

SEA EXPLORER POSITION PATCH
L to R: Assistant Crew Leader, on blue 1.50
Crew Leader, in white 1.75
Boatswain's Mate, on white 2.00
Boatswain, on blue 2.50

SEA EXPLORER POSITION PATCHES

Top row, L to R: Mate, on blue 2.50
    Skipper, on blue 3.00
    Ship Committee, on blue 3.00
    Ship Chairman, on blue 3.25

2nd row, L to R: Council Staff, on blue 3.50
    Council Committee, on blue 3.75
    Council Chairman, on blue 4.00

3rd row, L to R: Regional-National Staff, on blue 4.50
    Regional-National Committee, on blue 4.75
    Regional-National Chairman, on blue 5.00

Bottom row, L to R: 1 Star Strip (for Mate) 1.00
    Star and Bar Strip (for Skipper) 1.50
    2 Star Strip (for Council level position) 1.25

SEA EXPLORER POSITION PATCHES

Top row, L to R: Storekeeper, on blue 2.50
    Bugler, on blue 2.50
    Specialist, on blue 2.50
2nd row: Cabinet Officer strip, on blue 1.00
3rd row: Cabinet Officer strip, on white 1.00
Bottom row, L to R: Purser, on white 2.50
    Representative strip, on white 1.00
    Yeoman, on white 2.00

EXPLORER INSIGNIA
Top row, L to R: Explorer Insignia, 1940's emblem
Explorer Insignia, 1950's emblem
Explorer Insignia, 1960's emblem
Explorer Insignia, 1970's emblem

AIR SCOUT-EXPLORER INSIGNIA

Top: Air Explorer universal insignia, wings, 1950's 6.00

Bottom row, L to R: Aviation Exploring patch, 1970's ... 1.00
   Air Scout Insignia patch for blue jacket, 1940's 1.00
   AOPA Aviation Exploring Patch, 1970's 2.00

SPECIAL INTEREST EXPLORING INSIGNIA

Top: Law Enforcement Explorer patch, 1970's 4.00

Middle row, L to R: Aviation Exploring patch, 1970's 1.00
   Medical Explorer patch, 1970's 1.00

Bottom: Law Explorer patch, 1970's 1.00

SEA SCOUT EXPLORER INSIGNIA

Top row, L to R: Explorer E patch on navy felt, 1970's ... 2.50

1960's Explorer Emblem on navy felt, square cut 3.50

2nd row, L to R: Sea Explorer E Emblem navy felt, square cut, 1970's 2.50

1960's Explorer Emblem on white, square cut 3.50

3rd row, L to R: Explorer E Emblem on white, blue rolled edge, 1970's 1.50

Sea Scout Emblem, round on white twill, 1960's 2.00

Sea Scout Emblem round on blue twill, 1960's 2.00

4th row, L to R: Explorer E Emblem, on white, white rolled edge, 1970's 1.50

Seas Explorer E Emblem, round on blue, white rolled edge, 1970's 1.50

Bottom row, L to R: Sea Explorer E Emblem, on white, white rolled edge, 1970's 1.50

LONE SCOUT

Arrowhead shape patch in woven burlap, "LSA" in blue circle on yellow arrowhead, blue background, yellow cut edge, original 125.00

Note: A reproduction of this exists of woven cloth rather than burlap, has thin white backing.
white backing.

3" square cut heavy twill, red standing Indian in red circle, black lettering "LSS" at top, "BSA" at bottom 12.00

3" square cut khaki, red stainding Indian, in red circle, black lettering "LSS" at top, "BSA" at bottom 6.00

2" round on khaki, red standing Indian in red circle, black lettering "LSS" and "BSA", cut edge 3.00

Red standing Indian in red circle, black lettering "LONE SCOUT" at top, "BSA" at bottom 1.50

ALPHA PHI OMEGA

3" round, yellow emblem on dark blue twill, with tab 4.50

GIRL SCOUTS

2" trefoil shape, white "GS" on green felt, white cut edge 1.50

1 5-8 trefoil shape, white "GS" on green felt, white cut edge 1.25

2" white "GS" and trefoil on green felt, white cut edge 2.00

1¼" round, white "GS" and trefoil on green twill, green rolled edge, has white, green and copper ruffles at top of patch 1.00

3 5-8" shoulder patch, green "GIRL SCOUTS USA" on green, multi color shield above, green rolled edge (exist with yellow rolled edge) 1.00

3 5-8" shoulder patch, white "GIRL SCOUTS USA" on dark green twill, multicolor shield above, white rolled edge 1.00

2" round, white "GS" and trefoil on green felt, green rolled edge 2.00

2" round, green trefoil, red "Cadette" on white felt, green rolled edge 2.00

BROWNIES

2" oval, orange dancing brownie on brown copper felt, cut edge 2.00

3 5-8" shoulder patch, brown on brown, "Girl Scouts U.S.A.", brown rolled edge 1.00

3 5-8" shoulder patch, green "GIRL SCOUTS USA" on green, multicolor shield above, green rolled edge (exist with yellow rolled edge 1.00

2¾" brown strip type, "GIRL SCOUTS USA" in brown on brown, ... 1.00

2" round, orange trefoil, orange dancing brownie on brown felt, brown rolled edge 1.00

2" round, yellow trefoil, yellow dancing brownie on light brown felt, brown rolled edge 1.00

ROVER SCOUTS

30's, 1½" x 2" tenderfoot emblem over red fully embroidered circle, "ROVER SCOUT" in yellow (emblem extends above circle) cut edge 50.00

70's, same description as above but shield in the scout emblem and lettering "BSA" are not as finely done as the 30's patch 15.00

LONE SCOUT INSIGNIA

Top row, L to R: Lone Scout Insignia patch, woven burlap,
extremely rare 125.00
BSA Lone Scout medallion on square 6.00

Bottom row, L to R: BSA Lone Scout medallion, round, cut
edge 3.00
BSA Lone Scout medallion, round, rolled edge, 1980 ... 1.50

GIRL SCOUT INSIGNIA

Top row, L to R: Girl Scouts shoulder strip, green with green
border 1.00
Girl Scout trefoil patch, felt, 1 5-8" 1.35
Girl Scouts shoulder strip, green with white border ... 1.00

Bottom row, L to R: Girl Scout trefoil patch, green felt
...... 2.00
Cadette Girl Scout patch, 2" round 2.00
Girl Scout patch, 2" round 2.00
Cadette Girl Scout hat patch 1.00

WORLD SCOUTING

1 5-8" round, fleur de-lis inside rope circle with square knotted bottom on purple twill, purple cut edge 1.50

Same, 2" round with cut edge 4.00

Same, 3" round with cut edge 3.00

Same, 3" round with rolled edge 2.00

Same, 6" round (jacket), cut edge 8.00

U.S. FLAG (all 50 stars)

1st issue, 1⅝" x 2½", has dots for stars, blue cut edge 2.00

2nd issue, 1⅝ x 3", woven silk, blue rolled edge, rare 2.50

3rd issue, 1⅝" x 2½", blue cut edge .... .25

RANK
SCOUT RANK

1972-73, oval, brown tenderfoot emblem without eagle and shield on dull orange twill, brown rolled edge .... .50

TENDERFOOT

1910, emblem on square cut tan, back shows handsewn, top of emblem shorter than later series 40.00

1920, emblem on square cut tan, machine made appearance 15.00

1927, emblem on square cut tan, ridge in center of fleur de-lis top 8.00

1946, emblem with top ridge on khaki, cheese cloth back 5.00

1950, emblem on square cut khaki, no cheese cloth, usually edges folded .. 4.00

Early 60's, emblem on khaki twill, cut edge with border 1.00

Late 60's emblem on khaki cotton, polyester, cut edge with border .... .75

1970, emblem on khaki cotton, polyester, rolled edge 1.50

'72-'73, emblem on brown twill oval, yellow rolled edge .... .50

2nd CLASS (BE PREPARED bar)

1910 emblem, on square cut tan, handmade appearance 35.00

1927, emblem on square cut tan, machine made 8.50

1946, emblem on square cut khaki, cheese cloth on back 5.25

1950, emblem on square cut khaki, no cheese cloth (edges usually folded) . 4.25

Early 60's, emblem on khaki twill, cut edge with border 1.00

Late 60's, emblem on khaki cotton polyester, cut edge with border .... .75

1970, emblem on khaki cotton polyester, rolled edge 1.50

1972-73, yellow emblem on green twill, yellow rolled edge .... .50

1st CLASS (Tenderfoot and 2nd class combined into)

1910, emblem on square cut tan, 2nd class bar separated from tenderfoot, hand sewn, top of tenderfoot emblem is short and squatty, handmade appearance 50.00

1920, emblem on square cut tan, 2nd class bar joins tenderfoot emblem, machine made 22.00

1927, emblem on square cut tan, top of fleur de-lis has ridge in center 10.00

1946, emblem on square cut khaki, cheese cloth on back 7.00

1950, emblem on square cut khaki, no cheese cloth, edges usually folded .. 6.00

Early 60's, emblem on khaki twill, cut edge with border 1.00

Late 60's, emblem on khaki cotton polyester, cut edge with border .... .75

1970, emblem on khaki cotton polyester, rolled edge 2.00

'72-'73, oval yellow emblem on red twill .... .50

B.S.A. EARLY 1960's RANK PATCHES

Top row,d L to R: Tenderfoot 1.00
    2nd Class 1.00
    1st Class 1.00
Bottom row, L to R: Star 1.00
    Life .... .75
    Eagle 12.00

STAR (during part of teens, Star was above Life in rank)

1910, star emblem on square cut tan, hand made 35.00

1915, embroidered eagle on emblem faces wearer's left 29.00

1920, eagle faces right, machine made, double hanging knot 15.00

1927, emblem on square cut tan with single knot 10.00

1946, emblem on square cut khaki, cheese cloth back, cut edge 5.00

1950, emblem on square cut khaki, no cheese cloth on back 7.00

Early 60's, emblem on khaki twill, cut edge with border 1.00

Late 60's, emblem on khaki cotton poylester, cut edge with border .... .75

1970, emblem on khaki cotton polyester, rolled edge 2.00

'72-'73, oval, yellow star on blue twill, yellow rolled edge .... .50
    on white for Sea Scouts, square cut 8.00
    On navy blue for Sea Scouts, square cut 8.00

B.S.A. FIRST CLASS RANK PATCHES
Rop row, L to R: 1910 series 50.00
.1927 series 10.00
1946 series 7.00
Early 1960's series 1.00
Late 1960's series .... .75

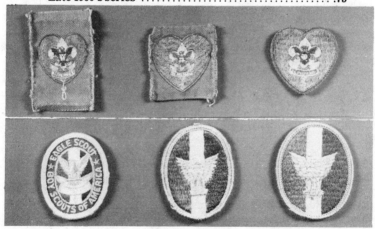

B.S.A. LIFE AND EAGLE RANK PATCHES
Top row, L to R: Life, 1920 .... 20.00
Life, 1927 .... 12.00
Life, 1960's .... .75
Bottom row, L to R: Eagle, 1960 .... 12.00
Eagle, late 1960's 10.00
Eagle, 1970 .... 8.00

LIFE

1910, emblem on square cut tan twill, handmade appearance 45.00

1915, emblem on square cut tan, double knot extends beyond heart 36.00

1920, emblem on square cut tan, single knot extends below heart 20.00

1927, emblem on square cut tan, knot completely within heart 12.00

1946, emblem on square cut khaki, cheese cloth back, cut edge 7.00

1950, emblem on square cut khaki, no cheese cloth back, cut edge 9.00

60's, fully embroidered emblem, heart shaped, red, cut edge .... .75

'72-'73, orange emblem on pale orange, orange rolled edge .... .50

   on white for Sea Scouts, square cut 15.00

   On navy blue for Sea Scouts, square cut 15.00

EAGLE

1911, emblem on square cut tan, handmade appearance 95.00

1917, emblem on square cut tan, machine made (minor variations on this were
used up to 1946) 36.00

1946, emblem on square cut khaki, used up to 1960 .... 22.00

1960, emblem on red, white, blue background, red twill border ring with
"EAGLE SCOUT BOY SCOUTS OF AMERICA" grey rolled edge 12.00

Late 60's, oval small eagle on red, white, blue background, fully embroidered,
grey rolled edge, straight tail feathers 10.00

1970, oval, eagle on red, white, blue background, fully embroidered, grey
rolled edge, (two minor variations exist) 8.00

'72-'73, oval, eagle on embroidered red, white, blue background border ring is
red twill, lettering "EAGLE SCOUT" white rolled edge, several minor
variations of this exist 6.00

   On white for Sea Scouts, square cut 50.00

   On navy blue Sea Scouts, square cut 50.00

HANDICAP SCOUTS (Special)

Special segments that fit around rank patch, small, unlettered segments such
as camping, citizenship, cooking, first aid, flag, hiking, ideals, knot typing,
swimming, symbol, each .... .50

CUB SCOUT

1930, WOLF, black on red felt, paw print, wide felt border 9.00

   BEAR, yellow on red felt, paw print 9.00

   LION, white on red felt, paw print, wide felt border 10.00

1940, same as 1930 but has cut edge, no excess border, WOLF 5.00

   BEAR 5.00

   LION 6.00

1950, WOLF, black on red twill, paw print shows as toe nails 1.50

   BEAR, yellow on red twill paw prints shows as toe nails 1.50

   LION, white on red twill, paw print shows as toe nails 2.00

1960, same as 1950 but paw print shows no toenails, WOLF 1.00

   BEAR 1.00

   LION 1.50

1967, BOBCAT, on blue twill cut edge, tenderfoot emblem .... .50

   WOLF, red twill, cut edge, tenderfoot emblem .... .50

   BEAR, on aqua twill, cut edge, tenderfoot emblem .... .50

1975, added WEBELOS, stylized "W" over flame on blue twill, tan border, cut
edge .... .75

1977, WEBELOS is same as '75 but has yellow cut edge .... .50

B.S.A. 1972 SERIES OF RANK PATCHES
Center: Scout Rank .... .50
   Handicapped Scout, segments in circle starting at top, going clockwise, flag, symbols, ideals, first aid, knot tying, swimming, camping, cooking, hiking, citizenship, each   .50

Outside ring starting at top going clockwise: Tenderfoot . .50
   2nd Class .... .50
   1st Class .... .50
   Star .... .50
   Life .... .50
   Eagle 6.00

ARROW OF LIGHT
(Highest Cub Right)
Arrow with sunrise on khaki twill, blue cut edge, very narrow patch in use until about 1970 .... 1.25
Replaced by patch of same design but on cotton polyester, that is much wider .... .50

SENIOR SCOUTS
1938, various segments were earned and these were worn around the universal emblem patch. All existed in 5 colors, tan, green, light blue, navy, and white, The segments are: Airman, Artisan, Artist, Citizen, Conservationist, Craftsman, Dairyman, Farm Manager, Forester, Gardener, Journalist, Livestockman, Naturalist, Poultryman, Radioman, Seaman and Sportsman
On tan 15.00
On green 10.00
On light blue 20.00
On white 18.00
On navy 18.00

EXPLORER SCOUTS
1942, Apprentice, 2'' round, yellow compass on green twill, tenderfoot emblem at top, says "EXPLORER SCOUT", green rolled edge 20.00
Woodsman, 2'' round, yellow compass on green twill, tenderfoot at top, white pine tree, says "EXPLORER SCOUT", green rolled edge 25.00
Frontiersman, 2'' round, yellow compass on green twill, tenderfoot emblem at top, white teepee, says "EXPLORER SCOUT" green rolled edge ... 25.00
Ranger, 2'' round, yellow compass on green twill, tenderfoot emblem at top, white powderhorn, says "EXPLORER SCOUT", green rolled edge .. 45.00
1950's, 1st series (all on blue twill)
Apprentice, odd shaped with wing, anchor and compass 5.00
Bronze Award, round, bronze wing, anchor and compass 10.00
Gold Award, round, yellow wing, anchor and compass 15.00
Silver Award, round, white wing, anchor and compass 26.00
1950's, 2nd series (all on red twill)
Apprentice, odd shape, wing, anchor and compass 3.00
Bronze Award, round, bronze wing, anchor and compass 4.50
Gold Award, round, yellow wing, anchor and compass 6.50
Silver Award, round, white wing, anchor and compass 22.00
1950's, 3rd issue
Silver Award, round, grey flying eagle on red, white, blue background over compass, tenderfoot at bottom wingtips extend beyond patch, black cut edge 28.00

AIR SCOUT-EXPLORER
1938, tenderfoot air scout candidate, blue, two blade propeller on square cut tan 18.00
2nd class air scout candidate, blue, three blade propeller on square cut tan 22.00
1st class air scout candidate, blue, four blade propeller on square cut tan 29.00
1942, Apprentice, wing shape on blue twill, single prop plane, blue cut edge, says "AIR SCOUTS" 26.00
Observer, wing shape on blue twill, two prop plane, blue cut edge, says "AIR SCOUTS" 30.00

Craftsman, wing shape on blue twill, three prop plane, blue cut edge, says "AIR SCOUTS" 38.00
Ace, wing shape on blue twill, four prop plane, blue cut edge, says "AIR SCOUTS" 50.00

2nd series: (same as 1942 series except all now says "Air Explorer")
Apprentice 15.00
Observer 22.00
Craftsman 30.00
Ace 45.00

3rd series: (same as 1942 series but dropped lettering and "ACE" rank)
Apprentice 15.00
Observer 18.00
Craftsman 24.00

SEA SCOUTS-EXPLORER
Note: All patches in two color scheme, blue on white and white on blue.

1912, Apprentice, 1 felt bar below sea scout emblem 12.00
Ordinary, 2 felt bars below sea scout emblem 26.00
Able, 3 felt bars below sea scout emblem 31.00

1954, Apprentice, 1 embroidered bar below sea scout emblem 1.00
Ordinary, 2 embroidered bars below sea scout emblem 2.00
Able, 3 embroidered bars below sea scout emblem 3.00

1954, Quartermaster patch, a plain sea scout explorer emblem with no bars (also used as Junior Assistant Mate) 4.00

GIRL SCOUT
Note: At one time, there was a Golden Eaglette rank which existed in pin form only.

1st Class, on tan 22.00
on green 7.50
2nd Class, on tan 15.00
On green 5.00

PROMOTIONAL
BOYS LIFE
Boys Life Arc, yellow or blue, cut edge (awarded for promoting "Boys Life"). If each family in the troop subscribed to **Boys Life**, the unit got patches . 3.00

Outlined Pedro patch, cut edge (Pedro is a donkey's head, cartoon image) and was awarded for selling "Boys Life" 5.00

"Boys Life" promotional patch, round, Pedro on yellow with green rolled edge
...... 1.25
Round, Pedro on white with red rolled edge 1.25
1975 100 percent Boys Life Unit patch 1.00
1976 Boys Life patch 1.00
1978, Boys Life patch 1.00

There was a red and white shoulder patch used in training films that said "Sunrise Council, Smithtown, U.S.A., rare 35.00

RECRUITING AND ROUNDUP
Council Issue 50-1.00
National Issue 1.00
National Issue 1.00-2.00
Strips 50-1.50

Top center group, clockwise from top: Wolf rank, 1950's . 1.50
    Lion rank, 1950's 2.00
    Webelos with insignia, narrow border, 1958 .... 1.50
    Lion Rank, 1950's 1.50
Left grouping, clockwise from top: .... Lion rank, 1960's 1.50
    Wolf rank, 1960's 1.00
    Webelos with insignia, wide border, 1962 .... 1.00
    Bear rank, 1960's 1.00
Bottom center group, top : Arrow of Light, narrow type,
    1940's-1960's 1.25
    Bottom: Arrow of Light, wide type, 1967 .... .50
Right grouping, clockwise from top: Bobcat rank, 1967 .... .50
    Bear rank, 1967 .... .50
    Webelos rank, 1975 .... .50
    Wolf rank, 1967 .... .75

EXPLORER RANK PATCHES. 1950's

Top row, L to R: Apprentice, on blue 5.00
    Apprentice, on red 3.00
2nd row, L to R: Bronze Award, on blue 10.00
    Bronze Award, on red 4.50
3rd row, L to R: Gold Award, on blue 15.00
    Gold Awrd, on red 6.50
Bottom: Silver Award, 3rd issue, 1950's (called "Flying
    Eagle") 32.00

SEA SCOUT ITEMS

Top row, L to R: Star Rank on Sea Scout white 8.00
    Life Rank on Sea Scout blue 15.00
2nd row, L to R: Jr. Leader green bar training patch on Sea
    Scout white 2.00
    Long Cruise patch on Sea Scout blue 3.00
    Red Long Cruise arc 1.00

SEA EXPLORER RANK PATCHES

L to R: Apprentice Seaman 1.00
    Ordinary Seaman 2.00
    Able Seaman 3.00
    Quartermaster 4.00

Florida 1974 Governor's Roundup set, each ... 1.00

BOYS LIFE PROMOTIONAL PROMOTIONAL PATCHES

Top: Boys Life arc segment 3.00

2nd row: Pedro patch, cut edge 5.00

3rd row, L to R: Pedro patch, on yellow 1.25
Pedro patch, on white 1.25

4th row, L to R: 1975 100 percent Boys Life patch 1.00
1976 Boys Life patch 1.00

Bottom row, L to R: 1977 Boys Life Patch 1.00
1978 Boys Life patch 1.00

B.S.A. NATIONAL ISSUE ROUNDUP PATCH
Top row, L to R: Sunrise Roundup, ca. late 1950s, cut edge
...... 2.00
   Touchdown for Boypower, 1970 .... 1.00
2nd row, L to R: Go Roundup, 1962 .... 1.00
   Scouting Rounds A Guy Out, 1967 .... 1.00
   Adventure Roundup, 1963 .... 1.00
   Follow The Rugged Road, 1966 .... 1.00
   Frontier Roundup, 1964 .... 1.00
   Follow The Rugged Road, 1965 .... 1.00

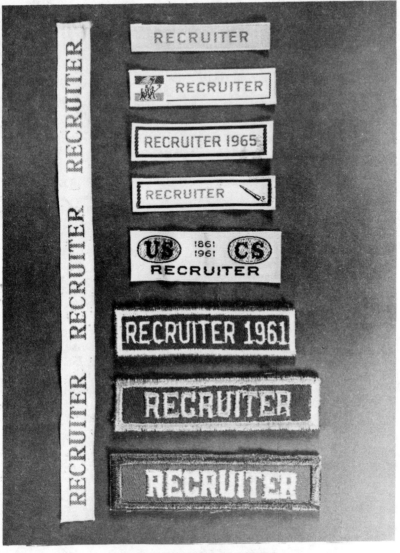

B.S.A. RECRUITER STRIPS

Left: Uncut strip of 3 on tan silk 3.50
Right, top to bottom: Plain "Recruiter" on tan, woven .... .50
1965 Follow the Rugged Road strip 1.00
1965 strip .... .75
1963 Adventure Roundup strip 1.00
1861-1961 U.S.-C.S. Recruiter strip .... .50
1961, Recruiter strip, white on red, cut edge .... .75
1960, Recruiter strip, yellow on red, cut edge 1.00
1959, Recruiter strip, white on red 1.00

OLD REGION SYSTEM
Started in 1921

Region One

1939, 1st, white felt, round, black outline, red lettering "ALL FOR ONE - ONE FOR ALL" shows map of region with Maine, blue; New Hampshire, yellow; Vermont, red; Massachusetts, purple; Connecticut, green; Rhode Island, orange 50.00

2nd, same except felt is thin and Massachusetts is light violet 40.00

3rd, same as 1st except felt is thick and Massachusetts is light violet 18.00

4th, same as 1st except now on white twill and patch has a rolled edge . . . 15.00

5th, same as 1st except on white twill and Rhode Island is red, rolled edge
. . . . . . 12.00

6th, round white twill, red lettering "REGION 1 BSA BOYPOWER TEAM", white rolled edge 11.00

7th, round white twill, red lettering "REGION 1 BSA BOYPOWER TEAM" black rolled edge 10.00

Region Two

1st, oval, black felt, red "NY" and "NJ", white "2", white cut edge 50.00

2nd, round khaki grey twill, outline of "2" and region are red, 2 and inner border are white, red at edge 40.00

3rd, 1946, round, blue twill, white star, white "REGION 2" red outline of region, blue "46", white cut edge (issued for 25th Anniversary of Region 2)
. . . . . . 28.00

4th, dome, red twill, white "2", black lettering "NEW YORK NEW JERSEY" black outline of "2", yellow statue with green outline, yellow cut edge . 18.00

5th dome, red twill, black lettering "NEW YORK NEW JERSEY PUERTO RICO" yellow cut edge 15.00

6th, dome, red twill, black lettering "NEW YORK NEW JERSEY PUERTO RICO" yellow rolled edge 15.00

7th, dome red twill, black lettering "NEW YORK NEW JERSEY PUERTO RICO VIRGIN ISLANDS", yellow rolled edge 10.00

Region Three

1st (1939), round, red twill lettering "BOY SCOUTS OF AMERICA REGION 3" outline of hand and circle, white hand and ring, blue cut edge 12.00

2nd, round, bright red twill 8.00

3rd, round, white twill, blue lettering 12.00

4th outline of hand and circle, white hand and sleeve, red stripes on sleeve, blue cut edge (this was made for use as a neckerchief patch) . . . .

Region Four

1st (1939), round, yellow felt, black printed "4", yellow powderhorn below
. . . . . . 40.00

2nd, round, red twill, white lettering "REGION BSA BUCKSKIN MEN", green "4", brown Ohio, yellow Kentucky, blue West Virginia, solid outline of states, yellow cut edge 22.00

3rd, round, red twill same as above but white broken outline of states, green "4", yellow cut edge 18.00

4th, round red twill, same as above but light green "4" 16.00

5th, round, red twill, same as above but light green "4", small Kentucky 15.00

6th, round, red twill, white lettering "REGION BSA BUCKSKIN MEN" yellow rolled edge 12.00

7th, round, red twill, yellow broken outline of states, white lettering "REGION BSA KY-OHIO-WEST VA", white space capsule, black smoke trail from capsule, yellow rolled edge 8.00

NOTE: There are slight mfg. errors of the last 6 listed with the lettering on some and are not considered issues. Two local issues have likenesses of Daniel Boone and are not to be confused with Region Issues.

Region Five
1937, round light brown felt acorn, yellow felt "5" on green felt 60.00

1941, round, yellow felt "V", red felt arrow on green felt 35.00

1944, shield shape, fully embroidered red, white, blue, yellow "V" and arrow, cut edge 20.00

1946, shield shape, fully embroidered, black "V" on black, black cut edge, 25th anniversary issue of region five 16.00

Shield shape, fully embroidered, red, white, blue, yellow "V" and arrow, brown cut edge 16.00

Shield shape, fully embroidered, red, white, blue, yellow "V" and arrow, brown rolled edge 10.00

Region Six
1924, black felt arm band with white felt "6" 65.00

1926, rectangle, black felt with white felt "6" 50.00

1939, round, two red circles, green lettering "BOY SCOUTS OF AMERICA" green North Carolina, red South Carolina, blue Georgia, orange Florida on white felt 35.00

same as 1939 but on white twill, red cut edge 22.00

Same as 1939 but on white twill, red rolled edge 18.00

Same as 1939 but fully embroidered white, red rolled edge 10.00

Note: Varieties will exist as to "thick" or "thin" states.

Region Seven
Shield shape, yellow "7" with rough stitch outline of "7", dark green states with white rough stitch outline of states, white lake on red twill, yellow cut edge 10.00

Shield shape, same as above but red shows through lake 8.00

Other variations with pale yellow "7", heavy outline of states, heavy red twill, wide yellow cut edge.

Region Eight
1939, round, white silk screened emblem on red felt 50.00

Round, multi-color cowboy, green grass, red lasso and lettering, "THE ACTIVE 8'ERS B.S.A." on light tan twill, black cut edge 30.00

Round, cowboy with red shirt, white pants, brown hat and horse, green "8", red lettering "GREAT CENTRAL WEST" on blue twill, black cut edge 25.00

Round, cowboy has blue shirt, white pants, brown horse, brown lasso, red lettering, "GREAT CENTRAL WEST" and "8" on light tan twill, black cut edge 15.00

Round, cowboy has blue shirt, white pants and head, brown horse, black hair, lasso and hat in hand, red lettering "GREAT CENTRAL WEST" on light tan twill, black cut edge 12.00

Same as above but cowboy has disconnected arm 15.00

Teardrop shape light blue cowboy on sturdy brown hourse, black lettering "GREAT CENTRAL WEST", red "8" on yellow twill, red flat rolled edge
.... 13.00

Teardrop, same as above but dark blue cowboy on thinner, yellow horse . 12.00

Teardrop, cowboy not detailed well around hair and ears, bronze horse on yellow twill, red rolled edge 11.00

Teardrop, cowboy has detailed hair and nose but no ear, brown horse on yellow twill, red rolled edge 10.00

Same as above but heavy, yellow twill 8.00

Five sided, brown cowboy and horse, brown outline of mountains and plateau, white clouds, green shrubbery on yellow twill, brown cut edge (this is a neckerchief patch) 15.00

Region Nine

1939, round, black bison and Lettering "REGION B.S.A.", yellow "9" embroidered over bison, black circle, all on yellow felt 50.00

1940, round, embroidered black bison and lettering "REGION B.S.A.", yellow "9" over bison, black circle on yellow muslin, black cut edge 30.00

1944-'45, same as above but on yellow twill ('44 is smaller than '45), each 25.00

1948, shield shape, brown "9" inside white star, star has dark blue outline, emblem of star (TEXAS), peace pipe, olive branch and shield with feathers (OKLAHOMA), red sun (NEW MEXICO), all on orange twill, red cut edge
.... 20.00

1949, shield shape, dark blue "9", all the rest is same as above 18.00

1950, shield shape, black bison with white "9" inside white star, brown peace pipe, has emblem described above, orange twill, red cut edge 15.00

1959, shield shape, black bison with white "9" inside white star, brown peace pipe, green olive branch, orange twill, red cut edge 12.00

1970, shield shape, black bison with white "9" inside white star, fully embroidered orange, red cut edge, has emblem 10.00

Region Ten

Round, black lettering "PAUL BUNYAN REGION TEN", red hat, black center and cut edge on white twill 25.00

Round, red center circle and hat, black lettering, black flat rolled edge, white twill 18.00

Round, black lettering "REGION TEN", black hair (none behind ear) and beard, black rolled edge, white twill 12.00

Round, same as above but has hair behind ear 11.00

Round, same as above except flesh colored face on off-white twill 10.00

Region Eleven

1939, round, white lettering "REGION ELEVEN THE PACIFIC NORTH-WEST", blue circles, blue "XI", red felt 30.00

Dome shape, white lettering "REGION ELEVEN NOR'WESTERS", yellow axe in maroon log, yellow cut edge, black twill 15.00

Dome shape, white lettering "REGION ELEVEN NOR'WESTERS", yellow axe in green log, yellow rolled edge on maroon twill, used as a neckerchief patch 10.00

Dome shape hat patch, axe in log, yellow cut edge, black twill 10.00

Dome shape, axe partially in log, yellow cut edge, black twill 15.00

Same as above but yellow rolled edge 10.00

Region Twelve
1924, oval, blue felt lettering "12th B.S.A. REGION" sewn on tan felt, black strap on back 65.00

Round, round blue felt on white felt, yellow "12" silkscreened on blue felt, white bull sewn on blue felt 50.00

Round, yellow and orange sunset over water, blue felt shows through sun and reads "12", all on blue felt 35.00

Round printed yellow and orange sunset over water, printed yellow "12", on blue felt 25.00

Round, round regional emblem silk screened in lime green on yellow felt square 35.00

Round, red lettering "SIEMPRE ADELANTE REGION TWELVE B.S.A.", black bull, bull has white hair on head and white smoke from nostrils, white above nose, black cut edge, white twill 22.00

Round, same as above but no white above nose and smoke from nostrils is grey and can barely be seen 18.00

Same as above but no hair on bull's head 15.00

Round, large red lettering and bull has small white eyes, rolled edge 11.00

Round, small red lettering and bull has large white eyes 10.00

Round, hat patch with lettering, and bull deisgn 10.00

Round, white leather, printed design, rare 20.00

Region Thirteen
Round, blue lettering "REGION BOY SCOUTS OF AMERCA" with blue inner circle, red center sewn on white twill, yellow "13CCCCCCC" on red cloth, blue cut edge 22.00

Round, same as above but red center is embroidered rather than cloth .. 18.00

Round, same as above but has blue rolled edge 15.00

Round, white continents, yellow rope, fleur de-lis, "AMERICAS" green outline of rope, on red twill, white cut edge (worn by professional scouters in Central and South America), rare 25.00

The B.S.A. has issued a souvenir set of last patch issued by the 1st 12 regions these have a plastic back, individually 1.00

Complete set 15.00

B.S.A. REGION PATCH
This photo shows a complete set of the reissue set issued by
the B.S.A. in 1972. Designs are the same as last issue of
each region, individually 1.00
Complete set of 12 .... 15.00

REGIONAL MANAGEMENT

EAST CENTRAL REGION
1st, pie-shaped, red lettering "EAST CENTRAL REGION", white lettering "AMERICA'S HEARTLAND", multi-color landscape scene on white twill, orange rolled edge 20.00
2nd, same as above but fully embroidered 12.00
3rd, round, same as above 6.00
4th, round jacket patch, same as above 8.00
5th, round, same as 3rd but with additional scout emblem at left 3.00

NORTH CENTRAL REGION
1st, square with rounded corners, fully embroidered blue, dark blue lettering, red and white stripes, yellow fleur de-lis, blue rolled edge 3.00

NORTH EAST REGION
Rectangle, fully embroidered, yellow center, blue lettering "NORTH EAST REGION", red lettering STILL A FRONTIER", red outline of fleur de-lis, red rolled edge 4.00
Round, fully embroidered, red lettering, white stars, yellow rolled edge, Scout Handsign in center 4.50
Same only now has Scout emblem in center 3.00

SOUTH CENTRAL REGION
Shield shape, fully embroidered, blue center, white lettering, white rolled edge, back has all white back stitching 3.25
Shield, same as above but has bright blue center with little back stitching 3.00

SOUTHEAST REGION
Shield shape, fully embroidered, yellow lettering, light blue center, design in yellow, blue and green, yellow rolled edge 5.00
Small shield shape, same design as above (for use as a hat patch) 6.50
Shield shape, yellow lettering and design on turquoise twill, plastic back, yellow rolled edge 4.00
Same only with addition of B.S.A. at bottom 3.00

WESTERN REGION
Round, fully embroidered, yellow lettering "WESTERN REGION BA", red lettering "NESW", white states, blue ocean, black rolled edge 3.00
Round, same as above but has plastic backing 2.00

SCOUT SHOW
Council Issue 75-2.00
Naitonal Issue 1.00-3.00

SPECIAL EVENTS
Bicentennial Events ....
National Eagle Scout Roundup, 1976 .... 6.00
1976 Scouting USA Bicentennial Washington DC 5.00
1976 Bicentennial Camp shoulder patch 6.00
1976 Eagle Scout Bicentennial jacket patch 12.00

NATIONAL JAMBOREE

1935 and 1937, CAUTION! Official pocket patches for these 2 Jamborees are known to have been counterfeited.

1935, Washington D.C., cancelled due to polio epidemic (items already issued) Round pocket patch, yellow outline of capitol, yellow, purple outlined outer circle on white felt 110.00

1937 Jamboree patch, Washington D.C. 95.00

COUNCIL ISSUE SCOUT SHOW PATCHES

Top row, L to R: 1958 Great Smoky Mountain Council Scout Exposition, cut edge 1.50

1973 Great Smoky Mountain Council Scout Show, rolled edge .... .50

2nd row, L to R: 1959, Great Smoky Mountain Council Scout-O-Rama, cut edge 1.50

1975 Great Smoky Mountain Council Scout-O-Rama, rolled edge .... .50

3rd row, L to R: 1962 Great Smoky Mountain Council Exposition, rolled edge 1.00

1976 Great Smoky Mountain Council Scout-O-Rama, rolled edge .... .75

Bottom row, L to R: 1972 Great Smoky Mountain Council Scout Show, rolled edge .... .50

1978 Great Smoky Mountain Council Expo, rolled edge . .50

U.S. NATIONAL JAMBOREE

1935-1937 National Jamboree, these patches are duplicated and re-produced. Done in 1974 and 1976, both by collectors and National Council.

1935, National Jamboree, Washington D.C., cancelled by polio epidemic, yet most items were issued prior to Jamboree and are very collectible. Official patch, 3" round felt, their are six known variations, basic value 90.00

1935 National Jamboree Committee patch, wide diamond, felt, blue 125.00

1935 National Jamboree set of 11 daily newspapers, 45.00 bound 55.00

1935 National Jamboree set of 3 official large decals 65.00

1935 National Jamboree, National Staff, neckerchief, purple, rare 225.00

1935 National Jamboree, large blue felt pennant, logo 45.00

1935 National Jamboree, Official Troop contingent flag, rare 110.00

1935 National Jamboree, ID, card, two-fold, with RR pass 15.00

1935 National Jamboree, half-moon, red felt, shoulder patches, contingent
.... 45.00

1935 National Jamboree official small decals, there are two 5.00

1935 National Jamboree Sectional Manual 25.00

1935 National Jamboree Leaders Guide Book 12.50

1935 National Jamoree Aerial photos, set of three, 8 x 10 .... 30.00

1935 National Jamboree Leaders neckerchief, red, stenciled logo 110.00

1935 National Jamboree Leaders neckerchief, blue, stenciled logo 110.00

1935 National Jamboree Boys Neckerchief, red (in camp), full square ... 65.00

1935 National Jamboree Boys Neckerchief, blue (out of camp) square
.... 70.00

1935 National and World Jamboree Book in Pictures, blue cover 35.00

1937 National Jamboree official 3" felt patch, (4 variations known) 75.00

1937 National Jamboree Leaders neckerchief, blue, white stencil 100.00

1937 National Jamboree Leaders neckerchief, red, white stencil 100.00

1937 National Jamboree Boys neckerchief, red, (in camp), square 50.00

1937 National Jamboree Boys neckerchief, blue (out of camp) square ... 60.00

1937 National Jamboree, two part ID card, with RR pass 20.00

1937 National Jamboree, Region 3, "Host" patch, canvas, stencil 50.00

1937 National Jamboree special Usher patch, felt 110.00

1937 National Jamboree set of three large decals, for all three 55.00

1937 National Jamboree small decals, their are three, each 6.00

1937 National Jamboree special Regional Contingent shoulder epalets (12)
.... 48.00

1937 National Jamboree special in Jamboree-to-World Jamboree epalet . 65.00

1937 National Jamboree "I'm Going" celloid button 15.00

1937 National Jamboree special, "Piasa Bird Council" coin 30.00

1937 National Jamboree "Regional Staff Bar" green felt 75.00

1937 National Jamboree "World Staff Bar" red felt 100.00

1937 National Jamboree "National Staff Bar" white felt 150.00

1937 National Jamboree, Special Guide, neckerchief, rare 125.00

1937 National Jamboree, large troop contingent flag, with logo 110.00

1937 National Jamboree large maroon pennant, with logo 35.00

1937 National Jamboree large bleu pennant, rare 45.00

1937 National Jamboree small blue pennant, (sold on the streets) 12.50

1937 National Jamboree Sachen Council, special brass slide 15.00

1937 National Jamboree slide, woggle, tri-color, scarce 10.00

1937 National Jamboree, set of 11 daily papers, 35.00 bound 40.00

1937 National Jamboree, special Tour Guide to NY, with logo, paper 20.00

1937 National Jamboree Leaders Guide Book, with logo 15.00

1937 National Jamboree Sectional Leaders Guide Book 20.00

1937 National Jamboree Special Contest Medal, tri-color ribbon, rare .. 300.00

1950 National Jamboree, proto-type patch, pre-jambroee, yellow twill ... 65.00

1950 National Jamboree, proto-type, post jamboree, blue-cut-edge 125.00

1950 National Jamboree, official pocket patch, canvas, (note 6 varieties) 28.00

1950 National Jamboree twill patch, official (note 4 varieties) 30.00

1950 National Jamboree large decal 15.00

1950 National Jamboree decal, large, on reverse, Trading Post B, rare
.... 25.00

1950 National Jamboree decal, slip-off-paper type, small 5.00

1950 National Jamboree official ID card 12.50

1950 National Jamboree small clutch pin, bronze 15.00

1950 National Jamboree special promotional pin, blue print on white 11.00

1950 National Jamboree official brass coin 15.00

1950 National Jamboree, key fob, on chain 10.00

1950 National Jamboree, special masonite plaque, with logo 12.50

1950 National Jamboree, Rayon-silk neckerchief, (note two varieties) ... 22.00

1950 National Jamboree, cotton neckerchief (note two varieties) 20.00

1950 National Jamboree Region 12, special contingent patch 10.00

1950 National Jamboree Region 6, continegent patch 12.00

1950 National Jamboree, official Troop Contingent flag, 3 x 5 .... 65.00

1950 National Jamboree large pennant, blue felt 25.00

1950 National Jamboree, medium size blue pennant 20.00

1950 National Jamboree, official issue T-shirt, in wrappers 20.00

1950 National Jamboree, official souvenir book, with logo 10.00

1950 National Jamboree, Special Leaders Award, Kneeling Washington in
lead, pedestal base, with appreciation, etc., rare 100.00

1950 National Jamboree, sterling ring, with logo 20.00

1950 National Jamboree, Bucktail Council Waterproof mat-safe 7.50

1953 National Jamboree official twill patch (note four known varieties) . 22.00

1953 National Jamboree, staff patch (note- "California" on patch), rare . 85.00

1953 National Jamboree, official "Jacket" patch, 6", scarce, 4 varieties . 55.00

1953 National Jamboree T-shirt, in wrappers 12.00

1953 National Jamboree silk neckerchief, ladies scarf-type, two varieties
.... 15.00

1953 National Jamboree large pennant, blue felt 22.00

1953 National Jamboree, special leaders award, bronze bell, with logo ... 45.00

1953 National Jamboree, special Regional and National Award, bronze wagon
.... 60.00

1953 National Jamboree, special "Chorous" neckerchief, rare 40.00
1953 National Jamboree Achievement Award card 7.50
1953 National Jamboree, "Going to the Jamboree" pin, tri-color 8.50
1953 National Jamboree small clutch pin, lapel 6.50
1953 National Jamboree ID card 7.60
1953 National Jamboree official decal, square 6.50
1953 National Jamboree sterling ring, with logo 12.50
1953 National Jamboree special promotional pin, gold-black letters 10.00
1953 National Jamboree souvenir book, with logo 7.50
1953 National Jamboree troop contingent flag, 3 x 5, with logo 65.00
1953 National Jamboree Sachem Council slide, brass 6.50
1953 National Jamboree masonite appreciation plaque 10.00
1953 National Jamboree small silk flag, with holder and staff 10.00
1953 National Jamboree official brass coin 8.50
1953 National Jamboree, key-fob, on chain 6.50
1953 National Jamboree Region 12 Host patch, note 4 varieties 15.00
1953 National Jamboree Region 4 Contingent coin, aluminum 7.50
1953 National Jamboree Region 5, contingent patch 6.50
1953 National Jamboree Region 6, contingent patch 7.50
1953 National Jamboree Max Silber bronze slide, (special presentation) . 60.00

1957 National Jamboree, pre-jamboree proto-type patch, yellow pants, on Washington, rare 110.00
1957 National Jamboree, offical 3'' twill patch, note 6 varieites 12.50
1957 National Jamboree, official Jacket patch, 6'', note 4 varieties 25.00
1957 National Jamboree, 2'' promotional pin, celloid, blue-white 5.00
1957 National Jamboree, small brass pin, clutch 6.00
1957 National Jamboree, brass coin 6.50
1957 National Jamboree, small silk flag, with staff and base, desk type ... 6.50
1957 National Jamboree, large leather, back-pack patch 15.00
1957 National Jamboree, large decal 5.00
1957 National Jamboree, ID, card 6.50
1957 National Jamboree, special Max Silber bronze belt buckle 50.00
1957 National Jamboree, Guide Arm Band, white felt, stencil logo 60.00
1957 National Jamboree, official cotton neckerchief, note 4 varieties 11.50
1957 National Jamboree Ladies silk scarf, with logo, red-pipiing 15.00
1957 National Jamboree, ladies silk scarf, blue piping 13.50
1957 National Jamboree Trading Post ID, leather 7.50
1957 National Jamboree Region 2, contingent patch 7.50
1957 National Jamboree Region 5, contingent patch, note 2 varieties 6.50
1957 National Jamboree Region 6, contingent patch, note 2 varieties 6.50
1957 National Jamboree, Region 7, metal slide 7.50
1957 National Jamboree, T-shirt, in wrappers 6.50
1957 National Jamboree, T-shirt, terry cloth, in wrappers 7.50
1957 National Jamboree, large or medium pennants, blue felt 9.50
1957 National Jamboree, Troop contingent flag, 3 x 5, with logo 45.00

1957 National Jamboree, sterling ring, with logo 10.00
1957 National Jamboree, poster, large, for Council use, promotional 20.00
1957 National Jamboree, sardines, in can, not opened 6.50
1957 National Jamboree, set of 7 daily papers, set 12.50
1957 National Jamboree, silk pillow case, with scene of Jamboree 15.00
1957 National Jamboree souvenir book, with logo 6.50
1957 National Jamboree, Sectional Leaders Guide Book 15.00
1957 National Jamboree, Leaders Guide Book 6.50
1957 National Jamboree stationary set, large or small 10.00
1957 National Jamboree, official hat patch, diamond shaped 10.00

1960 National Jamboree, official 3" patch, note 3 varieties 8.50
1960 National Jamboree, cotton neckerchief, note 3 varieties 8.50
1960 National Jamboree, special arena arm band 75.00
1960 National Jamboree, leather, back-sack patch 25.00
1960 National Jamboree, specail Conservation Crew, patch 75.00
1960 National Jamboree, Jacket patch, 6", note 2 varieties, borders 22.00
1960 National Jamboree brass coin 7.50
1960 National Jamboree, set of stationary, in wrappers .... 10.00..
1960 National Jamboree, set of stationary, in wrappers 10.00
1960 National Jamboree, brass coin, no finish, proto-type 35.00
1960 National Jamboree, small diamond hat patch, yellow-twill 10.00
1960 National Jamboree, T-shirt, in wrappers 7.50
1960 National Jamboree, contingent bus-banner, 3' x 15' 50.00
1960 National Jamboree, leaders appreciation lucite block, with logo 22.00
1960 National Jamboree, set of 7 daily papers, set 9.50
1960 National Jamboree, souvenir book 8.50
1960 National Jamboree, ladies silk scarf, with logo 12.50
1960 National Jamboree, troop flag, 3 x 5, with logo 40.00
1960 National Jamboree, special "Adventure Award" patch 75.00
1960 National Jamboree, sardines, in can, unopened 5.00
1960 National Jamboree, lapel pin, clutch 6.00
1960 National Jamboree, lapel pin, white enamel, rare 30.00
1960 National Jamboree, 1" sticker 3.00
1960 National Jamboree, 1" sticker 3.00

1960 National Jamboree, "I'm Going" button, celloid 5.50
1960 National Jamboree, ID, card 6.00
1960 National Jamboree, large decal, 3½ square 5.00
1960 National Jamboree, Region 1 visitors pass 4.00
1960 National Jamboree,d Region 1, small hand lense, souvenir 6.00
1960 National Jamboree, Region 9 contingent patch, 5" round 15.00
1960 National Jamboree, Region 6, contingent patch 6.50
1960 National Jamboree, Region 2, contingent patch 6.00
1960 National Jamboree, special Max Silber, bronze buckle 45.00
1960 National Jamboree, large or medum pennant, blue felt 7.50

1960 National Jamboree, Sectional Leaders Guide book, with logo 12.50

1960 National Jamboree Commisary Guide Book 10.00

1960 National Jamboree, Leaders Guide Book 6.50

1964 National Jamboree, official patch, gum-backed, note 5 varieties 6.00

1964 National Jamboree, official patch, cloth back, note 3 varieties 5.00

1964 National Jamboree, official patch, silk-open weave, note 5 varieties . 7.50

1964 National Jamboree, official cotton neckerchief, note 3 varieties 6.00

1964 National Jamboree, lapel pin, clutch type 3.00

1964 National Jamboree, ladies white scarf 5.00

1964 National Jamboree, small silk flag, base and staff 6.00

1964 National Jamboree, decal, large 4.00

1964 National Jamboree, stationary set in wrappers 4.50

1964 National Jamboree, special protection servies arm-band 30.00

1964 National Jamboree, special Health Services arm band 40.00

1964 National Jamboree silver coin 4.50

1964 National Jamboree, brass coin 3.00

1964 National Jamboree continental silver coin, commemorative 5.50

1964 National Jamboree, Trading Post leather ID, button-hole type 5.00

1964 National Jamboree ID card 5.00

1964 National Jamboree, Region 9 contingent patch 4.00

1964 National Jamboree, Region 5, contingent patch 5.00

1964 National Jamboree, Region 6, contingent patch 5.00

1964 National Jamboree, Regional or National stationary sheet and envelope
.... 6.00

1964 National Jamboree, Region 12, contingent patch 5.00

1964 National Jamboree, can of sardines, unopened 4.00

1946 National Jamboree, large or medium pennants, blue felt 7.50

1964 National Jamboree, Max Silber, bronze commemorative buckle 30.00

1964 National Jamboree, jacket patch, 6'', note 2 varieties 15.00

1964 National Jamboree, proto-type pocket patch, yellow FDL 75.00

1964 National Jamboree, Adventure Award patch 35.00

1964 National Jamboree, hat patch, white-twill, diamond 7.50

1964 National Jamboree, hat patch, STAFF, white twill 45.00

1964 National Jamboree, large leather patch, for back-sacks 15.00

1964 National Jamboree, official mug, first issued, is repro out, original . 40.00

1964 National Jamboree, T-shirt in wrappers 7.50

1964 National Jamboree, silk pillow case, blue fringe, logo 15.00

1964 National Jamboree, silk pillow case, blue fringe, logo 15.00

1964 National Jamboree, ladies appreciation lucite block, with logo 20.00

1964 National Jamboree, leaders appreciation lucite block, with logo 20.00

1964 National Jamboree, Bucktail Council, match safe, glass 5.00

1964 Nationa Jamboree, cuff links, enamel, logo 7.50

1964 National Jamboree, Creamer, sold in TP, with logo, limited 12.50

1964 National Jamboree, small dish, for safety pins, with logo, TP item ... 7.00

1964 National Jamboree set of Daily Journals, all 9.50

1964 National Jamboree, souvenir book 6.50
1964 National Jamboree, troop flag, 3 x 5, with logo 45.00
1964 National Jamboree, Sectional Leaders Guide Book 10.00
1964 National Jamboree, Leaders Guide Book 6.50
1964 National Jamboree, patch-pin combination, rare 50.00
1964 National Jamboree, Medical staff patch 75.00
1964 National Jamboree, special gate pass 4.50

1969 National Jamboree, official pocket patch, 4 varieties 6.50
1969 National Jamboree, cotton neckerchief, 5 varieties 6.50
1969 National Jamboree, Medical staff patch, gold-border variety 30.00
1969 National Jamboree, Medical staff patch, white ce, proto-type 60.00
1969 National Jamboree, small leather patch, 3 varieties 12.00
1969 National Jamboree, small leather no-roped edges, proto-type 50.00
1969 National Jamboree, large leather patches, 3 varieties 7.50
1969 National Jamboree, "Building to Serve" stripe, (wide game) two
varieties 8.00
1969 National Jamboree, hat patch, diamond type 6.00
1969 National Jamboree, stationary set, in wrappers 7.50
1969 National Jamboree, pennants, three different types, each 6.50
1969 National Jamboree, silver coin 3.00
1960 National Jamboree, brass coin 2.00
1969 National Jamboree, proto-type medallion, 51mm, Goldine Metal, 4mm
thick 100.00
1969 National Jamboree, clutch pin, lapel 2.50
1969 National Jamboree, cluth pin, enamel 3.00
1969 National Jamboree, jacket patch, 6'', 3 varieties 15.00
1969 National Jamboree, small silk flag, with staff and base 4.50
1969 National Jamboree, decal 2.00
1969 National Jamboree, souvenir neckerchief 2.50
1969 National Jamboree, ceramic cup, bowl, saucer, etc., each 3.50
1969 National Jamboree, Region 5, contingent patch 3.00
1969 National Jamboree, Region 6 Contingent patch, either variety 4.00
1969 National Jamboree, Region 9, contingent patch 5.00
1969 National Jamboree, Region 1, contingent neckerchief 5.00
1969 National Jamboree, Max Silber, bronze commemorative buckle 35.00
1969 National Jamboree, T-shirt, in wrappers 4.50
1969 National Jamboree, large bus banner, 3' x 15' 30.00
1969 National Jamboree, Leaders appreciation block, lucite 15.00
1969 National Jamboree, Leaders appreciation tape measure 10.00
1969 National Jamboree, set of daily journals, all 6.50
1969 National Jamboree, souvevir book 5.00
1969 National Jamboree, ladies silk scarf 4.00
1969 National Jamboree, Region 12 contingent patch 5.00
1969 National Jamboree, troop flag, large type, 3 x 5, with logo 27.50
1969 National Jamboree, zippo pocket knife 6.00

1969 National Jamboree, coaster set 5.00
1969 National Jamboree, staff horseshoe bolo, silver 8.50
1969 National Jamboree, antler bolo 7.50
1969 National Jamboree, Explorer enameled bolo 6.50

1973, Farragut State Park, Idaho, and Moraine State Park, PA, rectangular
  pocket patch, yellow twill, bronze rolled edge 3.00
  OA SERVICE CORPS EAST rectangular pocket patch, red embroidered
  "WWW" on yellow twill, bronze rolled edge 20.00
  Rectangular jacket patch, yellow twill, bronze rolled edge 5.00
  Rectangular leather jacket patch, embossed design 6.00
  Round AQUATICS STAFF patch, red lettering on yellow twill, green cut
  edge 12.00
  KYBO PATROL round pocket patch, black lettering on yellow twill, yellow
  rolled edge 15.00
  FRIENDSHIP segment, clasped hands on yellow twill, bronze rolled edge
  ...... 5.00

1973 semi-official issues, McBryde's Marauders Patch, rectangle 12.50
  TRADING POST A, rectangular yellow twill pocket patch, bronze rolled
  edge 20.00
  Same description for TRADING POSTS B, C, & D, each 25.00
  TRADING POST A, round fully embroidered pocket patch, black rolled
  edge 25.00
  Same description for TRADING POSTS B & C, each 25.00
  TRADING POST D, round yellow twill pocket patch (Jamboree East) 25.00
  TRADING POST A, round fully embroidered jacket patch, black rolled edge
  ...... 35.00
  Same description for TRADING POSTS B & C, each 30.00
  There are three segments (EAST, WEST & STAFF) which are rectangular
  yellow twill with black lettering, East 7.50
West 7.50
Staff 12.0

MEDICAL STAFF pocket patch, fully embroidered 15.00
  1973 East Hilton Lodge Patch, round 15.00
1973 East Hilton Lodge Patch, round 15.00

1977, Moraine State Park, PA, pocket patch; yellow fleur de-lis, "1977", and
  arrow; red top left corner and lettering "NATIONAL SCOUT JAMBOREE"
  blue lower right corner; black, red and yellow compass points; black "N";
  on white twill, yellow rolled edge 4.00
  Jacket patch, same design 6.00
  Leather patch for jacket, same design, embossed 7.00
1981 Fort A.P. Hill, Virginia, pocket patch, rounded square, orange twill
  backgroun pictures George Washington and silhouette of Scout, red rolled
  edge 75.00
  Pocket patch, same as above only fully embroidered orange background
  ...... 3.00
  Jacket patch, same design as 1st patch only larger 4.00
  Staff pocket patch, same design as 2nd patch except has wording "Staff"
  added 12.00
  Leather jacket patch, same design as others only has embossed design . 5.00

U.S. NATIONAL JAMBOREE STRIPS
Top, 1937, World Staff strip 200.00
    Center, 1937 Regional Staff strip 65.00
    Left, 1973 For Friendship segment 5.00
    Right, 1973 "West" strip 7.50

Sea Explorer Bay Jammer (a Bay Jammer is the Sea Explorer equivalent of a
    jamboree) 5.00
    Jamboree) 5.00-20.00
Rover Scout Moot (a moot is the Rover Scout equivalent of a jamboree)
    ...... 10.00-30.00

WORLD JAMBOREES
1920 World Jamboree-England
1920 World Jamboree US - Official Contingent Medal, with name, tri-color
    ribbon, with bronze medal, World 350.00
1920 World Jamboree US - Official Contingent patch, white felt, with red eagle,
    cut out, small variation 200.00
1920 World Jamboree, Daily news letters, set of 11 .... 50.00
1920 World Jamboree, Religious programs, each 10.00
1920 World Jamboree, official souvenir book, embossed cover 35.00
1920 World Jamboree, vast assortment of foreign pins, commemorating event,
    each 10.00
1920 World Jamboree,d Underwood official photo, 8 x 10, rare 20.00

1924 World Jamboree, official patch, small silk, Danish flag, with World
    Jamboree, and a number from 1-5000, rare 500.00
1924 World Jamboree, US Contingent Medal, with name, bronze 350.00

1924 World Jamboree, US Contingent patch, white felt, with red stenciling
.... 150.00
1924 World Jamboree, official souvenir book 75.00
1924 World Jamboree, official daily newspapers, set of 11, all 100.00
1924 World Jamboree, Baden-Powell Medallion, bronze, rare 450.00
1924 World Jamboree, limited ed, book, 6,000 copies, rare 75.00

1929 World Jamboree, official patch, square, tan, with name 200.00
1929 World Jamboree, US, Contingent Medal, with name, green ribbon . 150.00
1929 World Jamboree, US, Contingent patch, white felt, large, red stenciling
.... 75.00
1929 World Jamboree, set of daily newspapers, $25.00, bound 35.00
1929 World Jamboree, special issue souvenir book 35.00
1929 World Jamboree, official souvenir stick-pin, brass, with arrow 50.00
1929 World Jamboree, Religious propgramme 10.00
1929 World Jamboree, US Baggage tag 20.00
1929 World Jamboree, First Day cover, with seal 10.00
1929 World Jamboree, official Underwood photo, 8 x 10 .... 15.00
1929 World Jamboree, certificate of ID 22.00
1929 World Jamboree, varied foreign pins and contingent badges, each .. 15.00
1929 World Jamboree, re-rpint from the Times, on Jamboree 10.00

1933 World Jamboree, official patch, small brown silk, with leeping deer
.... 100.00
1933 World Jamboree, US Contingent medal, with name, green ribbon .. 500.00
1933 World Jamboree, US Contingent patch, white twill, with eagle, round
.... 50.00
1933 World Jamboree, silver stick pin, worn by scouts 45.00
1933 World Jamboree, ID, certificate 50.00
1933 World Jamboree, set of daily papers, for all 75.00
1933 World Jamboree, official Guide book, souvenir 55.00
1933 World Jamboree, Leaders appreciation certificate 30.00
1933 World Jamboree, coin or medallion, embossed, with BP profile 150.00

1937 World Jamboree, official patch, white twill, with medallion center, please
note that there are over 16 different patches, due to sub-camps, not colors
.... 200.00
1937 World Jamboree, US Contingent Medal, green ribbon, bronze medal
.... 150.00
1937 World Jamboree, US Contingent patch, 3'' round, brown rare 50.00
1937 World Jamboree, official set of daily papers, $40.00, bound 50.00
1937 World Jamboree, official silver stick-pin 45.00
1937 World Jamboree, official small sticker, green, nice 4.50
1937 World Jamboree, certificate of ID, embossed 30.00
1937 World Jamboree, Leaders certificate of appreciation 20.00
1937 World Jamboree, special BP, presentation medallion, to leaders .. 300.00
1937 World Jamboree, Guide book, souvenir type, embossed cover 35.00

U.S. NATIONAL JAMBOREE POCKET PATCHES

Top row, L to R: 1950 canvas patch 35.00
1964 embroidered patch 8.00
2nd row, L to R: 1950 embroidered patch 40.00
1964 woven patch, bright red border 11.00
1973 pocket patch 3.00
3rd row, L to R: 1953 pocket patch 25.00
1969 pocket patch 7.00
1977 pocket patch 4.00
Bottom row: 1957 pocket patch 20.00
1969 leather patch, small 14.00
1981 pocket patch, fully embroidered 3.00

1947 World Jamboree, official patch, red, silk, gauze backing, there are known to be over 22 different patches, sub-camps and service camps, all with French names, vary in value, due to sub-camps and service camps 110.00-150.00

1947 World Jamboree, US Contingent patch, 3'' twill, red eagle 22.00

1947 World Jamboree, US, Contingent neckerchief, yellow, stenciled 20.00

1947 World Jamboree, US ship-board menu's and guides, each 10.00

1947 World Jamboree, doilies, given at Jamboree, embossed with logo .. 10.00

1947 World Jamboree, set of daily papers, all 35.00

1947 World Jamboree, official ID card, with picture 22.00

1947 World Jamboree, souvenir book and Log 30.00

1947 World Jamboree, enameled stick pin, inscribed Franch 1947 .... 30.00

1947 World Jamboree, special 2'' bronze Medallion, given to leaders 300.00

1947 World Jamboree, promotional poster 35.00

1947 World Jamboree, promotional fold-out folder 10.00

1947 World Jamboree, ship-board deck plan and evacuation roster, US .. 10.00

1947 World Jamboree, official postage stamp, brown 7.00

1947 World Jamboree, First Day Cover, logo affixed, with stamp 8.50

1951 World Jamboree, official patch, leather, with out green letters 30.00

With green letters, and button loop, staff 40.00

1951 World Jamboree, semi-official patch, yellow twill, note repor's out . 20.00

1951 World Jamboree, US Contingent patch, 3'' white twill, eagle 15.00

1951 World Jamboree, US Contingent neckerchief, tri-color, eagle 10.00

1951 World Jamboree, set of daily papers, all 30.00

1951 World Jamboree, silver stick pin 25.00

1951 World Jamboree, Log or Guide book, souvenir type 20.00

1951 World Jamboree, official ID card, scarce 30.00

NATIONAL JAMBOREE JACKET PATCHES

Top L to R: 1957 .... 25.00
    1960 .... 22.00
Middle, L to R: 1964 .... 15.00
    1969 .... 15.00
Bottom, L to R: 1973 .... 5.00
    1977 .... 6.00

NATIONAL JAMBOREE JACKET PATCHES

Top, L to R: 1957, leather 25.00
 1953, embroidered 55.00
Bottom row, L to R: 1973, leather 6.00
 1977, leather 7.00

World Jamboree continued

1963, same patch as 1957 .... 12.00

1967 World Jamboree, the U.S. hosted this jamboree, pocket patch, rectangle
 with rope design border, blue twill background, cut edge 8.00
 Jacket patch, round purple twill, white fleur de-lis in center, white ring
 around edge, purple rolled edge 12.00
 leather patch, large embroidered design of the pocket patch 14.00

1971, blue twill hat patch, blue cut edge 12.00

1971, blue twill pocket patch, blue cut edge 8.00
 Blue twill pocket patch, blue cut edge 8.00
 Blue twill jacket patch, blue cut edge 10.00

1975, white twill pocket patch, yellow rolled edge ....
 White twill jacket patch, yellow rolled edge ....

1979, World Jamboree, (this jamboree was to have been held in Iran and was
 switched to Sweden), pocket patch, round, white twill, stylized flying eagle
 below stylized blue field of flag, lettering says "1979 IRAN", rolled edge
 ...... 50.00
 Pocket patch, same as above only lettering says "DALAJAMB 1979" .. 10.00
 Jacket patch, same design as above for Sweden 30.00

WORLD JAMBOREE PATCHES

Top row, L to R: 1963 W.J. Greece, Trading Post patch . 20.00

1979, WJ., Sweden-Official pocket patch 30.00

2nd row, L to R: 1975 W.J., Norway-Friendship Tour patch
...... 6.50

1979 W.J., Iran-Canadian Contingent Join In Jamboree
patch 8.00

3rd row, L to R: 1979 W.J., Sweden-U.S. Contingent Pocket
patchd 15.00

1979 W.J., Iran-Canadian Contingent pocket patch ... 10.00

1955 W.J., Canada-U.S. Contingent pocket patch 10.00

4th row, L to R: 1979 W.J., Sweden (spin off in Switzerland)
pocket patch 10.00

1963 W.J., Greece-Trading Post patch 20.00

1967 W.J. U.S.A.-Official pocket patch 8.00

Bottom row, L: 1971 W.J. Japan-Trading Post patch 5.00

Upper center: 1971 W.J., Iran-World Join-In Jamboree
patch 20.00

Lower center; 1975 W.J., Norway-World Join-In Jamboree
patch 5.00

R: 1971 W.J., Japan-Trading Post patch 5.00

194

WORLD JAMBOREE JACKET PATCHES
Top row, L to R: 1975 W.J., Norway-Official jacket patch
...... 10.00
1971 W.J., Japan-Official jacket patch 12.00
2nd row, L to R: 1967 W.J. U.S.A.-Official leather patch   14.00
1979 W.J. Sweden-Official jacket patch 30.00
1979 W.J., Sweden-U.S. Contingent jacket patch 15.00
1967 W.J., U.S.A.-Official jacket patch 12.00

GIRL SCOUT JAMBOREE

1965, Senior Girl Scout round-up patch 10.00

1974, NESA, National Conference, Ft. Collins CO, pocket patch 15.00

1976, NESA, National Conference, Washington DC, pocket patch 10.00

1978, NESA, National Conference, Nashville, TN, pocket patch 8.00

1980, NESA, National Conference, pocket patch 6.50

1982, NESA, National Conference, pocket patch 5.00

NATIONAL ORDER OF THE ARROW CONFERENCE (NOAC)

NOTE: There is a counterfeit 1974 NOAC set.

1940, pocket patch, arrowhead shape, red chenille background on white felt, lettering is white chenille "CTE". 120.00

Pocket patch for staff only, arrowhead shape, white "CTE", silk screened on puffy type red felt, rare 200.00

1946 patch, white felt, round, embroidered red design and lettering verified 100.00

1948, delegate patch, white round, red silk screened design and lettering 85.00

Staff patch, white twill round, red embroidered design and lettering, red cut edge 100.00

1950 patch, white twill oval, green, silver, red embroidered design, silver cut edge 60.00

1952 patch, red twill round, yellow, black, white embroidered design, red cut edge 45.00

BROTHERHOOD CHORUS patch, blue twill round, red cut edge and arrow, yellow lettering and design, black "37TH ANNIVERSARY WWW" 60.00

1954 patch, white twill shield, yellow, blue and red embroidered design, blue cut edge 40.00

1956 patch, white twill oval, multicolored embroidered design, blue rolled edge 30.00

1958 patch, white twill arrowhead, (including loop), yellow red, blue embroidered, blue cut edge 22.00

BROTHERHOOD CHORUS patch, white twill round, orange cut edge, black, white embroidered design 40.00

1961 patch, white twill shield, red, yellow, black embroiderd, black cut edge 22.00

BROTHERHOOD CHORUS patch, blue twill, round, red embroidered lettering, white rolled edge 35.00

1963, patch, fully embroidered arrowhead, multicolored design, brown cut edge 20.00

1965 patch, gray twill shield, multicolored embroidered design, blue cut edge 20.00

1967 patch, fully embroidered arrowhead, multicolored design, green cut edge 15.00

1969 patch, fully embroidered, multicolored embroidered emblem, blue rolled edge 12.00

1971 patch, fully embroidered arrowhead, multicolored design, white cut edge 12.00

1973 patch, white twill sexagon, multicolored embroidered design, white rolled edge 10.00

ORDER OF THE ARROW NOAC
AND INDIAN SEMINAR PATCHES

Rop row, L to R: 1978 O.A. Indian Seminar patch 20.00

1980 O.A. Indian Seminar patch 15.00

2nd row: 1940 N.O.A.C. Staff pocket patch 200.00

3rd row, L to R: 1952 N.O.A.C. pocket patch 45.00

1956 N.O.A.C. pocket patch 30.00

4th row: 1975 N.O.A.C. pocket patch 12.00

Bottom row, L to R: 1973 N.O.A.C. pocket patch 10.00

1977 N.O.A.C. pocket patch 6.00

NEWSROOM STAFF patch, fully embroidered rectangle, embroidered red with black lettering, black flat rolled edge 20.00
1975 jacket patch, fully embroidered sexagon, blue rolled edge 12.00
pocket patch, fully embroidered sexagon, blue rolled edge 8.00
1977 pocket patch, odd shaped, fully embroidered, stylized Indian chief in flame over campfire, white lettering, rolled edge 6.00
Jacket patch, same as above only larger 10.00

NATIONAL OA COMMITTEE
1956 NATIONAL COMMITTEE patch, white twill, blue lettering and rolled edge, red arrowhead, embroidered loop sewn to back 50.00
1973 NATIONAL CONFERENCE patch, fully embroidered round, white background, red rolled edge 28.00

NATIONAL ORDER OF THE ARROW INDIAN SEMINAR
1978, patch, round turquoise, twill with embroidered feathers hanging down, design is branch with smoking peace pipe, cut edge 20.00
1980, patch, round, blue twill, star sunburst design, dark blue, rolled edge 15.00

Military Events, Explorer encampments at military bases 2.50-5.00
Air encampments 5.00-10.00
Explorer flight or airlift 5.00-10.00
Naval cruise 3.00-10.00
Athletic Event, Usher patches exist for baseball and football games, Mardi Gras, Indianapolis 500, etc. General events 2.00-5.00
Events of National importance (bowls, etc.) 3.50-10.00

WORLD's FAIR
1939, New York World's Fair Service Corps Patch, round, orange twill, blue lettering and white lettering has "1939", blue cut edge 30.00
1940, same as above only says "1940" 30.00
1964-65, New York World's Fair, round, orange twill, blue rolled edge and black tab 10.00
New York World's Fair, odd shaped square, blue, rolled edge 10.00

STATE STRIPS
All are arc shaped segments.
Red on tan (Boy Scout), each 2.00
Red on khaki (Boy Scout), each 2.00
Yellow on blue (Cub Scouts), each 2.00
Brown on green (Explorers, each 4.00
Bright blue on light blue (Air Scouts), each 5.00
White on Navy (Sea Scout, each 4.00
Navy on White (Sea Scouts), each 4.00
White on red (All programs) 50-1.00

NOTE: There are a few red on tan full one half strip size strips known to exist for U.S. overseas territories. These are Alaska, Hawaii, Canal Zone, and Puerto Rico.

Red and white one half strips known for U.S. overseas territories and other parts of the world where U.S. bases exist.

There are a few red on tan full ½ strip size strips known to exist for U.S. overseas territories. These are Alaska, Hawaii, Canal Zone, and Puerto Rico each 30.00

Red and white ½ strips known for U.S. overseas territories and other parts of the world where U.S. bases exist: Agana, Aleutian Islands, Aruba, Austria, Belgium, Denmark, Dhahran, England, France, Far East Council, Germany, Great Britain, Greece, Guam, Guantanamo Bay, Iceland, Indonesia, Iran, Italy, Jakarta, Japan, Kobe, Kwajelein M.I., Libya, Mexico, D.F., Morocco, Netherlands, Norway, Okinawa, Pago Pago, Philippines, Poland, Saipan, Samoa, Saudi Arabia, South Korea, Spain, Switzerland, Taiwan, Thailand, Tokyo, Turkey, Vietnam, each 3.00-7.00

Red and white ¼ strips known to exist for U.S. overseas territories and areas of U.S. bases: Australia, Austl, Austria, Belgium, China, Cuba, Denmark, France, Germany, Greece, Guam, Hong Kong, Italy Iwo Jima, Japan, Kobe Korea, Libya, Lux Luxembourg, Morroco, Nepal, Netherlands, New Zealand, Norway, Okinawa, Peru, Phillipine Islands, Saigon, Saudi Arabia, Spain, Taiwan, Thailand, T. H., Tokyo, Venezuela, Viet Nam, Wake, Yugo., Yugoslavia, Laos, each 3.00-7.00

SUB UNIT INSIGNIA

Den numeral strips, yellow on blue twill, each .... .25

Patrol medallions, 1st set were 58 felt, black on red, no "BSA", each 12.00

2nd set were 73 felt, black on red, with "BSA", each 1.00-2.00

3rd set were 52 red twill, black on red, variations has all black backstitching

3rd set were 52 red twill, black on red, variations has all black backstitching each 3.00-3.50

With "BSA" gumback, each .... .60

With plastic back, each 1.00

With rubber back, each 1.50

35 multi-color with two variations of antelope, each .... .50

SPECIAL EVENT PATCHES
Top row, L to R: 1939, NY World's Fair Service Corps patch
...... 30.00
1940 NY World's Fair Service Corps patch 30.00
1964-65 NY World's Fair Service Corps patch 10.00
Bottom row, L to R: 1974 Gator Bowl Service Award patch
..... 4.00
1969 LSU Scout Usher patch 2.50

PERSONAL TENURE VETERAN SCOUT INSIGNIA
5 YEAR VETERAN
1915, white design, brown eagle, blue background on cloth 50.00

1920, fully embroidered, pale yellow design, white badge, brown eagle, purple
background on cloth 25.00

1925, fully embroidered, yellow badge and design, brown eagle, blue background on cloth 12.00

1952, fully embroidered (NO CLOTH), yellow design and badge, brown eagle,
blue background, yellow cut edge 5.00

10 YEAR VETERAN
1920, blue badge with yellow outline, yellow design, blue background on cloth
...... 26.00

1925, blue badge with yellow outline, blue circle, yellow design on cloth .. 15.00

1952, fully embroidered (NO CLOTH), yellow design and badge, brown eagle,
blue background, yellow cut edge 8.00

15 YEAR VETERAN
1925, blue badge with yellow outline, yellow design, blue circle on cloth .. 20.00

1952, fully embroidered (NO CLOTH), yellow design and badge, brown eagle, blue background, yellow cut edge 12.00

20 YEAR VETERAN
1930, blue badge with yellow outline, blue circle, yellow design on cloth .. 20.00

1952, fully embroidered (NO CLOTH), yellow design and badge, brown eagle, blue background, yellow cut edge 15.00

25 YEAR VETERAN
1935, blue badge with yellow outline, blue circle, yellow design (sewn with bullion thread) on cloth 28.00

1952, fully embroidered (NO CLOTH), yellow design and badge, brown eagle, blue background, yellow cut edge 15.00

1952, the following description is for the 30 YEAR, 35 YEAR, 40 YEAR, 45 YEAR, and 50 YEAR tenure patches: fully embroidered (NO CLOTH), yellow design and badge, brown eagle, blue background, yellow cut edge.

30 year 15.00

35 year 20.00

40 year 20.00

45 year 20.00

NOTE: Some veteran insignia is known to exist on Sea Scout white and also on Sea Scout blue. These are worth substantially more 40.00-60.00

UNIT TENURE
There are hundreds of patches named after historic trails: patches for trails

Grey, (silver), 25 year bar (plain) 1.00

Grey (silver), 25 year bar with black "25" .... .25

Yellow, (gold) 50 year bar (plain) 1.00

Yellow, (gold) 50 year bar with black "50" .... .25

TRAIL
There are hundreds of patches named after historic trails: patches for trails

that are no longer in existance 2.00-5.00

Patches for existing trails 1.00-3.00

Jacket patches for trails 4.00-15.00

TRAINING
Rectangular yellow twill with two green bars on scout emblem, red cut edge
...... 5.00

Octagonal shape, khaki twill, two green bars over red "JL", green cut edge
...... 1.25

Octagonal shape, white twill, two green bars over red "JL", red cut edge (for Sea Scouts) 2.00

Octagonal shape, khaki twill, two green bars over red "JL", "BSA" at top, green cut edge 1.00

Troop Leader Development, shield shape 1.50

Instructor patch, 2" round, khaki twill, red rolled edge 1.25

Instructor patch, same only on khaki cotton polyester 1.00

Aquatic Instructor, 2½" round, life ring over crossed oars on red twill, yellow rope border, cut edge 1.00

Trained strips embroidered rectangle, yellow on blue, blue cut edge 1.00
    Yellow on blue, yellow cut edge 3.00
    Blue on white, white cut edge 1.00
    White on blue, blue cut edge 1.00
    Brown on green, green cut edge 1.00
    White on red, red cut edge 1.00
    White on red, white cut edge 1.00
    White on red, woven silk 3.50
Wood Badge Strips, red twill rectangle, red cut edge, has ax in log 5.00
    Has beads on red twill 8.00
Commissioners Training patch, white embroidered arrow head, cut edge 3.50
    Yellow embroidered arrow head, cut edge 6.00
ALL OUT FOR SCOUTING, 2½" x 4¼", multicolor coat of arms on brown twill, says "FORWARD", yellow rolled edge, has button hanger 1.50
    Same as above but slightly larger, on white twill, lettering reads "Brownsea II" 4.00
Square Knots, rectangular, embroidered (worn above left breast pocket to represent medal earned).
Den Leader Training (Cub Scouting), both strands yellow on blue 2.00
Den Leaders Coach Training (Cub Scouting), blue and yellow strands on blue 2.00
Scouter Training Award, (Sea Exploring), both strands green on deep blue 2.00
Scouter Training Award, (Sea Exploring), both strands green on white ... 2.00
Scouter Training Award, (Exploring), both strands green on green 2.00
Scouter Training Award, (Scouting), both strands green on khaki 1.50
Scouter's Key, (Sea Exploring), green and white strands on deep blue 2.00
Scouter's Key, (Sea Exploring), green and white strands on white 2.00
Scouter's Key, (Exploring), green and white strands on green 2.00
Scouter's Key (Boy Scouting), green and white strands on khaki 1.75
Professional Scouters Training (Professionals), both strands black on tan 1.75
Religious Award (Scouter), both strands silver on purple 2.00
Religious Award, (Scouter), both strands purple on silver 2.00
Arrow of Light, (Cub Scouting), green and white strands on tan 1.50
Arrow of Light (Cub Scouting), green and red strands on khaki 3.00
Silver Award (Exploring), both strands white on fully embroidered red, white and blue 5.00
Silver Award, (Exploring), both strands grey on fully embroidered red, white and blue 10.00
Silver Award (Sea Exploring), yellow and red strands on deep blue ....
Silver Award, (Exploring), yellow and red strands on khaki 26.00
Silver Award, (Exploring), yellow and red strands on green 26.00
Quartermaster Scout, (Sea Exploring), both strands white on deep blue .. 5.00
Quartermaster Scout, (Sea Exploring), both strands blue on white 5.00
Quartermaster Scout, (Sea Exploring), both strands blue on khaki 6.00
Eagle Scout, (Sea Exploring), red, white and blue strands on deep blue .. 4.00
Eagle Scout, (Sea Exploring), red, white and blue strands on white 4.00
Eagle Scout, (Sea Exploring), red, white and blue strands on green 4.00

Eagle Scout, (Scouting), red, white and blue strands on khaki 3.00
Ranger Award, (Exploring), bronze and green strands on deep blue ... 100.00
Ranger Award, (Exploring), bronze and green strands on green 100.00
Ranger Award, (Exploring), bronze and green strands on khaki 90.00
Ace Award, (Air Scouting), red and blue strands on khaki 100.00
Ace Award, (Air Scouting), red and blue strands on blue 100.00
Distinguished Award of Merit, (District), both strands silver on purple ... 2.00
Distinguished Service, (OA), both strands white on red 8.00
Silver Beaver, (Sea Exploring), blue and white strands on deep blue 3.50
Silver Beaver, (Sea Exploring), blue and white strands on white 3.50
Silver Beaver, (Exploring), blue and white strands on blue 3.50
Silver Beaver, (Scouting), blue and white strands on khaki 3.00
Silver Antelope, (all, at regional level), orange and white strands on khaki
..... 5.00
Silver Buffalo, (all, at national level), red and white strands on khaki 8.00
Silver World, (all, at international level), design is not a knot but on globe with
stars on red and black stripes 15.00
Honor of Merit, yellow and blue strands on khaki 6.00
Honor Medal, both strands red on khaki, ... 8.00

B.S.A. SQUARE KNOTS
Top to bottom: District Award of Merit 2.00
    Silver World Award 15.00
    Scouters Training Award, on Explorer green 2.00

UNIT PATCHES

Boy Scout Troop patches 50-1.25

Explorer Post patches 1.00-2.00

Air Scout Squadron patches 5.00-10.00

Sea Scout, Explorer Ship patches 1.00-3.00

NOTE: Older issues, on felt, are worth slightly more.

UNIT NUMERALS

Boy Scouting, 1st, white on maroon felt with white border
   2nd, white on red felt
   3rd, white on red felt with embroidered white border (used after 1935 to
   denote a 25 year unit)
   4th, embroidered white on red

Cub Scouting, 1st, blue on yellow felt, diamond
   2nd, blue on yellow felt, square
   3rd, embroidered blue on yellow

Explorer, brown on green felt
   Embroidered brown on green

Air Scout, embroidered blue on light blue

Sea Scout, white on blue felt,
   Blue on white felt

Sea Explorer, embroidered white on blue
   Embroidered blue on white

ORDER OF THE ARROW

In any work of this kind, it is impossible to list every item ever made. This is especially true when it comes to Order of the Arrow patches issued by individual lodges. There have been some 770 different Order of the Arrow Lodges over the eyrs since the Order of the Arrow was founded in 1915. While collecting Order of the Arrow flap patches has been very popular for many years, it has remained a specialty primarily of those who belong to the Order.

In order to aid the layman in some way, we offer the following as guide:

Order of the Arrow patches and flaps can vary in value anywhere from $2.50 to $2,000.00.

Patches from Lodges no longer in existance are worth more than those from existing lodges.

Patches from lodges which restrict their patches will be worth more than those from lodges which do not.

Older issues will be worth more than more recent ones.

As a general rule, with exceptions, patches with twill background will be worth more than those which are fully embroidered.

As a general rule, with some exceptions, patches with cut edges will be older and be worth more than those with rolled edges.

Felt patches will generally be worth more than embroidered patches will be.

Chenille patches will, in general, be worth more than either felt or embroidered patches will be.

Collecting Order of the Arrow is not for the novice. If you collect this specialty, then take the time and trouble to get to really know it. There are many pitfalls. Almost every lodge has several highly respected collectors which can help you. The major dealers will also gladly assist you.

SEA EXPLORER PATCHES
Top row: Ship 264 Unit patch 1.00
2nd row, L to R: Spring Seamanship School, 2nd year patch
..... 1.00
    Chief Old Ox District 1976 Seven Seas patch 1.00
3rd row: 1961 Naval Cruise patch 3.50
Bottom row, L to R: Commodore Tole Heyday XVI patch
..... 1.00
    Bay Lakes Council 1975 Bay Jammer patch 5.00

O.A. LODGE FLAPS
Top row, L to R: Scaroyadi Lodge 472 flap patch, 12th issue
...... 5.50
    Potowatomie Lodge 63 flap patch (merged), 6th issue 18.00
2nd row, L to R: Unami Lodge 1, flap patch, 19th issue ... 5.00
    Woapink Lodge 167 flap patch, 5th issue 12.00
3rd row, L to R: Chippecotton Lodge (merged), 2nd issue
...... 60.00
    Pellissippi Lodge 230 flap patch, 13th issue (Bicentennial)
...... 8.00
    Wetassa Lodge 227 flap patch (merged), 7th issue ... 40.00
5th row, L to R: Baluga Lodge 538 flap patch (reissue of
original by sucessor) 15.00
    Shin-Go-Beek Lodge 334 flap patch, 6th issue 5.50
Bottom row, L to R: Pellissippi Lodge 230 flap patch, 5th
issue 10.00
    Tseyedin Lodge 65 flap patch, 9th issue (rare variation, cut
edge) 10.00

FLAGS, EQUIPMENT, ETC.

NOTE: Keep in mind that when it comes to equipment, while flags, knives and to some extent axes and first aid tins are highly collectible, most so called equipment is not. This is primarily because the collector likes to display his collection and needs room to do it. For example, if you happen to have a very old Boy Scout tent which could be identified as such, its value would still be little more than its re-sale value as a used tent, simply because almost no one collects such items.

Boy Scout Patrol flags, 1st issue, red silk screened patrol symbol on white muslin, 19" x 12" 6.00
2nd issue, embroidered black patrol symbol on red circle on white gabardine, 20" x 11" 4.50
3rd issue, embroidered black patrol symbol on yellow circle on white gabardine, 20" x 11" 2.00

Cub Scout Den flag, yellow numeral in yellow diamond on dark blue 1.00

Webelos Den flag, sylized fleur de-lis and flame emblem in yellow on dark blue 1.00

Explorer Crew flag, 1950's, white wings, anchor, compass emblem in red circle on white garbardine, 20" x 11" 7.50

FLAGS, STANDARD SIZE

Boy Scout Troop flags, 1st issue, top half red, bottom half white, has 1st class emblem, troop number, town and sometimes council, has V edge   10.00-15.00
2nd issue, top half red, bottom half white, has tenderfoot emblem, troop number, town and sometimes council, has straight edge 5.00-10.00

Cub Pack flags, 1st issue, top half yellow, bottom half dark blue, has "CUBS BSA" emblem in center, has pack number, town, and sometimes council
...... 10.00-15.00
2nd issue, same as above except center emblem says "CUB SCOUTS, BSA"
...... 5.00-10.00

Explorer Post Flags, 1950's, top half red, bottom half blue, with wings, anchor, compass emblem in center 25.00
1960's same except has circle V emblem in center 15.00
1970's, same except has stylized E emblem in center 10.00

Air Scout Squadron flag, top half red, bottom half dark blue, with Air Scout wings emblem in center 100.00

Air Scout Squdrom flag, top half red, bottom half dark blue, with Air Scout wings emblem in center 110.00

Sea Scout Ship flag, top half red, bottom half blue, with Sea Scout emblem in center 40.00

Sea Scout Commissioner Pennant, approx. 9" x 36" nautical type pennant with white felt S.S. on navy blue muslin 20.00

Brownie Troop flag, yellow dancing elf in trefoil on brown field with yellow band at each end. Has troop number at top, town name at bottom 5.00

Girl Scout Troop flag, top half blue, bottom half white with three leaf clover, G.S. in rope with square knot emblem in the center. White troop number on the blue tip and green town name on the bottom white 20.00
Top half blue, bottom half white with Girl Scout eagle, Trefoil emblem in center, troop number at tip, city and state at bottom 10.00

Left 2-3 has blue field, right ½ has white field, white lettering for troop number and town on blue field and green girl scout silhouette emblem on white field 5.00
World Association flag with troop number to left and town to right of three leaf clover world Girl Scout emblem 10.00
Girl Scout Troop Pennant, green felt pennant with Girl Scout emblem in white triangle at left and troop number in white on green field 3.50
B.S.A. District flag, Boy Scout seal emblem in yellow at center on a blue field, District name or member at tip, council name at bottom, all lettering yellow
1st issue 15.00
2nd issue 10.00
B.S.A. Council flag, Boy Scout seal emblem at center with council name at top and city and state at bottom, all in yellow on a blue field, 1st issue 25.00-50.00
2nd issue 20.00-35.00
Girl Scout Council flag, left 2-3 has blue field with white lettering of council name, etc., right ⅜ is white with green Girl Scout silhouette emblem ... 20.00
Boy Scout Camp flag, Boy Scout Seal emblem in center with camp name at top and council name at bottom, all in yellow on a blue field, 1st issue, has 1st class emblem in seal 20.00-35.00
2nd issue, has tenderfoot emblem in seal 15.00-25.00
Boy Scout Regional flag, 1sst issue, white 1st class seal emblem on purple with white region number at tip 75.00
2nd issue, white tenderfoot seal emblem on purple with white region number at tip 60.00
3rd issue, white tenderfoot seal emblem on purple with white region name at tip 45.00
Boy Scout Jamboree Troop Flags, top half red, bottom half white with jamboree emblem in center, has troop number in white on tip and council name and state in red on bottom:

1950 N.J.	115.00	1969 N.J.	40.00
1953 N.J.	100.00	1973 N.J.	35.00
1957 N.J.	85.00	1977 N.J.	30.00
1960 N.J.	75.00	1981 N.J.	25.00
1964 N.J.	50.00		

1935 Jamboree flag 150.00
1937 Jamboree flag 125.00
1935, 37" Jamboree, Headquarter Sect flag 200.00

FLAGS, MINIATURE

Boy Scout (1st class emblem) 2.00
Boy Scout (tenderfoot emblem) 1.00
Cub Scout 1.00
Explorer 1950's (wings, anchor, compass) 5.00
Explorer 1960's (circle V) 3.50
Explorer 1970's (stylized E) 1.25
Air Scout .... d 10.00-15.00
Sea Scout (1st class emblem on anchor) 7.50
Sea Explorer (stylized E on anchor) 3.00
Brownie 3.00
Girl Scout 1.00

National Jamboree, 1950 .... 45.00
1953 .... 30.00 1969 .... 15.00
1957 .... 25.00 1973 .... 10.00
1960 .... 22.50 1981 .... 8.50
1964 .... 18.00

Boy Scout Patrol Flag, 2nd issue "Pine Tree" patrol, black
on red circle on white gaberdine 4.50

B.S.A., In Memoriam flags, 8" x 12", has 1st class emblem in center and
lettering "In Memoriam" at top, all in white on blue 12.50
Same except has tenderfoot emblem in center 5.00

Scout Pennants, Boy Scout, 12" x 30", flocked yellow felt on heavy blue felt,
wording says "Boy Scouts of America" 10.00
12" x 30", yellow felt sewn on heavy blue felt, has BSA 1st class seal emblem
and wording "Boy Scouts" 10.00
12" x 30", flocked yellow felt on heavy blue felt, has BSA 1st class seal
and wording "Honor Patrol" 7.50
Same only 15" x 36" 6.50
12" x 30", flocked yellow felt on heavy blue felt, has BSA 1st class seal
emblem and says "Do a Good Turn Daily" 5.00
12" x 24", flocked yellow felt on heavy blue felt, has BSA 1st class seal and
emblem and says "Be Prepared" 5.00
Same only 9" x 18" 4.50
Silk screened yellow on thin blue felt, has tenderfoot emblem and wording
"Boy Scouts" 2.00
Silk screened yellow on thin blue felt, has tenderfoot emblem and wording
"Be Prepared" 1.50
Silk screened yellow on thin blue felt, has tenderfoot emblem and wording
"Do a Good Turn Daily" 1.50

Cub Scouts, yellow flocked felt on heavy blue felt, has "Cub B.S.A." emblem
Same except has Cub Scouts and pawprint emblem 5.00

Silk screened on yellow on thin blue felt, has Cub Scout tenderfoot sign emblem and says "Cub Scouts B.S.A." 1.50

Silk screened yellow on thin blue felt, has stylized W and flame Webelos emblem and wording "Webelos" 1.50

Explorers, has 1960's explorer emblem on green felt, has white lettering "Explorers" 6.00

Brownies, silk screened brown on thin yellow felt, has dancing elf in trefoil emblem and lettering "Brownie" 1.50

Girl Scout, white felt pennant with insignia for 1965 Senior Girl Scout Roundup and wording "Roundup" 8.00

Jamborees: All large pennants

1935 Jamboree	60.00	1964 N.J.	16.00
1937 Jamboree	50.00	1967 World Jamboree	12.50
1950 N.J.	35.00	1969 N.J.	12.00
1953 N.J.	30.00	1973 N.J.	10.00
1957 N.J.	25.00	1977 N.J.	8.50
1960 N.J.	20.00	1981 N.J.	7.50

MISCELLANEOUS SCOUT EQUIPMENT

Angling Outfit, 3 piece, black enamel, cork handled, steel rod with nickel plated reel seat, nickel plated reel, 75 feet of line, 6 steel hooks, spoon, 6 flies, sinkers, float, all in khaki carrying case 15.00

Bow and Arrow set 20.00

Snare Drum, 16" maple shell with fancy eagle 30.00

Snare Drum, 14" maple shell, no eagle 25.00

Prussian Pattern Drum (flat type) 15" nickel, plated shell 25.00

Boy Scout Bugle, brass, mouthpiece attached with chain 45.00-60.00

Same only chromed 45.00

NOTE: Variations known to exist with very fancy engraved scenes on them 85.00-100.00

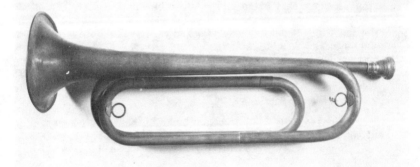

BSA Rexcraft Scout Bugle, brass 45.00

Bugle Cord, yard length with tassels 1.00

Trumpet and Drum Signal Call Brok 2.00

Universal Album for Trumpet and Bugle 2.00

Drum Fife, ebony wood with silver mountings 25.00

Crosby Model fife 18.00
Firemaking set, bow with leather thong, drill and drill socket, notched fire board, package of tinder 2.50

B.S.A. Rexcraft Scout Bugle, brass 35.00

Camp Blanket, khaki, cotton, stamped B.S.A., wool 15.00
Army Blanket, khaki, 50 percent wool, stamped with 1st class badge design 15.00
Water Proof Blanket, water proof sheet with brass grommets 2.50
Scout Sketching Case, drawing board, paper on rollers, brass compass with needle stop and slot, revolving cover, colored sketching pencils, wood ruler, folding sights 12.00
Microscope, brass 9" high, three lenses, power 110X, packed in wood box 15.00
100-Mile Pedometer, with BSA 1st class emblem on face 12.50
Pocket Signal Disk, made like two baseball score cards, turning disk gives code cross reference to letter in alphabet 5.00
Contest Cops (trophy style) 20.00
Contest Cops (trophy style), 5" high, silverplate 20.00
  7¼" high, silverplate 25.00
  10" high, silverplate 30.00
Scout Statuettes, 17" high, ivory finish 35.00
  Bronze finish 22.00
  Copper finish 20.00
First Aid kits, brown and black 1st aid kit, tin container with BSA 1st class emblem on cover, horizontal rectangle shape 6.00
  Kit, with contents 10.00
  Johnson and Johnson 1st aid kit, metal container, olive color, with red cross on green background and BSA 1st class emblem insignia on tip, has raised cut out type loops on back for running belt through, container only 4.50
  With contents 7.50
  Johnson and Johnson 1st aid kit, white plastic with red lettering, breast pocket size with curvature 2.50
Indian Beadcraft outfit, rectangular box with Indian, contains strings, loom racks, and beads 8.00
Scout Whittling set, box features wood carving of a deer on cover. Contains wood, instructions and whittling knife 8.00
Boy Scout Axes, fall size, double bladed 20.00
  Fall size, single blade 15.00
  ¾ size, single blade 10.00
  Hand axes were made in many styles and types over the years 5.00-18.00
Pocket Knives:
Boy Scout, Remington, 4 blades, brown bone handle 42.00
  Imperial, 4 blade with embossed 1st class emblem 12.00
  Imperial, 4 blade with raised 1st class shield shaped metal emblem ... 10.00
  Imperial, 4 blade with recessed 1st class shield shaped emblem under plastic 8.00
  Ulster, 5 blade with raised round tenderfoot emblem 8.00
  Ulster, 4 blade with raised round tenderfoot emblem 6.50
Cub Scout, Imperial, 4 blade with metal Cub emblem 8.50
  Imperial, 3 blade with recessed cub emblem under plastic 6.00

Top Row, L to R: Imperial 4 blade with embossed emblem
...... 7.50
B.S.A. Cook Kit folding knife, ca. 1930's 7.50
Non Scouting knife, says "Boy Scout" 10.00
Bottom row, L to R: Girl Scout Kutmaster 4 blade knife . 6.50
Girl Scout Camillus 3 blade knife 5.00
Cub Scout 3 blade knife 6.00

Girl Scout, Kutmaster, 4 blade with gold Girl Scout emblem under green
plastic handle 6.50
Camillus, 3 blade with silver colored raised emblem on black plastic handle
...... 5.00

213

B.S.A. Beadcraft outfit 8.00

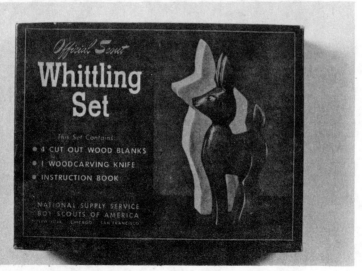

B.S.A. Scout Whittling Set 8.00

GIRL SCOUT CALENDARS

Prior to 1940	20.00	1975 to 1980	2.00
1940 to 1960	7.50-12.00	1981	1.25
1960 to 1975	5.00	1982	1.00

1918 Boy Scout Calendar, complete with all 12 sheets . . 60.00

1962 Boy Scout Calendar,
Norman Rockwell picture
"Pointing the Way" with
all 12 sheets, 8" x 14" 8.00

1960 Boy Scout Calendar,
Norman Rockwell pic-
Ture, "Growth of a Lead-
er" with all 12 sheets
(each page is a different
rockwell Scout picture),
8" x 14" 12.50

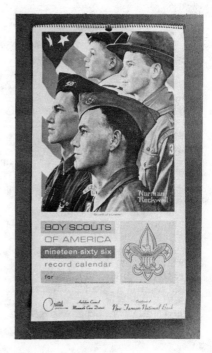

SCOUT CALENDARS

The Boy Scouts of America started issuing calendars in the early teens. Soon after Norman Rockwell began illustrating Boys' Life Magazine in the late teens, his talents were recognized by the B.S.A. and he began painting the pictures for their calendars. From the time he began this task he painted the calendar picture each year except 2 until shortly before his death. Calendars were issued in many sizes. Most early ones had single pictures with small tear off sheets below. Later, they were issued with a cover picture and flip type pages. Prices given will be for calendars with all 12 sheets attached and of the 16" x 30" size. For smaller sized calendars, adjust value downward slightly.

1912	100.00
1913	100.00
1914	75.00
1915	75.00
1916	75.00
1918	65.00
1919	65.00
1920	52.00
1921	52.00
1922	52.00
1924	41.00
1925 (N.R.)	62.00
1926 (N.R.) "A Good Turn"	50.00
1927 (N.R.) "Good Friends"	50.00
1928 (N.R.) "The Great Adventure"	45.00
1929 (N.R.) "Spirit of America"	45.00
1930	40.00
1931 (n.R.) "Scout Memories"	35.00
1932	35.00
1933 (N.R.)	35.00
1934	35.00
1935 (N.R.) "A Good Scout" (jubilee Edition)	40.00
1936 (N.R.) "The Campfire Story"	20.00
1937 (N.R.) "Scouts of Many Trails"	20.00
1938 (N.R.) "American Builds For Tomorrow"	30.00
1939 (N.R.) "The Scouting Trail"	20.00
1940 (N.R.) "A Scout is Reverent" (kneeling)	12.00
1941 (N.R.) "A Scout is Helpful"	12.00
1942 (N.R.) "A Scout is Loyal"	12.00
1943 (N.R.) "A Scout is Friendly"	12.00
1944 (n.R.) "We, too, Have a Job to do"	12.00
1945 (N.R.) "The Scout Oath"	12.00
1946 (N.R.) "A Guiding Hand"	12.00
1947 (N.R.) "All Together"	12.00
1948 (N.R.) "Man of Tomorrow"	12.00
1949	12.00
1950 (N.R.) "Our Heritage"	12.00
1951	12.00
1952	12.00
1953 (N.R.) "A Scout is Thrifty"	12.00
1954 (N.R.) "A Scout is Reverent" (sitting)	12.00
1955 (N.R.) "The Right Way"	12.00
1956 (N.R.) "The Scoutmaster"	12.00
1957	12.00

```
1958 .................................................................... 12.00
1959 (N.R.) "Tomorrow's Leader" ................................... 12.00
1960 (N.R.) "Ever Onward" ......................................... 10.00
1961 .................................................................... 10.00
1962 (N.R.) "Pointing The Way" ................................... 10.00
1963 .................................................................... 10.00
1964 (N.R.) "To Keep Myself Physically Strong" ................... 10.00
1965 .................................................................... 10.00
1966 (N.R.) "Growth of a Leader" ................................. 15.00
1967 .................................................................... 10.00
1968 (N.R.) "Scouting is Outing" ................................. 10.00
1969 (N.R.) "Beyond the Easel" ................................... 10.00
1970 ..................................................................... 8.00
1971 ..................................................................... 8.00
1972 N.R.) "Can't Wait" ............................................. 8.00
1973 ..................................................................... 8.00
1974 ..................................................................... 8.00
1975 ..................................................................... 8.00
1976 (n.R.) "Pictures of all Rockwell's Scout calendar pictures ....... 10.00
1977 ......................................................... 5.00
1978 ......................................................... 5.00
1979 ......................................................... 5.00
1980 ......................................................... 2.50
1981 ..................................................................... 2.25
1982 ..................................................................... 2.00
```

MISCELLANEOUS SCOUTING ITEMS

(Mugs, Glasses, Plates, License Plates, Magazines, Calendars, Prints, Etc.)
Among other things, this chapter will deal with several Norman Rockwell
items. As background on this famous artist, Mr. Rockwell started his career
as an illustrator for Boys' Life magazine. He remained a Scouter all of his life.
The originals of his Scout paintings are the property of the Boy Scouts of
America.

MUGS

Mugs, it is believed, were first issued in 1964 at the National Jamboree. Since
that time mug shapes and sizes have gone through somewhat of an evolution.
As a means of identifying a particular type of mug, collectors have begun to
designate particular shapes as 1st issue, 2nd issue, etc. (Please see photos for
specific style variations). A 5th type now coming into use with more regularity
is a plastic thermal mug.

SPECIAL NOTE: A few mugs are known to exist in left handed variations, as
    a general rule these are worth slightly more than a standard right handed
    mug, generally speaking any mug with a Norman Rockwell picture on it is
    worth from .50 to 1.00 more

```
District or Council activities (camporees, shows, roundups, etc.) ....... 1.50
District Mug ............................................................ 1.50
Camper and Special Award mugs ...................................... 1.50
Camp Mugs ............................................................. 1.50
Order of the Arrow Lodge Activity Mug .............................. 2.00
```

L to R: B.S.A. 1st Class Emblem Mug, 2nd issue 4.50
1966 Follow the Rugged Road Roundup Mug, 1st issue . 3.50

L to R: Great Trail Council, 1974 Century Club Mug with
Norman Rockwell design, 4th issue (dairy mug) 3.50
Tidewater Council Outstanding Leader Mug with Norman
Rockwell design, 3rd issue 3.25

Council Mug	2.00
Order of the Arrow Lodge Mug	2.25
Region Mug (repro set out)	2.00
Order of the Arrow Conclave Mug	2.25
National issue (themes)	2.00
National Bases	2.00
National Events	2.50
Rank	2.00
Norman Rockwell Thermal mugs	2.50
Pewter Steins	
Boy Scout Tenderfoot emblem	5.00
Girl Scout Trefoil emblem	5.00

Jamborees: NOTE: Repro set issued by BSA 1969.

1964 N.J.	25.00	1973 N.J. (4th issue)	4.25
1967 W.J. (2nd issue)	8.00	1975 W.J. (3rd issue)	5.00
1967 W.J. (3rd issue)	6.50	1977 N.J. (3rd issue)	4.00
1969 N.J. (2nd issue)	7.00	1977 N.J. (5th issue)	2.25
1969 N.J. (3rd issue)	6.00	1981 N.J. (3rd issue)	3.50
1973 N.J. (3rd issue)	4.00	1981 N.J. (5th issue)	2.00

GLASSES

A relatively new phenomena, it has yet to be ascertained whether or not many Scout glasses will be issued. See photos for a sample of some types now out.

L to R: North Central Region frosted glass stein 5.00
Gilwell Park glass 6.00
North Central Region frosted stem goblet 5.00

PLATES

1969 N.J. plate, blue ceramic with decal under plastic, 6" round 10.00

Baden-Powell plates, (at least 10 different) 45.00-65.00

Boy Scout scene plates, porcelain, 6⅝ round, ca. 1915-1920, bottom has "Dresden China" on it 75.00

Norman Rockwell Scout Plates:

No. 1 "Our Heritage (10½-Gorham) 60.00
No. 2 "A Scout is Loyal" (10½-Gorham) 60.00
No. 3 "A Good Sign All Over The World" (10½-Gorham) 55.00
No. 4 "The Scoutmaster" (10½-Gorham) 60.00
No. 5 "Pointing The Way" (10½-Gorham) 45.00
No. 6 "The Campfire Story (10½-Gorham) 45.00
No. 7 "Beyond The Easel" (10½-Gorham) 35.00
No. 8 "Can't Wait" (8¼-Gorham) 26.00

Baden-Powell Plate, lace design border with gold plate trim
...... 52.00

L to R: Norman Rockwell Scout Plate No. 1 (Gorham) "Our
Heritage" 60.00
Norman Rockwell Scout Plate No. 4 (Gorham) "The
Scoutmaster" 60.00

L to R: Norman Rockwell Scout Plate No. 3 (Gorham) "A
Good Sign All Over The World" 55.00
Norman Rockwell Scout Plate No. 2 (Gorham) "A Scout Is
Loyal" 60.00

LICENSE PLATES
1957, National Jamboree License plate from state of Michigan, License plate
No. 1, ... 35.00
Other numbers (these are extremely rare) 22.00
Tenderfoot emblem metallic decal on store design background license plate
...... 5.00

1957 National Jamboree Michigan License Plate, No. 30
...... 28.00

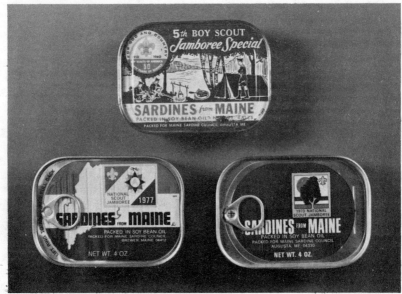

Top: 1960 National Jamboree can of sardines 10.00
Bottom row, L to R: 1977 National Jamboree can of sardines
...... 4.00
1973 National Jamboree can of sardines 4.00

L to R: Boy Scout Tenderfoot Emblem, bronze, pedestal type
paperweight 10.00
Boy Scout Wood badge paperweight 7.50

223

SARDINE CANS
These are collectible only so long as they remain unopened.

1957 National Jamboree can of sardines 14.00
1960 National Jamboree can of sardines 10.00
1964 National Jamboree can of sardines 8.00
1969 National Jamboree can of sardines 8.00
1973 National Jamboree can of sardines 5.00
1977 National Jamboree can of sardines 4.00
1981 National Jamboree can of sardines 4.00

PAPERWEIGHTS
Tenderfoot emblem paperweight, pedestal type, bronze, has tenderfoot
  emblem on front, fleur de-lis on reverse 10.00
Paperweight, composition imitation wood, pictures Scout with George
  Washington, lettering on top says "Be Prepared" merit badges carved
  around sides 20.00
Tenderfoot emblem paperweight, oxidized silver, 3¼ x 3¾" 5.00
Tenderfoot emblem paperweight, gold colored emblem on 2" x 2" white
  marble base 4.00
Same only on 4" x 4" white marble base 5.00
Pewter 1948 3 cent Boy Scout Stamp design on white marble base 7.50
Pewter 1960, 4 cent Boy Scout Stamp design on white marble base 7.50
Gold color Cub Scout emblem on 2" x 2" white marble base 5.00
Oxidized copper Cub Scout emblem paperweight, 2 x 2 .... 5.00
Girl Scout paperweight, kneeling Girl Scout feeding rabbit, case metal, black,
  ca. 1920's 25.00
Girl Scout Spinner top paperweight, antique finish, one side of spinning disc
  has Trefoil emblem, other side says "Thank You", 2" x 2", white marble
  base 3.50
Boy Scouter Woodbadge paperweight, copper color, ax in log on round base,
  ax detaches from log 7.50

SCOUT STATUES AND STATUETTES
Set of 5 miniature Scout statuette, 1½" high, starting fire, splitting log,
  carrying flag, signaling, hiking, value per set, painted 40.00
  Same as above but unpainted 20.00
Cast iron Scout figurines, hiking, 3" 10.00
Cast iron Scout figurines, saluting, 3" 11.00
  These 2 should be fully painted, those that are just plain tannish brown . 7.50
Lead Scout figurine, Saluting 3" 11.00
Lead Scout figurines, Signaling, 3½" 11.00
Lead Scout figurine, Frying Eggs, 3" 12.00
Lead Scout figurine, Hiking with Staff, 3" 12.00
MacKenzie Scout statuette, these stand about 7" high and have been used for
  many years. They come in different finishes and are made of cast pot metal.
  Those on plastic pedestals are not very old 13.00- 30.00
Moody Scout statue, ca. 1911, made of molded plaster type material, staff is
  hand carved wood, about 12" high 50.00

SET OF 5 MINIATURE SCOUT STATUETTES
L to R: Starting Fire 4.00
    Splitting Wood 4.00
    Carrying Flag 4.00
    Signaling 4.00
    Hiking 4.00

3'' CAST IRON
SCOUT
STATUETTES
L to R: Saluting
.... 14.00

Hiking 13.00

MacKenzie Scout Statue
.... 23.50

Moody Scout Statue, ca. 1911
.... 50.00

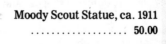

3" LEAD SCOUT FIGURINES

L. to R.: Saluting 11.00
Signaling 12.00
Frying Eggs 12.00

SCOUT PENNY BANK STATUE
L to R: Tunic style uniform ... 60.00
Neckerchief type uniform ... 50.00

Boy Scout Penny Bank Statues, cast iron, Scout is holding staff and has a
   shoulder roll bedpack and is wearing a backpack, coin slot is on top of
   backpack, constructed so as a single screw holds the two halves together,
   tunic style uniform 45.00
   Neckerchief style uniform 40.00
Norman Rockwell Cub statuette "Cub and Dog" 10½ high, plastic type
   material 25.00
Girl Scout bank, copper-bronze, 7" high, Girl Scout walking has double base,
   lower base says "Girl Scouts U.S.A." upper base has engraving plate . 15.00

Scouting cake decoration figurines, these are made of molded plastic, it is
believed that these were made in Taiwan sometime in 1950 or early 1960, Boy
   Scout sitting 1.00
   Cub Scout, sitting 1.00
   Girl Scout, kneeling 1.00
   Brownie Scout, standing 1.00
Steve Scout doll, made by Kenner Toy Company as pictured 15.00
   With additional equipment sets, etc. 20.00-35.00
Norman Rockwell Scout figurines, hand painted, brisque porcelain,
   "To Keep Myself Physically Strong," 6" 64.00
   "Good Friends", 5" 60.00
   "A Scout Is Helpful", 5½" 60.00
   "Scout Memories", 5½" 64.00
   "A Good Turn", 5½" 60.00
   "Can't Wait", 5¾" 60.00

Steve Scout Doll
.... 15.00

Norman Rockwell
Cub Scout with
dog 25.00

Girl Scout, copper
bronze 15.00

SPECIAL SCOUTING BOOKS

"Scouting For Boys" by Robert Baden Powell 7.50-75.00

"Aids to Scoutmastership" by Robert Baden Powell 10.00-60.00

The Boy Scout Encyclopedia 5.00

The Golden Anniversary Book of Scouting, illustrated by Norman Rockwell
...... 15.00

Boy's Life Treasury, Simon And Schuster, 1958 .... 5.00-7.50

The Scout Oath in Action by Walter MacPeck 4.00

The Scout Law in Action by Walter MacPeck 4.00

Resourceful Scouts in Action by Walter MacPeck, soft cover 1.00
    Hard cover 5.00

The Boy Scout Yearbook (published by B. Appleton and Co.)

    1915 The Boy Scouts Yearbook 15.00
    1916 The Boy Scouts Yearbook 12.00
    1917 The Boy Scouts Yearbook 12.00
    1918 The Boy Scouts Yearbook 12.00
    1919 The Boy Scouts Yearbook 12.00
    1920 The Boy Scouts Yearbook 11.00
    1921 The Boy Scouts Yearbook 11.00
    1922 The Boy Scouts Yearbook 11.00
    1923 The Boy Scouts Yearbook 11.00
    1924 The Boy Scouts Yearbook 11.00
    1925 The Boy Scouts Yearbook 11.00
    1926 The Boy Scouts Yearbook 11.00
    1927 The Boy Scout Yearbook 10.00
    1928 The Boy Scout Yearbook 10.00
    1929 The Boy Scout Yearbook 10.00

    NOTE: Add $5.00 if in Dust jackets, many with Rockwell covers.

1930 The Boy Scout Yearbook 10.00
1931 The Boy Scout Yearbook 10.00
1932 The Boy Scout Yearbook 10.00
1933 The Boy Scout Yearbook of Ghost and Mystery Stories 7.00
1934 The Boy Scout Yearbook of Stories of Brave Boys and Fearless Men
...... 7.00
1935 The Boy Scout Yearbook of Stories of Dogs 7.00
1936 The Boy Scout Yearbook of Sports Stories 7.00
1937 The Boy Scout Yearbook of Patriots and Pioneers 7.00
1938 The Boy Scout Yearbook of Fun In Fiction 7.00
1939 The Boy Scout Yearbook of Stories of Daring and Danger 7.00
1940 The Boy Scout Yearbook of Wild Animal Stories 6.00
1941 The Boy Scout Yearbook of Patriotic Stories 6.00
1942 The Boy Scout Yearbook of Stories of Boy Heroes 6.00
1943 The Boy Scout Yearbook of Stories of Adventurous Fliers 6.00
1944 The Boy Scout Yearbook of Stories of Boy Scouts Couragousness .. 6.00

NOTE: Most early yearbooks were undated. The date can be determined by looking at the copyright date (s) on the back of the title page. The latest date shown is the year of the particular yearbook.

BOYS' LIFE LIBRARY BOOKS
By Various Authors, Randon House, Publishers,
The Boy's Life Book of Horse Stories, 1963 .... 3.00
The Boy's Life Book of Mystery Stories, 1963 .... 3.00
The Boy's Life Book of Football Stories, 1963 .... 3.00
Mutiny in the Time Machine, by Donald Keith, 1963 .... 3.00
The Boy's Life Book of Outer Space Stories, 1964 .... 3.00
The Boy's Life Book of Baseball Stories, 1964 .... 3.00
The Boy's Life Book of Flying Stories, 1964 .... 3.00
The Boy's Life Book of Sports Stories, 1965 .... 3.00
The Boy's Life Book of Wild Animal Stories, 1965 .... 3.00
The Boy's Life Book of World War II Stories 2.00
The Boy's Life Book of Basketball Stories, 1966 .... 3.50
A Boy Scout With Byrd by Paul Siple 8.00
The Boy Scout Story by Will Oursler 7.50
Every Boy's Library series: These were a series of outstanding fiction with special printings sometimes by the B.S.A. - please see Fiction section.

Lone Scout of the Sky by James E. West, Variation 7/81, blue cover with scene
of Lindberg flying a plane 7.50
Variation 7/82, orange cover 4.00
Matching Mountains With The Boy Scout Uniform by Edward F. Rainer   11.00
Norman Rockwell's World of Scouting 15.00
Track Trails by Leonard Rossell 6.00

BOARD GAMES
The Boy Scout Progess Game, Parker Brothers, ca. 1924, in' original box,
complete with all contents 42.00
Bowling pins 35.00
Over 12 board games put out from 1912-32, all with litho boxes and
instructions, each 25.00-35.00
PRINTS
Norman Rockwell Scout prints, 11" x 14", each 5.00
Boxed set of 44 of above 100.00

Vanity Fair Prints, Portrait of Baden-Powell entitled "Mafeking" 40.00
 Portrait of Baden-Powell entitled "Boy Scouts" 40.00
NOTE: These are original limited edition prints dating to ca. 1911.

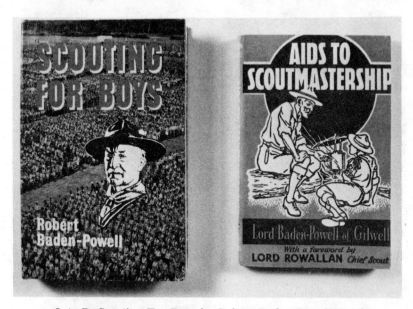

L to R. Scouting For Boys by Robert Baden Powell, hard
 bound with d-j 15.00
 Aids to Scoutmastership by Lord Robert Baden Powell,
 soft bound 10.00

L to R: Boy Scout Encyclopedia, 3rd printing with multicolored cover 5.00
 Golden Anniversary Book of Scouting with d-j, illustrated
 by Norman Rockwell 15.00

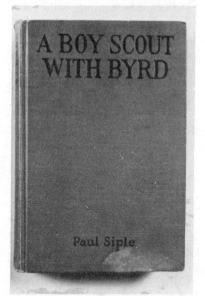

Boys' Life Treasury .... 5.00   Siple, Paul - A Boy Scout With Byrd

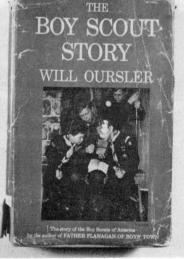

L to R: Tracks & Trails by Leonard Rossell 6.00
The Boy Scout Story by Will Oursler with d-j 7.50

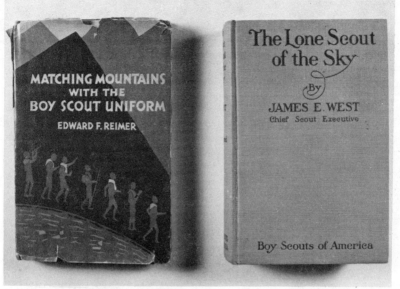

L to R: Matching Mountains with the Boy Scout Uniform by
Edward F. Reimer with d-j 11.00
Lone Scout of the Sky by James E. West, orange cover variety
...... 4.00

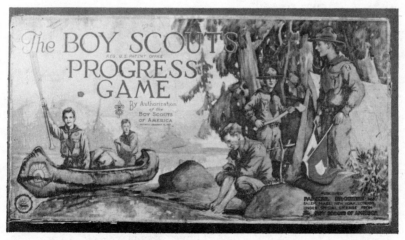

The Boy Scout Progress Game, Parker Bros., ca. 1924 ... 42.00

Vanity Fair lithograph print
of Baden-Powell, "Boy Scout"
...... 40.00

BOY's LIFE MAGAZINES
This is an official publication of the B.S.A. and intended for all boys and leaders
in all programs. Although sold by subscription only and not at news stands, in
1979 it ranked 38th in circulation among all U.S. Magazines published)
Volume 1 No. 1 (1911) 100.00
  1911-1912 .... 35.00
  1913-1915 .... 30.00
  1916-1918 .... 20.00
  1918-1921 .... 8.00
  1922-1929 .... 5.00
  1930-1935 .... 3.75
  1935-1940 .... 3.50
  1940-1949 .... 2.50
  1950-1959 .... 1.25
  1960-1965 .... 1.00
  1966-1974 .... .75
  1974-1982 .... .50

Note: Certain special issues such as Philmont, Jamboree's etc. are worth 25
cents more. For issues with Rockwell covers add 1.00-3.00

Boys' Life Magazine, January, 1938
.... 3.50

Boys' Life Magazine, June, 1951
.... 1.25

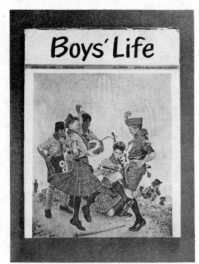

Boys' Life Magazine, February, 1963
with Norman Rockwell cover .. 4.50

Boys' Life Magazine, April, 1975
.... .50

SCOUTING MAGAZINE

(This is an official publication of the B.S.A. and is intended for only the adult leaders of all programs. Although sold by subscription only and not at newstands, in 1979 it ranked 53rd in circulation among all U.S. magazines published.)

Volume 1, No. 1 (1913)	50.00
1913-1915	20.00
1916-1921	10.00
1922-1929	5.00
1930-1940	2.00-2.50
1940-1949	1.50-1.75
1950-1959	1.25
1960-1965	1.00
1966-1974	.75
1975-1982	.50

Note: Certain special issues are worth .25 more. Issues with Rockwell covers are worth about 1.00-3.50 more.

EXPLORING MAGAZINES

This was an official publication of the B.S.A. and was intended for all Explorers and Explorer leaders.

Volume 1, No. 1	5.00
Late 1960's-1980	.50

Scouting Magazine, January, 1928, (has holes punched in it) 4.50

Scouting Magazine, April, 1937
.... 2.25

EXPLORING THE SCENE MAGAZINE

(This was an official publication of the B.S.A. and was intended for all Explorers and Explorer leaders)

It is generally believed that only 2 issues of this were published, in 1969, each
...... 1.00

SCOUT ADMINISTRATOR MAGAZINE
(This was an official publication of the B.S.A. and was intended for professional
  Scouters only)
  Volume 1, No. 1 (1935) 10.00
  Other issues 3.50

DAISY MAGAZINE
(This was an official magazine of the Girl Scouts of the U.S.A. and was intended
  for all Brownies and Brownies Leaders)
  Volume 1, No. 1 .... 5.00
  All other issues .... .50

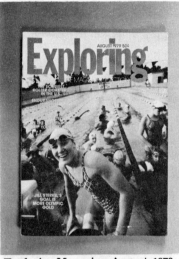

Exploring Magazine, August, 1979
.... .50

Exploring The Scene Magazine,
  Fall, 1969 .... 1.00

Daisy Magazine, Summer, 1978
.... .50

American Girl Magazine, May, 1979
.... .50

AMERICAN GIRL MAGAZINE
(This was an official magazine of the Girl Scouts of the U.S.A. and intended for all Girl Scouts and Girl Scout leaders. Although sold only by subscription and not at newstands, it ranked 94th in circulation in 1979 among all U.S. magazines published)

Issues prior to 1940	1.50
1940-1949	1.00
1950-1959	.75
1960-1982	.50

GIRL SCOUT LEADER MAGAZINE
(This is an official publication of the Girl Scouts of U.S.A. and is intended for all leaders in all programs)

Volume 1, No. 1, (1924)	35.00
1924-1925	7.00
1926-1929	3.00
1930-1939	2.00
1940-1949	1.25
1950-1959	1.00
1960-1969	.75
1970-1982	.50

LONE SCOUT MAGAZINE
(This was official publication of the Lone Scouts of America)

Volume ⅛, No. 1 (1915)	25.00
1915-1918 (weekly)	4.00
1919-1921 (bi-weekly)	3.50
1921-1925 (montly)	3.00

Special 50th Anniversary edition
(published by a group of former Lone Scouts
Special 50th Anniversary edition (published by a group of former Lone Scouts) October, 1965 .... 5.00

OTHER SCOUTING RELATED MAGAZINES
Life Magazine, July 24, 1950 (1950 National Jamboree issue) 10.00
Saturday Evening Post, July 23, 1960 (1960 National Jamboree issue) 6.00
National Geographic Magazine, September, 1956 (Philmont Scout Ranch) . 4.00

Girl Scout leader Magazine,
January, 1928   ..... 5.00

Girl Scout Leader Magazine,
March-April, 1978 .... .50

Lone Scout Magazine, October 5, 1918
.... 4.00

Lone Scout Magazine, October, 1965,
special 50th Anniversary edition
.... 5.00

Life Magazine, July 24, 1950 ... 10.00

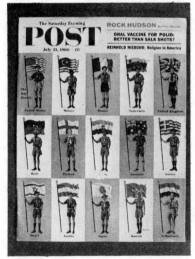

Saturday Evening Post Magazine,
July 23, 1960   .... 6.00

OTHER SCOUTING RELATED ITEMS

BOY SCOUT FICTION

Shortly after the Boy Scouts of America were founded, it became quite clear that this sort of an organization's time had come and that it was catching on fast. Publishers were quick to pick up on this and began to push story books into print about scouting to capitalize on this. By the late teens, several hundred such books were already in print. Needless to say, the Boy Scouts of America became quite concerned about the affect this may have on their fine public image. In 1906, the B.S.A. was awarded its federal charter by Congress and shortly thereafter began to go after some of the publishing houses. By 1922, the appearance of the new Scout fiction had slowed to a mere trickle. Other than some reprints which appeared in the 1930's, most Scout fiction was sanctioned by the B.S.A. Another factor contributing to this was that James E. West, Chief Scout Executive, hired Franklin Mathiens, in the teens to be the Scout librarian. Together, they got Percy Keese Fitzhugh, a somewhat respected writer of books to write a series of Scout fiction, with the activities of the Scouts therein toned down and more in line with what Scouting was all about. This he did with great success. His first book, Tom Slade, appeared in 1915. This series was named Tom Slade to compete with the then popular "Tom Swift" series. Eventually, the Pee Wee Harris, Tom Blakely, Westy Martin, and Mark Gilmore series were spun off into their own series.

Values given here are for books without dust jackets in fine condition. Add 25 cents to 50 cents for a dust jacket and adjust the value downward in 25 cent increments for declining condition. Books are listed by author, then title. In most cases the publisher is listed either in the heading or after the title.

Alsheler, Joseph A. The Shadow of the North, Appleton, 1917 (BSA copyright)

Ames, G.D. Boy Scout Campfires

Ames, Joseph B. (Century Publishing Co.)
The Clearport Boys	5.00
The Flying Mystery	4.50
The Mounted Troop	5.00
The Secret of Spirit Lake	5.00
Torrance from Texas, 1921	5.00
Under Boy Scout Colors, 1917	5.00

Barbour, Ralph Henry, The Mystery of the Rubber Boat, Appleton-Century, 1943 .... 4.50

Barclay, Vera C., Danny the Detective, Putnam, 1918 .... 4.50

The Best From Boy's Life Comics, by various authors, (Gilbertson World-Wide Publications)
Number 1, October 1957	2.00
Number 2, April 1958	2.00
Number 3, June, 1958	2.00
Number 4, July 1958	2.00
Number 5, October, 1958	2.00

Blaine, Capt. John, Saalfield Publishing Co.
The Boy Scouts in England, 1916	2.00
The Boy Scouts in Europe, 1916	2.00
The Boy Scouts in France, 1915	2.00
The Boy Scouts in Germany, 1916	2.00
The Boy Scouts in Italy, 1916	2.00
The Boy Scouts in the Netherlands, 1916	2.00
The Boy Scouts in Russia, 1916	2.00

The Boy Scouts in Serbia, 1916 .... 2.00
The Boy Scouts in Turkey, 1916 .... 2.00
The Boy Scouts on a Submarine, 1918 .... 2.00
The Boy Scouts on the Western Front, 1919 .... 2.00
The Boy Scouts with Joffre, 1919 .... 2.00

Boyton, Neil, The Silver Fox Patrol, Longmans, Green & Co., 1944 .... 4.00

Brereton, Captain F.S., Tom Stapleton, The Boy Scout, Caldwell Co. (no date)
...... 3.75

Brogan, S.D., Let the Coyotes, Howl, A Story of Philmont Scout Ranch, Putnam
1940 .... 6.00

Bruce, Brian, Cub Scouts, 1959, Golden Books, 1959 .... 3.50

Burgess, Thornton W., Penn Publishing Co.
The Boy Scouts in a Trapper's Camp, 1915 .... 4.50
The Boy Scouts of Woodcraft Camp, 1912 .... 4.00
The Boy Scouts on Lost Trail, 1914 .... 4.00
The Boy Scouts on Swift River, 1913 .... 4.00

Burritt, E.C. The Boy Scout Crusoes, Revell Publishing Co., 1916 .... 4.50

Burton, Charles P. (Holt Pubishing Co.)
The Boy Scouts of Bob's Hill 4.50
The Boy Scouts of Bob's Hill, 1912 .... 4.50
The Raven Patrol of Bob's Hill, 1917 .... 4.50

Carey, A.A. Boy Scouts at Sea, Little, Brown & Co., 1918 .... 5.00

Carter, Edward Champe, The Lone Scout, Cornhill Co., 1920 .... 4.75

Carter, Herbert, A.L. Burt Publishing Co.
The Boy Scouts Afoot in France, 1917 .... 2.00
The Boy Scouts Along the Susquehanna, 1915 .... 2.00
The Boy Scouts at the Battle of Saratoga 2.00
The Boy Scout's First Campfire, 1913 .... 2.00
The Boy Scouts in the Blue Ridge, 1913 .... 2.00
The Boy Scouts in Dixie, 1914 .... 2.00
The Boy Scouts in the Main Woods, 1913 .... 2.00
The Boy Scouts in the Rockies, 1913 .... 2.00
The Boy Scouts on Sturgeon Island, 1914 .... 2.00
The Boy Scouts on the War Trails in Belgium, 1916 .... 2.00
The Boy Scouts Through the Big Timber, 1913 .... 2.00

Carter, Russell, G.
Bob Hanson, Eagle Scout, (Penn Publishing), 1923 .... 2.50
Bob Hanson, First Class Scout, (Penn Publishing), 1922 .... 2.50
Bob Hanson, Scout, (Penn Publishing), 1921 .... 2.50
Bob Hanson, Tenderfoot (Penn Publishing), 1921 .... 2.50
Three Points of Honor, (Little Brown), 1929 .... 2.50

Case, John F., Banners of Scoutcraft, Lippincott Publishing Co., 1929 ...... 4.50

Chaffee, Allen, Elements, McLaughlin Bros., 1937 .... 4.25
Chaffee, Allen, Lost: Two Boys' Battle with the Elements, McLaughlin Bros.,
1937 .... 4.25
Lost River, Bradley, 1920 .... 4.25

Cheley, F.H. (Barse & Hopkins), The Boy Scout Trail Blazers, 1917 .... 4.00

Cochran, Rice E., Be Prepared: The Life and Illusions of a Scoutmaster, Sloan
Publishing Co., 1952 .... 3.50

Cody, H.A. Rod of the Lone Patrol, Doran, 1916 .... 4.00

Coe, Roland, The Little Scouts in Action, 1944 .... 3.00

Cororan, A.P., The Boy Scouts in Africa, 1923 .... 3.75

Corcoran, Brewer, The Page Co.
The Boy Scouts at Camp Lowell, 1922 .... 4.00
The Boy Scouts of Kandallville, 1918 .... 4.00
The Boy Scouts of the Wolf Patrol, 1920 .... 4.00
Crump, Irving, Boy Scout Firefighters (Barse and Hopkins), 1917 .... 4.00
Boy Scout Stories (Lantem Press), 1964 (Paperback) 2.50
Boys' Life Adventure Stories (Literary Guild), 1950 .... 5.00
Boys' Life Book of Scout Stories (Doubleday), 1953 .... 5.00
The Cloud Patrol (Grosset and Dunlap), 1929 .... 4.25
Craig of the Cloud Patrol, (Grosset & Dunlap), 1931 .... 4.25
The Pilot of the Cloud Patrol, (Grosset & Dunlap), 1929 .... 4.25
Scouts to the Rescue (Rand McNally), 1939 .... 3.75
Teen-Age Boy Scout Stories 3.00
Davis, Richard Harding, The Boy Scout, 1914 .... 4.50
The Boy Scout and Other Stories for Boys, 1920 .... 4.50
Dimock, A.W., Be Prepared, F.A. Stokes Co., 1919 .... 4.00
Douglas, Captain Alan (New York Publishing Co.), his original series was titled
the Hickory Ridge Boy Scouts as follows:
Hickory Ridge Boy Scouts Afloat, or Adventures on Watery Trails, 1917 .. 2.25
Hickory Ridge Boy Scouts the Camp Fires of the Wolf Patrol, 1913 .... 2.25
Hickory Ridge Boy Scouts Endurance Test or, How Clear Grit Won the Day,
1913 .... 2.25
Hickory Ridge Boy Scouts Fast Nine, or a Challenge from Fairfield, 1913   2.25
Hickory Ridge Boy Scouts Great Hike, or The Pride of the Khaki Troop, 1913
.... 2.25
Hickory Ridge Boy Scouts Pathfinder or, The Missing Tenderfoot, 1913 .. 2.25
Hickory Ridge Boy Scout Storm Bound, or a Vacation Among the Snow Drifts,
1915 .... 2.25
Hickory Ridge Boy Scouts Tenderfoot Squad, or Camping at Racoon Bluff,
1919 .... 2.25
Hickory Ridge Boy Scouts Under Canvas, or the Hunt for the Cartaret Ghost,
1915 .... 2.25
Hickory Ridge Boy Scouts Woodcraft, or How a Patrol Leader made Gook,
1913 .... 2.25
These were later reprinted by M.A. Donahue Publishing Co. and the titles were
altered to: (This reprint is known as The Victory Boy Scout series)
Afloat, or Adventures on Watery Trails 2.00
The Campfires of the Wolf Patrol 2.00
Endurance Test, or How Clean Grit Won the Day 2.00
Fast Nine, or A Challenge from Fairfield 2.00
Great Hike or Pride of the Khaki Troop 2.00
Pathfinder, or The Missing Tenderfoot 2.00
Storm Bound, or A Vacation Among the Snow Drifts 2.00
Tenderfoot Squad, or Camping at Raccoon Bluff 2.00
Under Canvas, or The Hunt for the Carteret Ghost 2.00
Woodcraft, or How a Patrol Leader made Good 2.00
Later these were reprinted again and the titles changed again:
Adventures on Watery Trails 2.00
Campfires of the Wolf Patrol 2.00
How Clear Grit Won the Day 2.00
A Challenge from Fairfield 2.00
Pride of the Khaki Troop 2.00
Missing Tenderfoot 2.00
A Vacation Among the Snow Drifts 2.00

Camping at Raccoon Bluff 2.00
The Hunt for the Carteret Ghost 2.00
How a Patrol Leader Made Good 2.00

L to R: Carter, Herbert, The Boy Scouts at the Battle of
Saratoga, A.L. Burt, Publisher 2.00
Crump, Irving, Boy Scout Stories, Lantern Press (paperback)
.......2.00

Dunn, J. Allen (Small, Maynard, and Co.), Jim Morse, Gold Hunter (copyright
B.S.A.) 3.00

Durston, George (Saalfield Publishing Co.) Durston represents another one of
the mazes in training the history of Scout fiction.

(These use a small format)
The Boy Scouts Afloat, 1921 .... 2.00
The Boy Scout Automobilists, 1921 .... 2.00
The Boy Scout Aviators, 1921 .... 2.00
The Boy Scouts Challenge, 1921 .... 2.00
The Boy Scouts Champion Recruit, 1921 .... 2.00
The Boy Scouts Defiance, 1921 .... 2.00
The Boy Scout Firefighters, 1921 .... 2.00
The Boy Scouts in Camp, 1921 .... 2.00
The Boy Scouts on the Trail, 1921 .... 2.00
The Boy Scout Pathfinders, 1921 .... 2.00
The Boy Scouts to the Rescue, 1921 .... 2.00
The Boy Scouts Victory, 1921 .... 2.00

These exist in a medium size and in a sightly larger edition, there is no
difference in value between these 2 sizes.
Boy Scouts Afloat, 1921 .... 2.00
Boy Scout Aviators, 1921 .... 2.00
Boy Scouts in Camp, 1921 .... 2.00

Boy Scouts on the Trail, 1921 .... 2.00
Boy Scouts to the Rescue, 1921 .... 2.00
Boy Scouts Victory, 1921 .... 2.00
These are a large-size edition with a picture on the cover.
A Boy Scouts Braver, 1927 .... 3.00
A Boy Scouts Campaign, 1927 .... 3.00
A Boy Scouts Discovery, 1927 .... 3.00
A Boy Scout on Duty, 1927 .... 3.00
A Boy Scouts Mission, 1927 .... 3.00
A Boy Scouts Secret, 1927 .... 3.00
Eaton, Walter P. (W.A. Wilde, Publisher)
Boy Scouts at Crater Lake, 1922 .... 2.50
Boy Scouts at The Grand Canyon, 1932 .... 2.50
Boy Scouts in Death Valley, 1939 .... 2.50
Boy Scouts in the Dismal Swamp, 1913 .... 2.50
Boy Scouts in Glacier Park, 1918 .... 2.50
Boy Scouts in the White Mountains, 1914 .... 2.50
Boy Scouts of Berkshire, 1912 .... 2.50
Boy Scouts of the Wild Cat Patrol, 1915 .... 2.50
Boy Scouts on Green Mountain Trail, 1929 .... 2.50
Boy Scouts on Katahidin Trail, 1929 .... 2.50
Peanut, Cub Reporter, 1916 .... 2.50
The Young Scoutmaster 2.50
Edwards, Lee (Grosset & Dunlap), Jerry Todd and The Bob Tailed Elephant,
1928 (dedicated to B.S.A.) 4.00
Jerry Todd, Editor in Chief, 1930 .... 4.00
Eldred, Warren L., St. Dunston Boy Scouts, (Lothrop, Lee, and Sheppard Co.),
1913 .... 4.50
Ellis, Edward (John C. Winston Co.), Around the Council Fire, 1913 ..... 4.50
The Boy Patrol on Guard, 1913 .... 4.00
English, J.W., Tailbone Patrol 4.50

EVERY BOYS LIBRARY
This is a series of 75 titles selected by the B.S.A. as being among the best
reading for Boys of Scout age. It was issued in three series. All bear the dates of
the 1st series. All were published by Grosset and Dunlap.
    1st series, varicolored covers with black and red embossed B.S.A.
    1st series, varicolored covers with black and red embossed B.S.A., 1st class
    seal emblem on the front cover and the spine.
    2nd series, same except embossed emblem is only on the front cover.
    3rd series, reprinted in the 1930's, these have various colored covers with a
    plain embossed emblem on the spine only, no emblem on the cover.
Note: Some sources reverse the order of the 1st and 2nd series.
Adventures in Beaver Stream Camp, by Major A.B. Dugmore, 1st series .. 6.00
    2nd series 5.50
    3rd series 4.50
Adventures of a Boy Scout, by Percy Keese Fitzhugh, 1st series 7.00
    2nd series 6.50
    3rd series 5.00

Cattle Ranch to College, by R. Doubleday, 1st series 5.50
   2nd series 5.00
   3rd series 4.00
College Yers, by Ralph D. Paine, 1st series 5.50
   2nd series 5.00
   3rd series 4.00
Crooked Trails, by F. Remington, 1st series 5.50
   2nd series 5.00
   3rd series 4.00
The Cruise of the Cachalot, by Frank T. Bullen, 1st series 5.50
   2nd series 5.00
   3rd series 4.00
The Cruise of the Dazzler, by Jack London, 1st series 5.50
   2nd series 5.00
   3rd series 4.00
Danny Fists, by Walter Camp, 1st series 5.50
   2nd series 5.00
   3rd series 4.00
Don Strong of the Wolf Patrol, by William Heyliger, 1st series 5.50
   2nd series 5.00
   3rd series 4.00
Don Strong, Patrol Leader, by William Heyliger, 1st series 5.50
   2nd series 5.00
   3rd series 4.00
For the Honor of the School, by Ralph Henry Barbour, 1st series 5.50
   2nd series 5.00
   3rd series 4.00
The Gaunt Gray Wolf, by Dillon Wallace, 1st series 5.50
   2nd series 5.00
   3rd series 4.00
Grit-A-Plenty, by Dillon Wallace, 1st series 5.50
   2nd series 5.00
   3rd series 4.00
A Gunner Aboard the "Yankee", From the Diary of Number Five of the After
   Port Gun, 1st series 6.50
   2nd series 6.00
   3rd series 5.00
The Guns of Europe, by J. Altsheler, 1st series 5.50
   2nd series 5.00
   3rd series 4.00
The Half-Back, by Ralph H. Barbour 5.50
   2nd series 5.00
   3rd series 4.00
Handbook for Boys, Revised Edition, by Boy Scouts of America, 1st series 35.00
   2nd series . . . . , ... 30.00
   3rd series 35.00
Handicraft for Outdoor Boys, by Dan Beard, 1st series 10.00
   2nd series 9.00
   3rd series 7.50

Redney McGaw: A Circus Story for Boys, Arthur E. McFarlane, 1st series . 5.50
  2nd series 5.00
  3rd series 4.00
The School Days of Elliot Gray, Jr., by Colton Maynard, 1st series 5.50
  2nd series 5.00
  3rd series 4.00
Scouting with Daniel Boone, by Everett T. Tomlinson, 1st series 5.50
  2nd series 5.00
  3rd series 4.00
Scouting with General Funston, by Everett T. Tomlinson, 1st series 5.50
  2nd series 5.00
  3rd series 4.00
Scouting with Kit Carson, by Everett T. Tomlinson, 1st series 5.50
  2nd series 5.00
  3rd series 4.00
Tecumseh's Young Braves, by Everett T. Tomlinson, 1st series 5.50
  2nd series 5.00
  3rd series 4.00
Three Years Behind the Guns, by Lieu Tisdale, 1st series 5.50
  2nd series 5.00
  3rd series 4.00
Through College on Nothing a Year, by Christian Gauss, 1st series 5.50
  2nd series 5.00
  3rd series 4.00
To The Land of the Caribou, by Paul Greene Tomlinson, 1st series 5.50
  2nd series 5.00
  3rd series 4.00
Tom Paulding, by Brander Mathews, 1st series 5.50
  2nd series 5.00
  3rd series 4.00
Tom Strong, Boy Captain, by Alfred Bishop-Mason, 1st series 5.50
  2nd series 5.00
  3rd series 4.00
Tom Strong, Washington's Scout, by Alfred Bishop-Mason, 1st series 5.50
  2nd series 5.00
  3rd series 4.00
Tommy Remington's Battle, by B.E. Stevenson, 1st series 5.50
  2nd series 5.00
  3rd series 4.00
Treasure Island, by Robert Louis Stevenson, 1st series 6.00
  2nd series 5.50
  3rd series 4.00
20,000 Leagues Under the Sea, by Jules Verne, 1st series 6.00
  2nd series 5.50
  3rd series 4.00
Under Boy Scout Colors, by J.B. Ames, 1st series 5.50
  2nd series 5.00
  3rd series 4.00
Ungava Bob: A Tale of the Fur Trappers, by Dillon Wallace, 1st series 5.50
  2nd series 5.00
  3rd series 4.00

Wells Brothers: The Young Cattle Kings, by Andy Adams, 1st series 5.50
   2nd series 5.00
   3rd series 4.00
Williams of West Point, by J.S. Johnson, 1st series 5.50
   2nd series 5.00
   3rd series 4.00
The Wireless Man: His Work and Adventures, by F.A. Collins, 1st series ... 5.50
   2nd series 5.00
   3rd series 4.00
The Wolf Hunters, by G.B. Grinnell, 1st series 5.50
   2nd series 5.00
   3rd series 4.00
The Wrecking Master, by R.D. Paine, 1st series 5.50
   2nd series 5.00
   3rd series 4.00
Yankee Ships and Yankee Sailors, by James Barnes, 1st series 5.50
   2nd series 5.00
   3rd series 4.00

Felsen, Henry Gregor, (Scribners), Anyone for Cub Scouts?, 1954 .... 3.00
   Cub Scout at Last, 1952 .... 3.00

Fennerd, Phyllis R., Heros, Heros, Heros, Franklin Watts Inc., 1956 ...... 3.00
Finnemore J., Boy Scouts in the Balkans, (Lippincott) 4.50
   Boy Scouts with the Russians, (Lippincott) 4.50
   The Wolf Patrol (MacMillan), 1924 .... 4.50
Fitzhugh, Percy Keese, The Adventures of a Boy Scout (Photoplay of Tom Slade) (Grosse & Dunlap) 12.50
   Along the Mohawk Trail or, Boy Scouts on Lake Champlain (Thomas Y. Crowell), 1913 .... 6.50
   For Uncle Sam Boss or Boy Scouts at Panama (Thomas Y. Crowell), 1913 ...... 6.50
   Hervey Willetts (Grossett & Dunlap), 1927 .... 3.50
   In the Path of La Salle, or Boy Scouts on the Mississippi (Thomas Y. Crowell), 1914 .... 6.50
   Lefty Leighton (Grosset & Dunlap), 1930 .... 3.75
   Mark Gilmore's Lucky Landing, 1931 (Grosset & Dunlap) 3.25
   Mark Gilmore, Scout of the Air, 1930 (Grosset & Dunlap) 3.25
   Mark Gilmore, Speed Flyer, 1931 (Grosset & Dunlap) 3.25
   The Parachut Jumper: A Tom Slade Story, 1930 .... 3.25
   Pee-Wee Harris, 1922 (Grosset & Dunlap) 3.00
   Pee-Wee Harris Adrift, 1922 (Grosset & Dunlap) 3.00
   Pee-Wee Harris: As Good as his Word, 1925 (Grosset & Dunlap) 3.00
   Pee-Wee Harris on the Briny Deep, 1928 (Grosset & Dunlap) 3.00
   Pee-Wee Harris in Camp, 1922 (Grosset & Dunlap) 3.00
   Pee-Wee Harris in Darkest Africa, 1929 (Grosset & Dunlap) 3.00
   Pee-Wee Harris Turns Detective, 1930 (Grosset & Dunlap) 3.00
   Pee-Wee Harris: Fixer, 1924 (Grosset & Dunlap) 3.00
   Pee-Wee Harris F.O.B. Bridgeboro, 1923 (Grosset & Dunlap) 3.00
   Pee-Wee Harris in Luck, 1922 (Grosset & Dunlap) 3.00
   Pee-Wee Harris: Mayor for a Day, 1926 (Grosset & Dunlap) 3.00
   Pee-Wee Harris and the Sunken Treasure, 1927 (Grosset & Dunlap) 3.00
   Pee-Wee Harris on the Trail, 1922 (Grosset & Dunlap) 3.00

Roy Blakeley's Adventures in Camp, (Grosset & Dunlap) 1920 .... 3.00
Roy Blakeley Up in the Air, (Grosset & Dunlap) 1931 .... 3.00
Roy Blakeley's Bee-Line Hike, (Grosset & Dunlap) 1922 .... 3.00
Roy Blakeley's Camp on Wheels, (Grosset & Dunlap) 1920 .... 3.00
Roy Blakeley's Elastic Hike, (Grosset & Dunlap) 1926 .... 3.00
Roy Blakeley's Funny Bone Hike, (Grosset & Dunlap) 1922 .... 3.00
Roy Blakeley's Go-As-You-Please Hike, (Grosset & Dunlap), 1929 .... 3.00
Roy Blakeley's Happy-Go-Lucky Hike, (Grosset & Dunlap) 1928 .... 3.00
Roy Blakeley at the Haunted Camp, (Grosset & Dunlap), 1922 .... 3.00
Roy Blakeley, His Story, (Grosset & Dunlap) 1920 .... 3.00
Roy Blakeley, Lost, Strayed or Stolen, (Grosset & Dunlap) 1921 .... 3.00
Roy Blakeley on the Mohawk Trail, (Grosset & Dunlap) 1925 .... 3.00
Roy Blakeley's Motor Caravan, (Grosset & Dunlap) 1922 .... 3.00
Roy Blakeley's Pathfinder, (Grosset & Dunlap) 1920 .... 3.00
Roy Blakeley's Roundabout Hike, (Grosset & Dunlap) 1926 .... 3.00
Roy Blakeley's Silver Fox Patrol, (Grosset & Dunlap) 1920 .... 3.00
Roy Blakeley's Tangled Trail, (Grosset & Dunlap) 1924 .... 3.00
Roy Blakeley's Wild Goose Chase, (Grosset & Dunlap) 1930 .... 3.00
Skinny McCord, (Grosset & Dunlap), 1928 .... 3.25
Spiffy Henshaw, (Grosset & Dunlap) 1929 .... 4.00
The Story of Terrible Terry, (Grosset & Dunlap), 1930 .... 4.50
Tom Slade at Bear Mountain, (Grosset & Dunlap), 1925 .... 3.00
Tom Slade at Black Lake, (Grosset & Dunlap) 1920 .... 3.00
Tom Slade, Boy Scout, (Grosset & Dunlap), 1915 .... 3.00
Tom Slade with the Boys over There, (Grosset & Dunlap(1918 .... 3.00
Tom Slade with the Colors, (Grosset & Dunlap), 1918 .... 3.00
Tom Slade's Double Dare, (Grosset & Dunlap), 1922 .... 3.00
Tom Slade with the Flying Corps, (Grosset & Dunlap), 1919 .... 3.00
Tom Slade, Forest Ranger, (Grosset & Dunlap), 1926 .... 3.00
Tom Slade at Haunted Cavern, (Grosset & Dunlap), 1929, (rare) 10.00
Tom Slade, Motorcycle Dispatch Bearer, (Grosset & Dunlap) 1918 ...... 3.00
Tom Slade on Mystery Trail, (Grosset & Dunlap) 1921 .... 3.00
Tom Slade in the North Woods, (Grosset & Dunlap), 1927 .... 3.00
Tom Slade on Overlook Mountain, (Grosset & Dunlap), 1923 .... 3.00
Tom Slade Picks a Winner (Grosset & Dunlap), 1924 .... 3.00
Tom Slade on the River, (Grosset & Dunlap), 1917 .... 3.00
Tom Slade on a Transport, (Grosset & Dunlap), 1918 .... 3.00
Tom Slade at Shadow Isle, (Grosset & Dunlap), 1928 .... 3.00
Tom Slade at Temple Camp, (Grosset & Dunlap), 1917 .... 3.00
Tom Slade on a Transport, (Grosset & Dunlap), 1918 .... 3.00
Westy Martin, (Grosset & Dunlap), 1924 .... 3.00
Westy Martin in the Land of the Purple Sage, (Grosset & Dunlap), 1929 .. 3.00
Westy Martin on the Mississippi, (Grosset & Dunlap), 1930 .... 3.00
Westy Martin on the Old Indian Trails, (Grosset & Dunlap), 1928 .... 3.00
Westy Martin in the Rockies, (Grosset & Dunlap), 1925 .... 3.00
Westy Martin on the Sante Fe Trail, (Grosset & Dunlap), 1926 .... 3.00
Westy Martin in the Sierras, (Grosset & Dunlap), 1931 .... 3.00
Westy Martin in the Yellowstone, (Grosset & Dunlap), 1924 .... 3.00
Out West with Westy Martin, (Grosset & Dunlap), 1924, 4 volume collection
containing: Westy Martin, Westy Martin in the Rockies, Westy Martin in the
Yellowstone, Westy Martin on the Sante Fe Trail 7.50
Wigwag Wiegand, 1929 (Grosset & Dunlap) 3.25

Fletcher, Major A.L. (M.A. Donohue & Co.):
Boy Scout Pathfinders; or, The Strange Hunt for the Beaver Patrol, 1913 ... 3.00
   Boy Scout Rivals; or, A Leader of the Tenderfoot Patrol, 1913 .... 3.00
   Boy Scouts in Alaska; or The Camp on the Glacier, 1913 .... 3.00
   Boy Scouts in Norther Wilds; or, the Signal from the Hills, 1913 .... 3.00
   Boy Scouts in the Coal Caverns; or, Light in Tunnel Six, 1913 .... 3.00
   Boy Scouts in the Everglades; or The Island of Lost Channel, 1913 .... 3.00
   Boy Scouts on Old Superior; or, The Tale of the Pictured Rocks, 1913 ..... 3.00
   Boy Scouts on the Great Divide; or, the Ending of the Trail, 1913 .... 3.00
   Boy Scouts Signal Sender; or, When Wig Wag Knowledge Paid, 1913 ..... 3.00
   Boy Scouts Test of Courage; or, Winning the Merit Badge, 1913 .... 3.00
   Boy Scouts Woodcraft Lesson; or, Proving their Mettle in the Field, 1913 . 3.00

Gardner, L.S. (Watts Inc.), Bill Martin, Cub Scout, 1952 .... 3.00
   From Bobcat to Wolf, the Story of Den 7, Pack 4, 1952 .... 3.00
Garfield, J.B. (Viking), Follow my Leader, 1957 .... 3.00
Garis, Howard R. (Little Brown), Chad of Knob Hill, 1929 .... 3.00
Garth, John (Barse & Hopkins), Boy Scouts on the Trail, 1920 .... 3.50
Gendron, Val (Longmens, Green & Co.), Behind Zuni Masks, 1929 .... 4.00
Gillman, C.L. (Buzza Publishers), The Fox Patrol on the River, 1912 ...... 4.50
Gilly bear, (Gabriel Sons), Billy Boy Scout, 1916 .... 4.50
Gordon, Paul (Holt), The Scout of the Golden Cross, 1920 .... 4.50
Grant, Captain Allan (Doran), In Defense of Paris, 1915 .... 4.00
Griggs, Edward, (Saalfield Publishing Co.), A Boy Scout Hero, 1921 .... 3.00
   A Boy Scout on the Trail, 1921 .... 3.00
   A Boy Scout Patriot, 1921 .... 3.00
   A Boy Scouts Adventure, 1921 .... 3.00
   A Boy Scouts Chance, 1921 .... 3.00
   A Boy Scouts Courage, 1921 .... 3.00
   A Boy Scouts Daring, 1921 .... 3.00
   A Boy Scouts Destiny, 1921 .... 3.00
   A Boy Scouts Holiday, 1921 .... 3.00
   A Boy Scouts Struggle, 1921 .... 3.00
   A Boy Scouts Success, 1921 .... 3.00
Hanes, DeWitt, (A.L. Burt), The Big Opportunity, 1934 .... 3.75
Hendrick, Edward P., The 7th Scout, 1938 .... 4.25
Heyliger, William, Beanball Bill and Other Stories (Grosset & and Dunlap),
  1930 .... 4.50
   Don Strong, American (D. Appleton), 1920 .... 4.50
   Don Strong, of the Wolf Patrol (D. Appleton), 1916 .... 4.50
   Jerry Hicks and His Gang (Grosset & Dunlap), 1929 .... 4.50
   Jerry Hicks, Explorer (Grosset and Dunlap, 1930 .... 4.50
   Jerry Hicks, Ghost Hunter (Grosset & Dunlap), 1929 .... 4.50
SOS Radio Patrol (Dodd, Mead), 1942 .... 4.50
   Yours Truly, Jerry Hicks (Grosset & Dunlap), 1929 .... 4.50
Holland, Rupert S. (Lippincott), Blackbeard's Island 4.00
   The Boy Scouts of Birchbark Island, 1911 .... 4.50
   The Boy Scouts of Snowshoe Lodge, 1915 .... 4.50
   The Sea Scouts of Birchbark Island, 1936 .... 5.00

Hornibrook, Isabel K., Captain Curly's Boy (Houghton Mifflin) 5.00
    Coxwain Drake of the Sea Scouts (Houghton Miffline), 1920 .... 5.00
    Drake and the Adventurers Cap (Little, Brown), 1922 .... 5.00
    Drake of Troop One (Houghton Mifflin), 1916 .... 4.50
    Lost in Maine Woods (Houghton Mifflin) 4.50
    Scout Drake in War Time (Little Brown) 4.50
    A Scout of Today (Houghton Mifflin), 1913 .... 4.50

Fitzhugh, Percy Keese, Roy Blakeley, Pathfinder, Grosset & Dunlap (shown in a gray cover variation) 3.25

Jonathan Norton, The Movie Scout, Goldsmith Publishers, 1934, with d-j 3.75

Houston, Edwin J. (David McKay Co.), Our Boy Scouts in Camp, 1912 ..... 4.25

Huntington, Dedwar (Lilco), The Forest Pilot, 1915 .... 4.00

Hyde, Elizabeth A. Watson (Rand McNally), Little Brothers to the Scouts, 1917
      ...... 4.25

Jackerns, Raymond, Three Amateur Scouts 4.25

Jackson, The Paleface Redskins 4.00

James, Will (World), Horses I've Known, 1945 (BSA Copyright) 3.50
    Smoky (BSA Copyright) 3.50

Jenkins, Marshall (D. Appleton and Co.), A Freshman Scout at College, 1914
      ...... 4.25

The Doings of Troop 5, 1914 .... 4.25
    The Jackel Patrol of Troop 5, 1915 .... 4.25
    The Norfolk Boy Scouts, 1916 .... 4.25
    Troop 5 at Camp, 1914 .... 4.25

Jonathan, Norton H., (Golsmith Publishing Co.), The Lost Empire, 1934 ... 4.00
    The Movie Scout, 1934 .... 3.50
    The Mystery of the Midnight Flyer 4.00
    The Speedway Cyclone, 1934 .... 4.00

Kanton, MacKinley, Follow Me Boys (Grosset & Dunlap), 1954 .... 6.50
   God and my Country (World), 1954 .... 5.00
   God and my Country (Bantam), 1955 .... 3.00
Note: This also appears in Spring, 1954 edition of Readers Digest Condensed
Books.

Keane, Thomas J. (Meade & Co.), Lubbers Afloat, 1932 .... 5.00

Kipling, Rudyard, Land and Sea Tales for Scouts and Guides (MacMillan) . 6.50
   Land and Sea Tales for Scouts and Scouters (Doubleday), 1923 .... 5.00

Kohler, J.H. (Alladin), Daniel in the Cub Scout Den, 1951 .... 3.00
   Razzberry Jamboree 3.00

Lamar, Ashton, When Scout Meets Scout; or the Aeroplane Spy, 1912 ...... 4.25

Leonard, Edward, Truck Simms, Fortyniner (BSA Copyright) 3.50

Lerrigo, C.H. Boy Scouts of the Robin Hood Patrol (Barse & Hopkins), 1927 4.75
   Boy Scouts of the Round Table Patrol (Barse & Hopkins), 1924 .... 4.75
   Boy Scouts on Special Service (Little Brown), 1922 .... 4.75
   Boy Scouts to the Rescue (Barse & Hopkins), 1920 .... 4.00
   Boy Scout Treasure Hunters (Barse & Hopkins), 1917 .... 4.00
   Merry Men of the Robinhood Patrol (Barse & Hopkins), 1927 .... 4.75

Lyons, K., The Vagabond Scout; or Adventures of Duncan Dunn, 1931 ..... 4.50

Maitland, Major Robert, (Saalfield)
Note: Although this series is commonly known as the Maitland series, several
titles were authored by George Durston. The books are in the small size format.
   The Boy Scout Automobilists, 1912 .... 2.00
   The Boy Scout Aviators, 1912 .... 2.00
   The Boy Scout Fire Fighters, 1912 .... 2.00
   The Boy Scout Pathfinders, 1912 .... 2.00
   The Boy Scouts Afloat, 1912 .... 2.00
   The Boy Scouts Before Belgrade, 1915 .... 2.00
   The Boy Scouts Challenge, 1912 .... 2.00
   The Boy Scouts Champion Recruit, 1912 .... 2.00
   The Boy Scouts Defiance, 1912 .... 2.00
   The Boy Scouts in Camp, 1912 .... 2.00
   The Boy Scouts in Front of Warsaw, 1916 .... 2.00
   The Boy Scouts in the War Zone, 1919 .... 2.00
   The Boy Scouts on the Trail, 1912 .... 2.00
   The Boy Scouts Test, 1916 .... 2.00
   The Boy Scouts to the Rescue, 1912 .... 2.00
   The Boy Scouts Under Fire in France 2.00
   Boy Scouts Under the Kaiser, 1915 .... 2.00
   The Boy Scouts Under the Red Cross, 1916 .... 2.00
   The Boy Scouts Under the Stars and Stripes, 1918 .... 2.00
   The Boy Scouts Victory, 1912 .... 2.00
   The Boy Scouts with King George, 1915 .... 2.00
   The Boy Scouts with the Allies, 1915 .... 2.00
   The Boy Scouts with the Cossacks, 1915 .... 2.00

Mathius, Franklin K. Boy Scouts Book of Adventureous Youth, 1941 ...... 10.00
   Boy Scouts Book of Campfire Stories (Appleton), 1921 .... 10.00
   Boy Scouts Book of Good Turn Stories (Scriber), 1931 .... 10.00
   Boy Scouts Book of Stories (Appleton), 1919 .... 10.00
   Boy Scouts Courageous (Barse & Hopkins), 1918 .... 10.00
   Boy Scouts Own Book (Appleton), 1924 .... 10.00
   Chuckles and Grins (Grosset and Dunlap), 1928 .... 9.00
   Coming Through (Appleton), 1927 .... 6.50

Coming Through (Grosset & Dunlap), 1927 .... 5.00
Flying High (Grosset and Dunlap), 1930 .... 6.50
Hitting the Trail (Grosset & Dunlap), 1930 .... 6.50
Laugh, Boy, Laugh (Grosset & Dunlap), 1930 .... 9.00
The Ransom of Red Chief and Other O'Henry Stories for Boys (Doubleday),
1918 .... 8.00
Skyward Ho! (Grosset & Dunlap), 1930 .... 6.50
Wild Animal Trails (Grosset & Dunlap), 1928 .... 9.00
McKall (Beneficto Publishing), Buttons and the Boy Scouts, 1958 .... 4.25
McCormick, Wilfred, Eagle Scout (Grosset & Dunlap), 1952 .... 3.50
Eagle Scout (Putnam), 1952 .... 3.50
McLane, F. Moirlton (Barse & Hopkins) The Boy Scouts of the Lighthouse
Troop, 1917 .... 3.25
Michelson, Florence, (Whitman) Lassie and the Cub Scout, 1966 .... 3.00
Mills, Joe)Sears and Co.) A Mountain Boyhood, 1926 (BSA Copyright) 4.00
Oswald, Lewis A., The Traditions of Troop One 3.75

McLane, F. Moirlton, The Boy Scouts of the Lighthouse Troop
(Barse & Hopkins, 1917) 3.25

Otis, James (Thomas Y. Crowell), Boy Scouts in a Lumber Camp, 1913 .... 3.75
Boy Scouts in the Maine Woods, 1911 .... 3.50
Palmer, Don, (Cupples & Leen) The Boy Scout Explorers at Emerald Valley,
1955 .... 3.00
The Boy Scout Explorers at Headless Hollow, 1957 .... 3.00
The Boy Scout Explorers at Treasure Mountain, 1955 .... 3.00
Park, George F. (McBride Co.) Dick Judson, Boy Scout Ranger, 1916 ...... 4.00
Parker, Capt. Thomas D. (USN) (Wilde Co.) The Cruise of the Deep Sea Scouts,
1917 .... 5.00
Parkinson, G.A. (Winston) David, the Chief Scout 4.50
Payson, Lt. Howard (Pen name of J.H. Goldfarb) (Hurst & Co.)
The Boy Scouts and the Army Airship, 1911 .... 2.00
The Boy Scouts at the Canadian Border, 1918 .... 2.00
The Boy Scouts at the Panama Canal, 1913 .... 2.00
The Boy Scouts at the Panama-Pacific Exposition, 1915 .... 2.00
The Boy Scouts Badge of Courage, 1917 .... 2.00
The Boy Scouts Campaign for Preparedness, 1916 .... 2.00
The Boy Scouts for Uncle Sam, 1912 .... 2.00
The Boy Scouts Mountain Camp, 1912 .... 2.00
The Boy Scouts of the Eagle Patrol, 1911 .... 2.00
The Boy Scouts on Belgian Battlefields, 1915 .... 2.00
The Boy Scouts on the Range, 1911 .... 2.00
The Boy Scouts under Fire in Mexico, 1914 .... 2.00
The Boy Scouts under Sealed Orders, 1916 .... 2.00
The Boy Scouts with the Allies in France, 1915 .... 2.00
Pashke, (Roy Publishing) Black Sheep patrol, 1946, ... 3.75
By Various Authors (G.P. Pritnam's Sons) The Pedro Books
Ahead of Their Time 4.00
Best from Boys' Life No. 1, 1970 .... 4.00
The Cub Book 4.00

Boy Scouts of the Life Saving Crew, 1914 .... 2.00
Boy Scouts of the Naval Reserve, 1914 .... 2.00
Boy Scouts of Pioneer Camp, 1914 .... 2.00
Boy Scouts of the Signal Corps, 1914 .... 2.00
Boy Scouts on Picket Duty, 1914 .... 2.00
Boy Scouts on the Roll of Honor, 1916 .... 2.00
Boy Scouts with the Motion Picture Players, 1915 .... 2.00
Boy Scouts with the Red Cross, 1915 .... 2.00

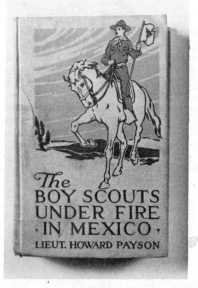
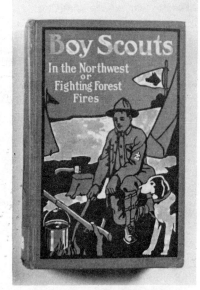

L to R; Payson, Lt. Howard, The Boy Scouts Under Fire in
   Mexico (Hurst & Co.) 2.00
Ralphson, G. Harvey, Boy Scouts in the Northwest, or
   Fighting Forest Fires (Donahue Publishing Co.) 2.00

Sherman, Harold T. (Grosset & Dunlap) Fight 'em Big Three, 1925, (BSA
   Copyright) 2.25
Sherman, Capt. V.T. (Donohue Publishing Co.)
   A Lot Patrol; or Scout Tactics to the Front, 1913 .... 2.25
   An Interrupted Wig Wag; or, A Boy Scout Trick, 1913 .... 2.25
   Boy Scouts with Joffre; or, The Trenches in Belgium, 1913 .... 2.25
   Capturing a Spy; or, A New Peril, 1913 .... 2.25
   Scouting the Balkans in a Motorboat; or, An Escape from the Dardanelles,
   1913 .... 2.25
   The Boy Scout Signal; or, The Camp on the Cliff, 1913 .... 2.25
   The Call of the Beaver Patrol; or A Break in the Glacier, 1913 .... 2.25
   The Perils of an Air Ship; or, Boy Scouts in the Sky, 1913 .... 2.25
   The Runaway Balloon; or, The Beseiged Scouts, 1913 .... 2.25
   The War Zone of the Kaiser; or, Boy Scouts of the North Sea, 1913 ..... 2.25

Sherwood, Elmer H. (Whitman Publishing Co.), Lucky and His Friend Steve
..... 3.50

Lucky and His Travels 3.50
Lucky Finds a Friend 3.50
Lucky in the Northwest 3.50
Lucky on an Important Mission 3.50
Lucky, The Boy Scout, 1916 .... 3.50
Lucky, The Young Navy Man, 1917 .... 3.50
Lucky, The Young Soldier, 1917 .... 3.50
Lucky, The Young Volunteer 3.50
Ted Marsh and the Enemy 3.50
Ted Marsh on an Important Mission 3.50
Ted Marsh, The Boy Scout 3.50
Ted Marsh, The Young Volunteer 3.50

Smith, Leonard K., Boy Scouts to the Rescue (Little, Brown), 1939 .... 4.00
Corley of the Wilderness Trails (Saalfield), 1937 .... 4.00
Corley takes the Scout Trail (Appleton), 1930 .... 4.00
Phil Burton, Sleuth (Saalfield), 1937 .... 3.75
Scouting on Mystery Trail (MacMillan) 4.00
Tommy of Troop Six (Saalfield), 1937 .... 4.00

Sterling, Dorothy (Doubleday) The Cub Scout Mystery, 1952 .... 3.00

Sterling, Gray (Marshall Jones Co.) The Tooth of Time: A Philmont
Adventure, 1955 .... 8.00

Stone, Gordon, (Graham Co.) Tommy Tip Top and his Boy Scouts, 1914 .... 4.50

Stuart, Gordon (pen name for H.S.Saylor) (Reilly & Britton)
Note: After his death in 1913, the name was used by G.N. Madison and H.
Bedford Jones, who completed the Boy Scouts of Air Series.
The Boy Scouts of the Air at Cap Peril, 1921 .... 3.25
The Boy Scouts of the Air at Eagle Camp, 1912 .... 3.25
The Boy Scouts of the Air at Greenwood School, 1912 .... 3.25
The Boy Scouts of the Air in Belgium, 1915 .... 3.25
The Boy Scouts of the Air in Indian Land, 1912 .... 3.25
The Boy Scouts of the Air in the Dismal Swamp, 1920 .... 3.25
The Boy Scouts of the Air in the Lone Star Patrol, 1916 .... 3.25
The Boy Scouts of the Air in the Northern Wilds, 1912 .... 3.25
The Boy Scouts of the Air on Baldcrest, 1922 .... 3.25
The Boy Scouts of the Air on Flathead Mountain, 1913 .... 3.25
The Boy Scouts of the Air on the French Front, 1918 .... 3.25
The Boy Scouts of the Air on the Great Lakes, 1914 .... 3.25
The Boy Scouts of the Air with Pershing, 1919 .... 3.25
A Thief in the Night 3.25
A Wild Night on Lost Island 3.25
B.P. Ranch in Indian Land, 1936 .... 3.25
Hal Kenyon Disappears 3.25
Tex Loses His Temper, 1936 .... 3.25
Wolf Patrol on the Great Lakes, 1936 .... 3.25

Thurston, T.I. (Revell Publishing) Billy Burns of Troop 5, 1916 .... 4.00
The Scoutmaster of Troop 5, 1912 .... 4.00

Tull, J.B. (Educational Supply) Winning the Bronze Cross 4.50

Victor, Ralph (A.L. Chatterton) Boy Scouts Air Craft, 1912 .... 2.50
Boy Scouts Canoe Trip, 1911 .... 2.50
Boy Scouts in the Black Hills, 1913 .... 2.50
Boy Scouts in the Canadian Rockies, 1911 .... 2.50

Girl Scouts in the Magic City 2.50
Girl Scouts in the Redwoods 2.50
Girl Scouts in the Rockies 2.50
Vandercrook, Girl Scouts in Beechwood Forest 3.50
Marksmanship for Boys, 1915 .... 20.00
Reynolds; Baden-Powell, 1970 .... 10.00
Rover Scouts, 1932 .... 13.50
Scouting in Education, 1921 .... 20.00
Boy Scouts in the North Woods, 1913 .... 4.50
Boy Scouts Motorcycles, 1911 .... 4.50
Boy Scouts on the Yukon, 1912 .... 4.50
Boy Scouts Patrol, 1911 .... 4.50

The Victor Books were also published by Platt and Peck, publishers and these bear the same dates.
Boy Scouts Air Craft, 1912 .... 4.00
Boy Scouts Canoe Trip, 1911 .... 4.00
Boy Scouts in the Black Hills, 1913 .... 4.00
Boy Scouts in the Canadian Rockies, 1911 .... 4.00
Boy Scouts in the North Woods, 1913 .... 4.00
Boy Scouts Motorcycles, 1911 .... 4.00
Boy Scouts on the Yukon, 1912 .... 4.00
Boy Scouts Patrol, 1911 .... 4.00

Walden, Walter (Barse & Hopkins) Boy Scouts Afloat, 1918 .... 4.50

Wallace, Dillen (Revell Publishing) Troop "One" of the Labrador, 1920 ... 4.25

Warren, George A. (Cupples & Leon) The Banner Boy Scouts, 1912 .... 2.00
The Banner Boy Scouts Afloat, 1913 .... 2.00
The Banner Boy Scouts in the Air, 1937 .... 2.00
The Banner Boy Scouts Mystery, 1937 .... 2.00
The Banner Boy Scouts on a Tour, 1912 .... 2.00
The Banner Boy Scouts Snowbound, 1916 .... 2.00

These were also printed by World Publishing Co. although not confirmed, it is believed that the World Publishing editions are reprints published sometime in the 1930's.

Watts, Mabel (Rand McNally) Cub Scout, 1954 .... 3.00

Webster, Frank V. (Cupples & Leon) 3.25

White, Stuart Edward (Doubleday), Daniel Boone, Wilderness Scout, 1922 (BSA Copyring) 4.50

Wilder, James Austin, The Pine Tree Patrol, 1918 .... 4.75

Willis, Charles E. (Dietz Publishing) Scouts of '76, 1924, (dedicated to BSA) 4.50

Wilson John F. (McMillan) Scouts of the Desert, 1920 .... 4.25
Tad Sheldon, Boy Scout, (Sturgis & Walton Co.), 1913 .... 4.50
Tad Sheldon's Fourth of July, (McMillan), 1913 .... 4.5

Wirt, Mildred A. (Cupples & Leon), Dan Carter and the Cub honor, 1953 .... 3.00
Dan Carter and the Great Carved Face, 1952 .... 3.00
Dan Carter and the Haunted Castle, 1951 .... 3.00
Dan Carter and the Money Box, 1950 .... 3.00
Dan Carter and the River Camp, 1949 .... 3.00
Dan Carter, Cub Scout, 1949 .... 3.00

Wright, Jack (World Syndicate Publishing Co.)
The Scout Patrol Boys and the Hunting Lodge Mystery, 1933 .... 3.00
The Scout Patrol Boys at Circle U Ranch, 1933 .... 3.00

The Scout Patrol Boys Exploring in Yucatan, 1933 .... 3.00
The Scout Patrol Boys inthe Frozen South, 1933 .... 3.00
Walden, Walter (Barse & Hopkins) Boy Scouts Afloat, 1918 .... 4.50o

GIRL SCOUT FICTION

Blanchard, Girl Scouts of Red Rose Troop 3.50
Blancard, From Tenderfoot to Golden Eaglet 4.00
   From Tenderfoot to Golden Eaglet 4.00
Galt, Katherine, Girl Scouts at Home 3.00
   Girl Scouts Rally 3.00
   Girl Scouts Triumph 3.00
Garis, Girl Scouts at Bellaire 3.50
   Girl Scouts at Camp Comalong 3.50
   Girl Scouts at Sea Crest 3.50
   Girl Scout Pioneers 3.50
LaVelle, Helen, Girl Scouts at Camp 3.00
   Girl Scouts at Miss Allen's School 3.00
   Girl Scouts Canoe Trip 3.00
   Girl Scouts Captain 3.00
   Girl Scouts Director 3.00
   Girl Scouts Good Turn 3.00
   Girl Scouts Motor Trip 3.00
   Girl Scouts on the Beach 3.00
   Girl Scouts Rivals 3.00
   Girl Scouts Vacation Adventure 3.00
Roy, Girl Scouts at Dandalion Camp 3.50
   A Garden Scout 3.50
   Girl Scouts in Arizona and New Mexico 3.50
   Girl Scouts in the Adirondacks 3.50
   Girl Scouts in the Magi
   Girl Scouts in Mystery Valley 3.50
   Girl Scouts of the Eagles Wing 3.50
   Girl Scouts of the Round Table 3.50
Wirt, Mildred, Brownie Scouts at the Circus 3.00
   Brownie Scouts at Silver Beach 3.00
   Brownie Scouts at Windmill Farm 3.00
   Girl Scouts at Singing Sands 3.00

OTHER SCOUTING RELATED BOOKS AND PUBLICATIONS

In addition to the fiction, and although technically not Scouting, works of Scoutings' grants are considered Scouting related and are highly collectible. Among those whose works fall in this group are:

   Olave Lady Baden-Powell
   Sir Robert Baden-Powell
   Daniel Carter Beard
   William S. Boyce
   William "Bill" Boyce
   Juliette Low
   Ernest Thompson Seton (went by Ernest E. Seton-Thompson prior to 1901)
   Julia Seton
   Dr. James E. West

This applies not only to works by these people, but, also to works about them. Too, several were great artists and illustrated books by others. These are also considered Scouting related.

Sir Robert Baden-Powell

Birds and Beasts in Africa, Mac Mitlan, 1928 .... 20.00
   Bond, the Baden Powell Story, 1955 .... 8.00
   Boy Scouts Scheme, 1907 .... 35.00
   The Cub Book, 1917 .... 15.00
   Freedman, Scouting With Baden-Powell, 1967 .... 7.00
   Lesson of a Lifetime, Holt, 1933 .... 18.00
   Scouting on Two Continents, by Major Frederick R. Bucknam, 1926 .... 10.00
   The Scouts First Book 1921 .... 20.00
   Sea Scouting and Seamanship for Boys, 1939 .... 20.00
   Steps to Girl Guiding, 1920 .... 15.00
   What Scouts Can Do, 1921 .... 20.00
   Yarns for Boy Scouts, 1909 .... 20.00

Daniel Carter Beard

   American Boys Book of Birds and Brownies of the Woods, Lippincott, 1923
   ...... 15.00
   American Boys Book of Bugs, Butterflies, and Beetles, Lippincott, 1916 15.00
   American Boys Book of Signs, Signals and Symbols, Lippincott, 1918 ... 18.00
   American Boys Book of Wild Animals, Lippincott, 1921 .... 15.00
   American Boys Handybook of Complore and Woodcraft, Lippincott, 1920
   ...... 12.00
   American Boys Handybook, What to Do and How to Do It, Sabners, 1882 15.00
   Animal Book and Campfire Stories, Moffat, 1907 .... 20.00
   Daniel C. Beard, The Man and His Books, 1915 .... 18.00
   Black Wolf Pack, 1922 .... 15.00
   Boat Building and Boating, 1911 .... 10.00
   Boy Heroes of Today, Benver, Warner & Putman, 1932 .... 15.00
   Boy Pioneers Sons of Daniel Boone, 1909 .... 20.00
   Buckskin Book for Buckskin Men and Boys, 1929 .... 25.00
   Dan Beard, Boy Scout, by M.E. Mason 3.00
   Dan Beard, Boy Scout Pioneer, by Jerry Siebert (paperback) 3.00
   Dan Beard Talks to Scouts, Garden City, 1940 .... 20.00
   Do It Yourself, Lippincott, 1925 .... 15.00
   Field and Forest Handybook, New Ideas for Out of Doors, 1906 ...... 12.00
   Hardly a Man is Now Alive, Doubleday, 1939 .... 10.00
   Jack of all Trades, New Ideas for American Boys, 1900 .... 10.00
   Moonlight and Six Feet of Romance, Webster, 1892 .... 8.50
   Outdoor Handybook, American Boy's Book of Sport, 1896 .... 18.00
   Shelters, Shacks and Shantics, 1914 .... 15.00
   The Story of Dan Beard, by Robert N. Webb 5.00
   Twain, Mark, A Connecticut Yankee in King Arthur's Court (editions
   illustrated by Beard) 8.00
   Twain, Mark, Huckleberry Finn (editions illustrated by Beard) 7.50
   Twain, Mark, Pudd'inhead Wilson (editions illustrated by Beard) ... 6.50
   Twain, Mark, Tom Sawyer (editions illustrated by Beard) 7.50
   Twain, Mark, Tom Sawyer Abroad (editions illustrated by Beard) 7.00
   Wisdom of the Woods, Lippincott, 1926 .... 20.00

William "Bill" Hillcourt

Baden-Powell: Two Lives of a Hero, Putnam, 1964 .... 25.00

Bill Hillcourt also wrote the 1st edition Patrol Leaders Handbook, and the 9th
   edition Boy Scout Handbook.

L to R: Mason, Miriam E., Dan Beard, Boy Scout (shown in
library binding) 3.00
Webb, Robert N., The Story of Dan Beard, with dust jacket
...... 5.00
Siebert, Jerry, Dan Beard, Boy Scout Pioneer (soft cover)
...... 3.00

Juliette Low
Choate and Ferris, Juliette Low and the Girl Scouts, 1928 .... 10.00
De Leuw, The Girl Scout Story (paperback) 3.50
Pace, Juliette Low, Girl Scout, 1941 .... 4.50
Schultz and Lawrence, Lady from Savannah, The Life of Julette Low, 1958
...... 10.00

Ernest Thompson Seton
Animal Heroes, Scribners, 1905 .... 10.00
Animals Worth Knowing, Doubleday, 1926 .... 12.50
Arctic Prairies, Scribners, 1911 .... 22.00
Bannertoil, 1922 .... 15.00
Billy, The Dog That Made Good, Hoddes, 1930 .... 15.00
Biography of a Grizzly, Century, 1900 .... 10.00
Biography of a Silver Fox, Century, 1909 .... 10.00
Biography of an Arctic Fox, Appleton Century, 1937 .... 18.00
Cute Coyote and Other Stories, Hodder, 1930 .... 10.00
Ernest Thompson Seton's American by Florida A. Wiley (ed), 1954 .... 10.00
The Forester's Manual, Doubleday, 1912 .... 45.00
Great Historic Animals, 1937 .... 12.50
Johnny Bear, Lobo, and Other Stories, 1935 .... 8.50
Kraz and Johnny Bear, 1902 .... 12.00
Library of Pioneering and Woodcraft (6 volumes), Doubleday, 1925 ...... 45.00
Lives of Game Animals (4 volumes), Doubleday, 1925-1928 .... 150.00
Lives of the Hunted, 1901 .... 8.00
Lobo, Benjo, The Racing Mustang, 1930 .... 10.00

Lobo, Rag, and Vixen, 1899 .... 12.00
Monarch, the Big Bear, 1904 .... 20.00
Preacher of Cedar Mountain, Doubleday, 1917 .... 12.00
Rolf in the Woods, Doubleday, 1911 .... 15.00
Sign Talk, Doubleday, 1918 .... 50.00
The Ten Commandments of the Animal World, 1907 .... 18.00
Trail of the Artist Naturalist, 1940 .... 35.00
The Trail of the Sandhill Stag, 1899 .... 12.00
Two Little Savages, Doubleday, 1916 .... 10.00
Wild Animals at Home, Doubleday, 1913 .... 10.00
Wild Animals I Have Known, 1898 .... 11.00
Woodland Tales, Doubleday, 1921 .... 15.00
Many of Seton's books have been reprinted many times and some have even
been published in paperback form. Values shown are for early editions in
hardbound form. Paperbacks are substantially less.

Julia Seton
Animal Tracks and Hunter Signs, Doubleday, 1958 .... 12.00
By A Thousand Fires, Doubleday, 1967 .... 20.00
Gospel of the Redman, Doubleday, Page and Co., 1936 .... 8.00

James E. West
Making the Most of Yourself, 1941 .... 8.50

CHAPTER 10

This last chapter is intended solely as a reference guide to various useful information to help you, the user of this guide, find specific information to help learn more about items, such as where they are from. What other items may be related to it or from the same area.

ALPHABETICAL LIST OF COUNCILS
BOY SCOUTING

In 1976 the National Council directed that all insignia had to be identified as belonging to the Boy Scouts of America. To do this all insignia made from that date had to have as part of the design either 1, the Scout emblem, 2, Scouting-USA, or 3, Boy Scouts of America, or its initials, BSA.

This requirement was effective in each individual council when its then present stock of insignia was exhausted. This included those patches stockpiled at one of three BSA supply centers. As a result of this new directive each council that presently did not meet the new requirements and all RWS council would issue a new CSP.

There would prove to be exceptions to this assumption. Some councils would re-order independently of National Council and not make the change. This, however, would be the exception.

Chester County would be the first exception and the resultant RWS would have a rolled edge. In doing so Chester County would be the third council to have a rolled edge RWS. The other two were central Connecticut prior to its merger with Quinnipiac; and Orange County prior to its CSP.

As time and events change so does the structure and needs of the local council. As a result many councils merge, are absorbed by another, or even change its name to reflect the group it represents. This constant fluid motion has been present since Scouting's beginning. Here we are concerned only with those councils that have issued a CSP.

MERGED OR NAME CHANGE CSP'S

COUNCIL	DATE
Canal Zone	1979
Central South Carolina	1978
Chautauqua County	1973
Copper	1977
Elk Lick	1973
Grand Valley	1974
Grayback	1974
Kaw	1974
Lebanon County	1970
Lonesome Pine	1979
Olympic Area	1974
Pheasant	1978
Pinellas Area	1978
Pioneer Trails	1973
Red River Valley	1973
Riverside County	1972
Seneca	1975
Susquehanna Valley Area	1974
Timber Trails	1975
Union	1980

Washington Trails		1972	
Wyo-Braska		1974	
Yellowstone Valley		1973	

This list gives you a historical view of some past events in the reorganization of Councils. For the collector it lists some CSP's that may be a bit more difficult to obtain. This does not mean you will not be able to add them to your collection. It simply means that you can't expect to trade a current CSP "one for one" for them. Some are more difficult than others.

Several councils had CSP's that were harder to obtain even before merging. Grand Valley is a prime example. Their first two CSP's were rare before merging with timber trails. Especially difficult was their first issue (dark blue border).

We will continue to discover new shoulder insignia as more and more people become interested in the hobby. As we have more interest more of us will ask questions about older items and material that could possibly have been worn on the shoulder. We should be cautioned, however about early labels on questionable patches. An accepted erroneous label is very difficult to remove. It is better to remove from our collection of CSP's an item that was a pocket patch than to have a pocket patch in our CSP collection. If a patch was in fact a pocket insignia then it should be in a collection of such patches.

OLD REGION CODES
There were 12 regions through 1972. These regions were designated by number.

NEW REGION CODES.
There are now 6 regions with geographic names.
EC - East Central
SC - South Central
NE - Northeast
SE - Southeast
NC - North Central
W - Western

COUNCIL NAME	LOCATION	DATES	LODGE
Abraham Lincoln	Springfield, IL	25	132
Adirondack	Plattsburgh, NY	24	364
Admiral Robert E. Peary	Johnstown, PA	36-69	441
Adobe Walls	Pampa, TX	29	341
Aheka	Passaic, NJ	39-72	359
Akron Area	Akron, OH	21-70	151
Alameda	Alameda, CA	21	379
Alabama-Florida	Dothan, AL	64	224
Alamo Area	San Antonio, TX	25	060
Alapaha Area	Valdosta, GA	60	545
Alaska	Anchorage, AK	46-54	355
Alexander-Hamilton	Union City, NJ	37-67	440
Alfred W. Dater	Glenbrook, CT	39-72	521
Algonquin	Framingham, MA	25	487
Alhtaha	Wayne, NJ	42-72	449
Allegheny	Pittsburgh, PA	43-66	057
Allegheny County West	Pittsburgh, PA	29-42	057
Allegheny Highlands	Mayville, NY	73	165
Allegheny Trails	Pittsburgh, PA	67	057

COUNCIL	LOCATION	DATES	LODGE
Aloha	Honolulu, HI	57	567
Ambraw-Wabash	Decatur, IL	29-53	167
Andrew Jackson	AL	26-29	
Andrew Jackson	Jackson, MS	37	260
Annawon	Taunton, MA	30	245
Anthony Wayne Area	Fort Wayne, IN	25	075
Anthracite	Hazelton, PA	33-69	316
Apache	Miami, AZ	22-34	
Appalachian	Beckley, WV	46-55	416
Appalachian	Bluefield, WV	56	416
Appalachian Trails	Pottsville, PA	41-69	125
Arbuckle Area	Ardmore, OK	46	190
Arrowhead	Memphis, TN	24-27	
Arrowhead	Watertown, SD	34-42	
Arrowhead	Champaign, IL	34	052
Arrowhead Area	San Bernardino, CA	34-72	478
Atlanta Area	Atlanta, GA	21	129
Atlantic Area	Atlantic City, NJ	21	423
Attakapas	Alexandria, LA	22	264
Audubon	Owensboro, KY	51	367
Aurora	Aurora, IL	21-55	106
Baden-Powell	Dryden, NY	75	546
Badger	Fond Du Lac, WI	26-73	061
Baltimore Area	Baltimore, MD	21	012
Battle Creek Area	Battle Creek, MI	21-52	315
Bay Area	Galveston, TX	37	113
Bay Shore	Lynn, MA	37-65	158
Bay Lakes	Menasha, WI	73	061
Bayonne	Bayonne, NJ	21	014
Beaumont	Beaumont, TX	21-41	036
Bergen	Rivers Edge, NJ	69	484
Berkeley-Contra Costa Co.	Berkeley, CA	35-50	
Berkshire	Pittsfield, MA	57-68	507
Bershire County	Pittsfield, MA	23-54	507
Berrien-Cass Area	St. Joseph, MI	29-39	
Bethlehem Area	Bethlehem, PA	21-68	476
Birmingham Area	Birmingham, AL	21	050
Black Beaver	Chickasha, OK	25-27	
Black Beaver	Lawton, OK	34	281
Blackhawk Area	IL	25-27	
Blackhawk Area	Rockford, IL	35	140
Black Hills Area	Rapid City, SD	30	171
Black Warrior	Tuscaloosa, AL	22	481
Blair-Bedford Area	Altoona, PA	30-69	347
Bloomfield-Nutley	Rutherford, NJ	29-34	
Blue Grass	Lexington, KY	29	480
Blue Mountain	Walla Walla, WA	23	336
Blue Ridge	Greenville, SC	34	185
Blue Ridge	Roanoke, VA	53-72	456
Blue Ridge Mountains	Roanoke, VA	72	161
Blue Water	Port Huron, MI	39	180
Boise Area	Boise, ID	21-50	365
Boston	Boston, MA	21	195
Boulder Dam Area	Las Vegas, NV	44	312
Bristol	Bristol, CT	21-66	471

COUNCIL	LOCATION	DATES	LODGE
Bronx	New York City, NY	21-66	004
Bronx	New York City, NY	67	004
Bronx Valley	Mount Vernon, NY	23-58	047
Brooklyn	Brooklyn, NY	21-66	024
Brooklyn	Brooklyn, NY	67	024
Bryce Canyon	Ephraim, UT	24-35	
Buckeye	Massillon, OH	53-58	377
Buckeye	Canton, OH	59	377
Bucks County	Doylestown, PA	27	033
Buckskin	Charlestown, WV	49	475
Bucktail	Du Bois, PA	30	139
Buffalo Area	Buffalo, NY	21-48	159
Buffalo Area	Buffalo, NY	49-66	159
Buffalo Bill (Area)	Davenport, IO	29-66	313
Buffalo Trace	Olney, IL	53-54	167
Buffalo Trace	Evansville, IN	55	422
Buffalo Trail	Midland, TX	23	141
Burlington County	Willingboro, NJ	22	076
Butler-Armstrong	Butler, PA	29-48	168
Buttes Area	Marysville, CA	24	395
Cachalot	New Bedford, MA	35-71	509
Cache Valley	Logan, UT	22	514
Caddo Area	Texarkana, TX	37	232
Cahokia Mound	Granite City, IL	25	126
Calcassieu Area	Lake Charles, LA	30	166
Calumet	Munster, IN	66	110
California Inlabd Empire	Redlands, CA	73	127
Calvin Coolidge	Bellow Falls, VT	37-64	493
Cambridge	Cambridge, MA	21	131
Camden County	W. Collingswood, NJ	21	077
Canadian Valley	Shawnee, OK	27-46	192
Canal Zone	Balboa, CZ	23-59	391
Canal Zone	Balboa, CZ	60-79	391
Cape Cod	Hyannia, MA	25	393
Cape Fear Area	Wilmington, NC	34	331
Capitol Area	Austin, TX	34	099
Cascade Area	Salem, OR	26	259
Catalina	Tucson, AZ	22	494
Cayuga County	Auburn, NY	24	247
Cedar Rapids Area	Cedar Rapids, IO	29-41	
Cedar Valley Area	Austin, MN	29-36	053
Cedar Valley Area	Albert Lea, MN	37-68	053
Central Connecticut	Meriden, CT	29-78	274
Central Florida	Orlando, FL	22	326
Central Georgia	Macon, GA	23	358
Central Indiana	Indianapolis, IN	42-72	
Central Iowa	Marshalltown, IO	25-42	
Central Minnesota	St. Cloud, MN	26	031
Central North Carolina	Albemarle, NC	37	188
Central Ohio	Columbus, OH	30	093
Central Oklahoma	Oklahoma City, OK	30-38	133
Central South Carolina	Columbia, SC	29-78	221
Central South Dakota	Huron, SD	28-42	
Central Union	Fanwood, NJ	21-22	010

COUNCIL	LOCATION	DATES	LODGE
Central Washington Area	Yakima, WA	42-53	301
Central West Virginia	Clarksburg, WV	41	527
Central Wyoming	Casper, WY	34	356
Chamorro	Agana, GM	70-73	565
Charleston Area	Charleston, WV	21-48	
Charter Oak	Hartford, CT	33-72	558
Chatham County	Savannah, GA	23-41	119
Chattahoochee	GA	24-49	204
Chattahoochee	Columbus	64	204
Chattanooga County	Chattanooga, TN	21-43	
Chautauqua County	Mayville, NY	42-73	165
Chautauqua Lake Area	Mayville, NY	34-41	165
Chehaw	Albany, GA	39	353
Cherokee	Burlington, NC	23	163
Cherokee Area	Bartlesville, OK	25	288
Cherokee Area	TN	26-27	
Cherokee Area	Chattanooga, TN	44	293
Chester County	West Chester, PA	21	022
Chicago Area	Chicago, IL	21	007
Chickasaw	Ardmore, OK	30-45	190
Chickasaw	Memphis, In	25	406
Chief Cornplanter	Warren, PA	53	255
Chief Cornstalk	Logan, WV	44	350
Chief Logan	Chillicothe, OH	44	350
Chief Okemos	Lansing, MI	34	374
Chief Paducah	Paducah, KY	25-39	
Chief Seattle	Seattle, WA	54	502
Chief Shabbona	Sycamore, IL	27-30	
Chief Shabbona	St. Charles, IL	34-67	120
Chippewa Valley	Eau Claire, WI	29	337
Chippewa Area	Sault St. Marie, MI	29-44	250
Chisholm Trail	Abilene, TX	26	330
Choctaw Area	LA	23-27	
Choctaw Area	Meridian, MS	35	193
Choctaw Area	McAlester, OK	26-71	320
Choccolocco	Anniston, AL	21	135
Cimmarron Valley Area	Cushing, OK	24-47	283
Cincinnati Area	Cincinnati, OH	21-56	462
Circle Ten	Dallas, TX	29	101
Clark AFB	Angeles City, PI	59-65	538
Clarion & Venango Counties	Oil City, PA	25-41	
Clinton Valley	Pontiac, MI	37	029
Coastal Carolina	Charleston, SC	41	
Coastal Empire	Savannah, GA	42	119
Cochise County	Douglas, AZ	22-63	177
Cogioba	Clarksville, KY	34-48	
Colonel Drake	Oil City, PA	42-72	256
Columbia County	Hudson, NY	29-44	027
Columbiana	Lisbon, OH	53	472
Columbiana County	East Liverpool, OH	26-52	472
Columbia Montour	Bloomsburg, PA	37	018
Columbia Pacific	Portland, OR	66	442
Comanche Trail	Brownwood, TX	34	295
Concho Valley	San Angelo, TX	26	199

COUNCIL	LOCATION	DATES	LODGE
Conquistador	Roswell, NM	53	078
Corn Belt	Bloomington, IL	25-72	063
Cornhusker	Lincoln, NB	29	492
Cornstalk	Logan, WV	53-53	210
Coronado Area	Salina, KS	39	434
Copper Country	Houghton, MI	34-44	
Copper	Safford, AZ	62-77	551
Covered Wagon	Omaha, NB	30-64	445
Crater Lake	Central Point, OR	25	421
Creek Nation Area	Okmulgee, OK	27-56	154
Creve Coeur	Peoria, IL	29-73	191
Crescent Bat Area	Los Angeles, CA	22-72	225
Crossroads of America	Indianapolis, IN	72	021
Cumberland	Middleboro, KY	49-62	435
Cumberland County	Bridgeton, NJ	21-43	
Custaloga	Sharon, PA	69-71	251
Dade County	Miami, FL	21-44	
Dan Beard	Covington, KY	52-54	155
Dan Beard	Cincinnati, OH	57	462
Dan Beard	Scranton, PA	47-61	543
Daniel Boone	KY	24-27	
Daniel Boone	Ashville, NC	25	134
Daniel Boone	Reading, PA	37-69	005
Daniel Webster	Manchester, NH	29	220
Dayton-Miami Valley Area	Dayton, OH	29-48	
Delaware	Muncie, IN	24-72	512
Delaware Valley Area	Easton, PA	33-68	058
Del-Mar-Va	Wilmington, DE	37	020
Delta Area	Clarksdale, MS	25	345
Denver Area	Denver, CO	21	383
Desert Trails	El Centro, CA	60	532
De Soto Area	El Dorado, AR	24	399
Detroit Area	Detroit, MI	21	162
Direct Service	Mexico City, MX	55-67	446
Direct Service	North Brunswick, NJ	67	555
Du Page Area	Wheaton, IL	29	041
Dutchess County	Hyde Park, NY	21	443
Eagle Rock	Montclair, NJ	31-75	515
East Boroughs	Wilkinsburg, PA	21-73	067
East Carolina	Kinston, NC	34	117
East Mississippi	West Point, MS	25-36	
East Texas Area	Tyler, TX	34	072
East Valley Area	Munhall, PA	73	067
Eastern Arkansas Area	Jonesboro, AR	35	413
Eastern Connecticut	Norwich, CT	29-71	297
Eastern New Mexico Area	Roswell NM	25-52	078
Eastern Oklahoma	Muskogee, OK	49	328
Egyptian	Carbondale, IL	29-30	
Egyptian	Herrin, IL	41	240
Elgin Area	Elgin, IL	21-57	279
Elk Lick	Bradford, PA	47-73	455
Elmira Area	Elmira, NY	21-46	
Erie County	Buffalo, NY	22-48	
Erie County	Erie, PA	36-43	046

COUNCIL	LOCATION	DATES	LODGE
Essex	Newark, NJ	75	515
Ethan Allen	Rutland, VT	65-72	398
Evangeline	Lafayette, LA	24	563
Evanston	Evanston, IL	21-68	248
Evanston North Shore	Glenco, IL	69-70	040
Evergreen	Everett, WA	41	305
Fall River	Fall River, MA	21-45	124
Fairfield	Norwalk, CT	73	313
Far East	Tokyo, JA	61	498
Fellsland	Winchester, MA	33-58	261
Fenimore Cooper County	White Plains, NY	22-50	246
Finger Lakes	Geneva, NY	24	417
Firelands Area	Sandusky, OH	25	205
Fitchburg Area	Fitchburg, MA	21-64	319
Flint River	Griffin, GA	30	324
Forest Lakes	Scranton, PA	62	542
Fort Armstrong Area	Rock Island, IL	46-58	504
Fort Hamilton	Hamilton, OH	35-58	306
Fort Orange	Albany, NY	24-62	181
Fort Orange-Uncle Sam	Loudonville, NY	63-70	181
Fort Simcoe	Yakima, WA	54	301
Fort Stanwix	Rome, NY	29-68	500
Fort Steuben Area	Steubenville, OH	29	289
Fort Worth Area	Fort Worth, TX	27-48	
Forty Niner	Stockton, CA	57	342
Four Lakes	Madison, WI	29	146
Four Rivers	Paducah, KY	47	499
Fox River Valley	Elgin, IL	58-72	279
Fox Valley	St. Charles, IL	26-30	
French Creek	Erie, PA	72	046
Fruit Belt Area	Kalamazoo, MI	37-72	203
Fulton County	Gloversville, NY	23-36	
Gamehaven	Rochester, MN	25	026
Gateway Area	La Crosse, WI	25	381
General Greene	Greensboro, NC	47	070
General Herkimer	Herkimer, NY	35	294
General Sullivan	Towanda, NY	27	030
Genesee	Batavia, NY	26	339
George H. Lanier	West Point, GA	50	273
George Rogers Clark	New Albany, IN	27	065
George Washington	Trenton, NJ	37	002
Georgia-Alabama	Columbus, GA	34-63	204
Georgia-Carolina	Augusta, GA	41	087
Glouster-Salem	Woodstown, NJ	24-67	411
Gitche Gumee	Superior, WI	30-59	174
Golden Empire	Sacramento, CA	37	354
Grand Canyon	Flagstaff, AZ	22-27	
Grand Canyon	Flagstaff, AZ	44	503
Governor Clinton	Loudonville, NY	71	181
Grand Valley	Grand Rapids, MI	37-75	079
Grayback	Redlands, CA	52-74	380
Great Plains Area	Minot, ND	29-73	183
Great Rivers	Columbia, MO	61	426

COUNCIL	LOCATION	DATES	LODGE
Great Salt Lake	Salt Lake City, UT	61	520
Great Salt Plains	Enid, OK	29	213
Great Smokey Mountain	Knoxville, IN	45	230
Great Southwest Area	Albuquerque, NM	77	066
Great Trail	Akron, OH	71	151
Great Trails	Dalton, MA	69	507
Great Western	Van Nuys, CA	72	566
Greater Cleveland	Cleveland, OH	29	017
Greater Lowell	Lowell, MA	66	451
Greater Lowell Area	Lowell, MA	29-54	451
Greater New York	New York City, NY	52-66	
Greater New York	New York City, NY	52-66	
Greater New York	New York City, NY	67	
Greater Niagra Frontier	Buffalo, NY	67	159
Green Mountain	Rutland, VT	29-64	398
Green Mountain	Essex Junction, VT	73	351
Greensboro Area	Greensboro, NC	21-46	070
Greenwich	Greenwich, CT	22	427
Guam	Agana, GM	51-54	
Gulf Coast	Corpus Christi, TX	29	307
Gulf Coast	Pensacola, FL	39	
Gulf Ridge	Tampa, FL	39	085
Gulf Stream	West Palm Beach, FL.	37	237
Hampden County	Springfield, MA	23-60	083
Hampshire County	Northampton, MA	22-29	
Hampshire-Franklin	Northampton, MA	30-68	556
Harding Area	Marion, OH	26	121
Harrisonburg Area	Harrisonburg, PA	21-47	011
Harrison Trail	Lafayette, IN	41-73	173
Hawk Mountain	Reading PA	70	005
Hawkeye Area	Cedar Rapids, IO	52	467
Headwaters Area	Hibbing, MN	29	196
Heart of America	Kansas City, KS	74	147
Heart O'Texas	Waco, TX	29	327
Hendrick Hudson	Ossining, NY	22-50	086
Herkimer County	Herkimer, NY	21-34	
Hiawatha	Syracuse, NY	69	410
Hiawatha Area	Marquette, MI	34-44	156
Hiawathaland	Marquette, MI	45	156
Holyoke Area	Holyoke, MA	23-48	277
Homestead District	Munhall, PA	21-51	130
Honolulu	Honolulu, HI	21-39	
Hoosier Hills Area	Du Pont, IN	29-73	290
Hoosier Trails	Bloomington, IN	73	212
Housatonic	Denby, CT	22	553
Hudson	Jersey City, NJ	37-67	037
Hudson Delaware	Middleton, NY	58	064
Hudson-Hamilton	Union City, NJ	68	037
Huroquois	Wheeling, NJ	25-65	323
Hutchison River	New Rochelle, NY	62-73	015
Idaho Panhandle	Coeur D'Alene, ID	29	311
Illowa	Bettendorf, IO	67	170
Imprial Yuma Area	El Centro, CA	29-59	532
Indian Nations	Tulsa, OK	57	138

COUNCIL	LOCATION	DATES	LODGE
Indian Trails	Janesville, WI	29-65	302
Indian Trails	Norwich, CT	71	010
Indian Waters	Columbia, SC	78	221
Indianapolis & Cent. Indiana	Indianapolis, IN	36-41	
Indianhead	St. Paul, MN	55	257
Inland Empire	Spokane, WA	34	415
Iowa City	Iowa City, IO	21-39	
Iowa River Valley	Iowa City, IO	41-51	344
Iron Range Area	Iron Mountain, MI	26-30	198
Iron Range	Virginia, MN	29-31	
Iroquois	Rome, NY	69	034
Istrouma Area	Baton Rouge, LA	24	479
Jayhawk Area	Topeka, KA	29	429
Jefferson Lewis	Watertown, NY	34	357
Jim Bridger	Rock Springs, WY	46-47	
Jim Bridger	Rock Springs, WY	48	529
Johnny Appleseed Area	Mansfield, OH	26	513
Juniata Valley	Lewiston, PA	29	103
Kalamazoo Fruitland	Kalamazoo, MI	29-35	
Kansas City Area	Kansas City, MO	21-74	
Kanza	Hutchinson, KS	46	321
Kaskaskia	Belleville, IL	37-64	115
Katahdin Area	Bangor, ME	29	211
Kaw	Kansas City, KS	29-74	147
Kedeka	Aurora, IL	56-67	106
Keemoshabee	New Britain, CT	53-66	234
Kenosha County	Kenosha, WI	29-61	153
Kenosha	Kenosha, WI	61-72	153
Kern County	Bakersfield, CA	22-65	303
Kettle-Moraine	Sheboygan, WI	35-73	501
Keystone Area	Harrisburg, PA	48	011
Kewanee Area	Kewanee, IL	39	045
Kickapoo Area	Vicksburg, MS	27-37	
Kikthawenund	Anderson, IN	35-72	222
Kilauea	Hilo, HI	41-72	454
Kit Carson	Albuquerque, NM	27-34	
Kit Carson	Albuquerque, NM	55-76	066
Kno-Co-Ho-Tus	Chshocton, OH	29-46	
Knoxville	Knoxville, TN	34-42	
Kootaga Area	Parkersburg, WV	33	201
Lake Agassiz	Grand Forks, ND	33-73	371
Lake Bonneville	Roy, UT	51	561
Lake Huron Area	Auburn, MI	72	089
Lake of the Ozarks	Jefferson City, MO	37-72	216
Lake Shore	Dunkirk, NY	29-41	187
Lake Superior	Duluth, MN	60	526
Lancaster County	Lancaster, PA	24-70	519
Lancaster-Lebanon	Lebanon, PA	71	039
Land O'Lakes	Jackson, MI	37	206
Last Frontier	Oklahoma City, OK	39	133
Lawrence County	New Castle, PA	22-73	419
Lebanon County	Lebanon, PA	25-70	039
Lehigh (County)	Allentown, PA	30-68	044
Lewis-Clark	Lewiston, ID	46	400

COUNCIL	LOCATION	DATES	LODGE
Lewiston Trail	Lockport, NY	37	409
Licking County	Newark, OH	22	420
Lincoln Trails	Decatur, IL	39	167
Llano Estracado	Amarillo, TX	41	486
Logan Boone Mongo Area	Logan, WV	35-52	210
Lone Star Area	Paris, TX	29-54	428
Lone Tree	Haverville, MA	26	539
Lonesome Pine	Pikeville, KY	34-79	241
Long Beach Area	Long Beach, CA	21	
Long Rivers	Hartford, CT	73	
Long Rivers	Hartford, CT	73	059
Long Trail	Burlington, VT	33-73	351
Longhorn	Fort Worth, TX	49	489
Longs Peak	Greeley, CO	29	464
Louisville Area	Louisville, KY	21-53	123
Los Angeles Area	Los Angeles, CA	21	252
Louis Agassiz Fuertes	Ithaca, NY	29-75	456
Lower Rio Grande Valley	Mercedes, TX	27-46	272
Madison County	Oneida, NY	23-68	034
Mahoning Valley	Youngstown, OH	27	396
Mammoth Cave	Bowling Green, KY	49-51	
Mammoth Cave	Bowling Green, KY	49-51	405
Manhattan	New York City, NY	21-66	082
Manhattan	New York City, NY	67	082
Marin (County)	San Rafael, CA	23	533
Mascoutah Area	Jacksonville, IL	26-35	
Mason Dixon	Hagerstown, MD	56	317
Massasoit	Fall River, MA	46-72	
Massillon	Massillon, OH	33-52	
Mattatuck	Waterbury, CT	35-72	217
Maui County	Wailuku, HI	41	554
Mauwehu	Ridgefield, CT	52-72	389
McKeesport & Af'd Territory	McKeesport, PA	39-50	
McKean-Potter-Cameron	Bradford, PA	37-46	
McKinley Area	Canton, OH	34-58	377
Mecklenburg County	Charlotte, NC	42	459
Mercer County	Farrel, PA	29-68	251
Meshingomesia	Marion, IN	29-73	269
Mesquakie Area	Clinton, IO	37-58	376
Miami Valley	Dayton, OH	49	495
Mid Fairfield	Norwalk, CT	35-51	
Mid Fairfield	Norwalk, CT	35-51	389
Mid-Iowa	Des Moines, IO	70	450
Mid Valley	Peckville, PA	33-61	542
Mid-America	Omaha, NB	65	097
Middle Tennessee	Nashville, TN	49	111
Middlesex	Edison, NJ	29-68	287
Middlesex County	Middletown, CT	24-72	059
Midnight Sun	Fairbanks, AK	60	549
Milwaukee County	Milwaukee, WI	21	231
Mineral Area	Bonne Terree, MO	30-39	
Minneapolis Area	Minneapolis, MN	21-22	016
Minneapolis Area	Minneapolis, MN	29-51	016
Minnesota Valley Area	Mankato, MN	27-68	069

COUNCIL	LOCATION	DATES	LODGE
Minsi Trails	Lehigh Valley, PA	69	044
Minuteman	Stoneham, MA	59	261
Minuteman	MA	29-30	
Mishawaka	Mishawaka, IN	22-51	314
Mission	Santa Barbara, CA	29	090
Mississippi Valley	East St. Louis, IL	37-64	081
Missiuri Kansas	Joplin, MO	29-35	
Missouri Valley	Bismark, ND	29-73	052
Mobile Area	Mobile, AL	21	322
Moby Dick	New Bedford, MA	72	529
Modoc	Klamath Falls, OR	37	437
Mohegan	Worchester, MA	55	525
Mohican	Glens Falls, NY	27	048
Mo-Kan	Joplin, MO	36	091
Moline Area	Moline, IL	21-58	170
Monadnock	Gardner, MA	24	329
Monmouth	Oakhurst, NJ	21	071
Monongahela Valley	Munhall, PA	52-71	130
Montana	Great Falls, MT	74	300
Moraine Trails	Butler, PA	73	168
Morris-Sussex	Dover, NJ	24	168
Mon-Yough	Munhall, PA	71-72	130
Montgomery (County)	Montgomery, AL	21-46	179
Montgomery County	Amsterdam, NY	30-35	
Monterey Bay Area	Salinas, CA	34	531
Mound Builders Area	Middletown, OH	33	145
Mount Baker	Bellingham, WA	29	325
Mount Diablo	Walnut Creek, CA	51	468
Mount Lassen Area	Chico, CA	24	485
Mount Ranier	Tacoma, WA	48	348
Mount Tom	Holyoke, MA	49-59	277
Mount Whitney Area	Visalia, CA	29	102
Mountaineer Area	Fairmount, WV	29	550
Mountainview	Boise, ID	51-67	365
Muscadawın	Flint, MI	27-35	365
Muskegon			
Muskingum Valley	Muskegon, MI	21-43	
Muskogee	Zanesville, OH	57	424
Narrangansett	Muskogee, OK	21-48	328
Nashua Valley	Providence, RI	30	534
Nashville Area	Lancaster, MA	65	309
Nassau County	Nashville, TN	21-48	111
Nathan Hale	Roslyn, NY	21	412
National Capitol Area	New Britain, CT	67-72	234
National Trail	Washington, DC	37	470
Nebraska Panhandle Area	Wheeling, WV	66	323
Nemaculin Trails	Scottsbluff, WV	29-35	
Netseo Trails	Washington, PA	64-66	242
Nevada Area	Paris, TX	55	428
New Bedford & Fairhaven	Reno, NV	29	346
New Britain Area	New Bedford, MA	21-34	
New Orleans Area	New Britain, CT	21-52	234
Niagara Falls Area	Metairie, LA	21	397
	Niagara Falls, NY	21-43	

COUNCIL	LOCATION	DATES	LODGE
Niagara Frontier	Niagara Falls, NY	44-66	284
Nicolet Area	Green Bay, WI	35-73	194
North Bay	Peabody, MA	66	505
North Bergen (County)	Hackensack, NJ	21-38	
North Central Montana	Great Falls, MT	29-73	300
North Central Washington	Wenatche, WA	29	335
North Essex	Lawrence, MA	25	490
North Florida	Jacksonville, FL	39	200
North Iowa	Mason City, IO	29-38	
North Orange	Anaheim, CA	66-73	430
North Shore	Salem, MA	25-65	505
North Shore Area	Highland Park, IL	26-68	040
North Star	Duluth, MN	37-59	526
Northeast Georgia	Athens, GA	22-30	
Northeast Georgia	Athens, GA	35	243
Northeast Ohio	Painsville, OH	29	114
Northeast Illinois	Glencoe, IL	71	040
Northeast Iowa	Dubuque, IO	35	074
Northern Arizona	Prescott, AZ	29-34	
Northern Indiana	South Bend, IN	73	573
Northern Kentucky	Newport, KY	29-51	155
Northern Lights	Fargo, ND	74	027
Northern Litchfield County	Torrington, CT	29-47	
Northern New Mexico	Albuquerque, NM	35-54	066
Northern Oklahoma	Ponca City, OK	29-30	
Northern Oklahoma	Ponca City, OK	37-47	148
Northern Orange County	Anaheim, CA	46-65	430
Northwest Georgia	Rome, GA	34	318
Northwest Suburban	Arlington Heights, IL	26	175
Northwest Texas	Wichita Falls, TX	37	035
Norwela Area	Shreveport, LA	23	149
Norumbega	Waban, MA	21	414
Nottawa Trails	Battle Creek, MI	53-72	315
Oakland Area	Oakland, CA	21-63	375
Oakland	Pontiac, MI	29-36	
Oak Plain	Waukegan, IL	42-72	215
Occoneechee	Raleigh, NC	29	104
Ocean County	Toms River, NJ	41	535
Ogden Area	Ogden, UT	34-50	
Okaw Valley	Belleville, IL	65	081
Okefenokee Area	Waycross, GA	26	229
Old Baldy (Area)	Claremont, CA	22	098
Old Colony	East Walpole, MA	21-68	164
Old Colony	Brockton, MA	69	164
Old Dominion Area	Suffolk, VA	29	483
Old Hickory	Winston-Salem, NC	42	118
Old Hickory Area	Bogalusa, LA	24-30	
Old Kentucky Home	Louisville, KY	54	
Olympic Area	Bremerton, WA	56-74	530
Onandaga	Syracuse, NY	41-68	516
Onandaga Cortland	Syracuse, NY	34-39	
Onandaga County	Syracuse, NY	21-30	
Orange County	Santa Ana, CA	73	013
Orange County	Santa Ana, CA	21-43	

COUNCIL	LOCATION	DATES	LODGE
Orange County	Middletown, NY	22-30	
Orange County	Port Arthur, TX	21-26	
Orange Empire (Area)	Santa Ana, CA	44-72	298
Orange Mountain	Orange, NJ	21-30	
Orange Mountain	Orange, NJ	49-75	362
Orange-Sullivan	Middletown, NY	34-57	064
Oranges-Maplewood Area	Orange, NJ	34-48	362
Oregon Trail	Eugene, OR	44	253
Ore-Ida	Boise, ID	35	266
Oregon-Idaho	Nampa, ID	29-34	
Oswego County	Oswego, NY	27-68	410
Otetiana	Rochester, NY	43	099
Otschodela	Oneonta, NY	27	402
Ottawa-Allegan	Holland, MI	29-48	
Ouachita Area	Hot Springs, AR	26	366
Ouachita Valley	Monroe, LA	25	254
Overland Trails	Grand Island, NB	54	517
Ozarks	Springfield, MO	41-65	042
Ozarks Empire Area	Springfield, MO	41-65	042
Palmetto Area	Spartanburg, SC	35	270
Panama Canal	Balboa, CZ	79	391
Pasadena-San Gabriel Valley	Pasadena, CA	29-50	488
Passaic Valley	Wayne, NJ	73	359
Patterson Area	Patterson, NJ	21-41	449
Paul Bunyan	Midland, MI	51-72	469
Pee Dee Area	Florence, SC	29	116
Peninsula	Newport News, VA	29	463
Penn Mountains	Plymouth, PA	70	223
Penn's Woods	Winber, PA	70	275
Pequot	New London, CT	35-71	388
Pere Marquette Area	Ludington, MI	26-34	
Petaluma Section	Petaluma, CA	21-43	
Phesant	Huron, SD	43-78	460
Philadelphia	Philadelphia, PA	21	001
Philippine Islands	Manila, PI	24-37	
Piankeshaw	Danville, IL	26	055
Piasa Bird	Wood River, IL	30	094
Piedmont	Piedmont, CA	21	466
Piedmont	Gastonia, NC	24	560
Piedmont Area	Lynchburg, VA	33-72	161
Pikes Peak	Colorado Springs, CO	25	
Pine Burr Area	Hattiesburg, MS	37	404
Pine Tree	Portland, ME	33	271
Pine Tree	ME	25-29	
Pine Tree Area	Marshall, TX	29-30	
Pinellas Area	Seminole, FL	35-78	340
Pioneer Trails	Elkhart, IN	35-72	142
Pioneer Trails	Butler, PA	49-73	168
Pioneer Valley	West Springfield, MA	61	083
Pokagon	Hammond, IN	37-43	110
Pokagon Trails	Hammond, IN	44-65	110

COUNCIL	LOCATION	DATES	LODGE
Pomeraug	Bridgeport, CT	37-72	408
Pontotoc County	ADA, OK	21-45	
Pony Express	St. Joseph, MO	34	
Portage Trails	Ann Arbor, MI	51-73	088
Portland Area	Portland, OR	21-65	442
Potawatomi Area	Chicago Heights, IL	25-30	
Potawatomi Area	Waukesha, WI	34	280
Potawattomi Trails	Harvey, IL	38-44	122
Pottawatomie Area	Shawnee, OK	22-26	
Pottawattomi	Michigan City, IN	26-72	452
Potomac	Cumberland, MD	37	540
Prairie	Galesburg, IL	41	038
Prairie Gold Area	Sioux City, IO	19	438
Puerto Rico	San Juan, PR	31-51	506
Puerto Rico	San Juan, PR	52-60	506
Puerto Rico	Rio Piedras, PR	65	506
Puerto Rico	San Juan, PR	61-64	506
Pushmataha Area	Columbus, MS	37	169
Put-Hat-Sen Area	Findlay, OH	30	382
Quannapowitt	Malden, MA	33-58	447
Quapaw Area	Little Rock, AR	27	160
Queens	New York City, NY	21-66	049
Queens	New York City, NY	67	049
Quincy	Quincy, MA	21-65	370
Quinnipiac	Hamden, CT	35	369
Quivira	Wichita, KS	41	458
Racine County	Racine, WI	29-72	524
Rainbow	Morris, IL	26	197
Raritan	Pert Amboy, NJ	27-68	009
Red Jacket	Brockport, NY	34-42	
Red River	Dennison, TX	48	209
Red River Valley	Fargo, ND	25-73	176
Redlands Area	Redlands, CCA	45-51	380
Redwood Area	Eureka, CA	23	262
Richmond Area	Richmond, VA	21-23	003
Richmond Area	Richmond, VA	27-41	003
Ridgewood & Glen Rock	Glen Rock, NJ	22	286
Rio Grande Area	Albuquerque, NM	26-34	
Rio Grande	Harlingen, TX	47	272
Rip Van Winkle	Kingston, NY	50	028
Riverside (County)	Riverside, CA	21-72	127
Roanoke Area	Roanoke, VA	21-52	456
Robert E. Lee	Petersberg, VA	26-30	
Robert E. Lee	Richmond, VA	53	003
Robert E. Lee-Virginia	Richmond, VA	42-52	003
Robert Treat	Newark, NJ	34-75	178
Rochester Area	Rochester, NY	21-42	095
Rockland County	Stony Point, NY	24	444
Rock Island Area	Rock Island, IL	21-45	
Rocky Mountain	Peublo, CO	29	536
Roosevelt	Phoenix, AZ	24-61	432
Sabine Area	Port Arthur, TX	29-69	062
Sac-Fox	Moline, IL	59-66	170

COUNCIL	LOCATION	DATES	LODGE
Sachem	Lexington, MA	26-58	496
Sagamore	Logansport, IN	73	173
Saginaw Bay Area	Saginaw, MI	61-71	089
Saint Clair Area	Port Huron, MI	29-38	
Saint Joseph Valley	South Bend, IN	30-51	182
Saint Lawrence	Canton, NY	39	461
Saint Lawrence County	Canton, NY	22-38	
Saint Louis Area	St. Louis, MO	21	051
Saint Paul Area	St. Paul, MN	21-24	
Saint Paul Area	St. Paul, MN	29-54	257
Salt Lake City Area	Salt Lake City, UT	21-50	
Samoset (Area)	Wausaw, WI	7A	096
Sam Houston Area	Houston, TX	37	137
San Diego County	San Diego, CA	21	436
San Fernando Valley	Van Nuys, CA	21	228
San Frnacisco Area	San Francisco, CA	21-65	282
San Francisco Bay Area	Oakland, CA	65	282
San Gabriel Valley	Pasadena, CA	51	488
San Joaquin-Calveras	Stockton, CA	29-56	342
San Mateo County (Area)	San Mateo, CA	34	528
Santa Clara (County)	San Jose, CA	35	439
Santa Fe Trail	Garden City, KS	46	372
Santa Lucia Area	San Luis Obispo	39	304
Saratoga County	Ballston Spa, NY	24	268
Sargeant Floyd Area	Sioux City, IO	39-72	474
Saukee	Quincy, IL	35	136
Sauk Trails	Gary, IN	41-65	189
Scenic Trails	Traverse City, MI	39	152
Schenectady	Schenectady, NY	21	019
Scioto Area	Portsmouth, OH	33	109
Scranton Area	Scranton, PA	21-46	
Seattle Area	Seattle, WA	21-53	
Sekan Area	Independence, KS	26-29	
Sekan Area	Independ, KS	37-71	
Seneca	Olean, NY	29-75	547
Sequoia	Fresno, CA	25	548
Sequoyah	Johnson City, TN	30	184
Shawnee	Lima, OH	26	238
Shenandoah	Winchester, VA	29	276
Sherman Area	Sherman, TX	34-65	056
Silverado Area	Vallejo, CA	23	263
Silver Bow	Butte, MT	27-43	
Sinnissippi	Beloit, WI	66	226
Sioux	Sioux Falls, SD	29	105
Sir William Johnson	Gloversville, NY	37	418
Siwanoy (County)	New Rochelle, NY	22-57	015
Siwanoy-Bronx Valley	New Rochelle, NY	58-61	015
Snake River Area	Twin Falls, ID	24	363
Sonoma-Mendocino Area	Petaluma, CA	44	537
South Central Minnesota	Fairbault, MN	29-45	144
South Florida	Miami, FL	45	265
South Jersey	Bridgeton, NJ	44-66	107
South Plains (Area)	Lubbock, TX	25	150

COUNCIL	LOCATION	DATES	LODGE
Southeast Alabama	Dothan, AL	35-63	224
Southeast Alaska (Area)	Juneau, AK	56	523
Southeast Iowa Area	Burlington, IO	30-35	
Southeast Kansas Area	Independence, KS	30-35	
Southeast Missouri	Cape Girardeau, MO	30	100
Southeast Wisconsin	Racine, WI	72	008
Southeast Ohio	Chillicothe, OH	33-42	
Southern Indiana Area	Evansville, IN	34-54	422
Southern Iowa	Ottumwa, IO	29-69	453
Southern Minnesota Area	Albert Lea, MN	29-36	053
Southern New Jersey	Vineland, NJ	67	107
Southern Sierra	Bakersfield, CA	66	303
Southern West Virginia Area	Bluefield, WV	29-55	416
Southwest Florida	Fort Myers, FL	67	564
Southwest Iowa	Council Bluffs, IO	35-64	097
Southwest Kansas Area	Hutchinson, KS	29-45	
Southwest Michigan	Kalamazoo, MI	73	373
Southwestern Michigan	St. Joseph, MI	41-73	373
Squanto	Brockton, MA	37-68	518
Stanford Area	Palo Alto, CA	41	207
Starved Rock Area	La Salle, IL	26-73	143
State Line Area	Beloit, WI	35-65	226
Staten Island	New York City, NY	29-65	112
Staten Island	New York City, NY	67	112
Steuben Area	Bath, NY	34	186
Steuben County	Bath, NY	22-30	
Stonewall Jackson	Staunton, VA	27	258
Suffolk County	Medford, NY	21	360
Sullivan Trails	Elmira, NY	47	394
Summer Trails	Bay City, MI	27-60	214
Sunny Land	Sarasota, FL	26	552
Susquehanna	Williamsport, PA	74	343
Susquehanna Valley Area	Sunbury, PA	27-74	343
Susquenango	Binghamton, NY	25	172
Suqanee River Area	Tallahassee, FL	25	239
Tacoma Area	Tacoma, WA	27-47	348
Tahoe Area	Auburn, CA	24-69	511
Tall Corn Area	Des Moines, IO	30-34	
Tall Corn Area	Des Moines, IO	34-69	450
Tall Pine	Flint, MI	37	218
Tamarack	Rutherford, NJ	35	084
Tecumseh	Springfield, OH	29	292
Tendoy Area	Pocatello, ID	34	407
Tennessee Valley	Huntsville, AL	24	310
Teton Peaks	Idaho Falls	25	544
Texoma Valley	Sherman, TX	66	056
Thatcher Woods Area	Oak Park, IL	41	334
Theodore Roosevelt	Phoenix, AZ	62	432
Three G	Safford, AZ	45-61	551
Three Rivers	Logansport, IN	37-73	425
Three Rivers	Beaumont, TX	70	578
Tidewater	Norfolk, VA	35	349
Timber Trails	Timber Trails, MI	44-75	401
Timpanogas	Provo, UT	22-35	

COUNCIL	LOCATION	DATES	LODGE
Tioughnioga	Cortland, NY	41-75	
Tippecanoe	Lafayette, IN	35-39	173
Toledo Area	Toledo, OH	29	522
Tomahawk	Coshocton, OH	48-56	448
Tom Sawyer Area	Hannibal, MO	29-35	
Transatlantic	Heidelberg, GR	59	482
Trinity-Neches	Beaumont, TX	42-69	036
Tri-State Area	Huntington, WV	35	457
Tri-Trails	North Platee, NB	54	510
Tri-Valley	South Bend, IN	52-72	182
Troy Area	Troy, NY	46	267
Trumbull County	Warren, OH	23-47	
Tukabatchee	Montgomery, AL	47	179
Tulsa (County) Area	Tulsa, OK	21-56	133
Tumwater Area	Olympia, WA	26	392
Tunxis	Torrington, CT	48-72	491
Tuscarora	Goldsboro, NC	23	296
Twin City	East Chicago, IN	25-69	352
Twin Harbors Area	Hoquiam, WA	30	285
Twin Lakes	Oshkosh, WI	35-73	244
Twin Valley	Mankato, MN	69	053
Two Rivers	St. Charles, IL	68	106
Ulster County	Kingston, NY	21-30	028
Ulster-Greene	Kingston, NY	34-49	028
Uncle Sam	Troy, NY	47-62	267
Union	Elizabeth, NJ	29	431
Upper Cumberland Area	Middleboro, KY	29-48	431
Upper Mohawk	Utica, NY	37	465
U.S. Grant (Area)	Freeport, IL	27-73	227
Utah National Parks	High Point, NC	23	208
Valley	Appleton, WI	25-73	233
Valley Forge	Valley Forge, PA	36	043
Valley Trails	Saginaw, MI	37-61	089
Ventura County	Camarillo, CA	21	291
Verdugo Hills	Glendale, CA	22	249
Vigilante	Butte, MT	44-73	299
Viking	Minneapolis, MN	52	016
Virgin Islands	St. Thomas	65	562
W.D. Boyce	Peoria, IL	73	023
Wabash Valley	Terre Haute, IN	34	128
Wachusett	Leominster, MA	21-64	309
Walker-Lamar	Jasper, AL		
Wallamet	Eugene, OR	34-43	
Wapsipinicon	Waterloo, IO	29-70	108
Warren County	Warren, PA	21-52	255
Washington Area	Hagerstown, MD	41-54	317
Washington County	MD	27-39	
Washington-Greene Counties	Washington, PA	30-63	242
Washington-Irving	White Plains	51-73	246
Washington-Trails	Erie, PA	44-72	046
Wastenaw-Livingston	Ann Arbor, MI	35-50	088
Watchung Area	Plainfield, NJ	26	068
Maubeek Area	Cedar Rapids, IO	42-51	

COUNCIL	LOCATION	DATES	LODGE
Waubonsie Boyer Area	Council Bluffs, IO	26-34	
Waumegesako	Manitowoc, WI	41-73	073
West Branch	Williamsport, PA	35-74	384
West Central Florida	Seminole, FL	78	340
West Georgia	La Grange, GA	46-63	333
West Michigan Shores	Grand Rapids, MI	75	266
West Suburban	La Grange, IL	21	157
West Tennessee Area	Jackson, TN	24-30	
West Tennessee Area	Jackson, TN	41	235
Westark Area	Fort Smith, AR	6	559
Westchester-Putnam	White Plains, NY	74	015
Western Alaska	Anchorage, AK	55	355
Western Colorado	Grand Junction, CO	42	541
Western Kentucky Area	Owensboro, KY	29-50	367
Western Montana	Missoula, MT	24-73	361
Western Reserve	Warren, OH	48	368
Westmoreland-Fayette	Greensburg, PA	37	006
White River	Bloomington, IN	27-73	212
Whitewater Valley	Hagerstown, IN	35-72	308
Wigwam	Galesburg, IL	34-39	
William Penn	Indiana, PA	33-69	275
Will Rogers	Ponca City, OK	48	148
Windham-Windsor (Counties)	Bellows Falls, VT	26-35	
Winnebago	Waterloo, IO	39	108
Winston-Salem Area	Winston-Salem, NC	21-41	118
Wolverine	Dundee, MI	25-73	332
Wolverine	Ann Arbor, MI	73	088
Worchester Area	Worchester, MA	21-54	
Wyo-Braska	Scottsbluff, NB	37-74	403
Wyoming Valley	Kingston, PA	25-69	223
Yakima Valley Area	Yakima, WA	25-41	
Yellowstone Valley	Billings, MT	29-73	390
Yocona Area	Tupelo, MS	26	202
Yonkers	Yonkers, NY	21-54	032
Yohogonia	McKeesport, PA	51-70	497
York-Adams (Area)	York, PA	33	386
York County	North Berwick, ME	27-35	
Yosemite Area	Modesto, CA	37	378
Yucca	El Paso, TX	37	378
Zane Trace Area	Zanesville, OH	29-56	424

ALPHABETIC LISTING OF ORDER OF THE ARROW LODGES
WITH LODGE NUMBERS

A

399	ApBooik-Paa-Gun
376	A-Me-Qua
380	A-Tsa
237	Aal-Pa-Tah
393	Abake Mi-Sa-Na-Ke
393	Abake Mi-Sa-Na-Ki
223	Acahela
427	Achewon Netopalis
282	Achewon Nimat
565	Achsin
037	Achtu
135	Achunanchi
422	Acorn
357	Adirondack
156	Ag-Im
257	Agaming
509	Agawam
477	Ah Wa Ge
058	Ah-Pace
213	Ah-Ska
139	Ah'Tic
359	Aheka
540	Ahtuhquog
430	Ahwahnee
473	Aiaouez
060	Aina Topa Hutsi
033	Ajapeu
351	Ajapeu
210	Ajudimo
232	Akela Wahinapay
269	Akonequa
179	Alabama
545	Alapaha
179	Alibamu
455	Allegewi
055	Allemakewink
083	Allogagan
088	Allohak
542	Amad'ahi
441	Amadahi
470	Amangamek-Wipit
390	Amangi Mos
470	Amanquemack
505	Amiskwi
339	Amo'Chk
424	Amochol
067	Anicus
100	Anpetu-We
078	Antelope
410	Aola

246	Apachedotte
107	Apatukwe
277	Apinakwi Pita
189	Aposa Achomawi
300	Apoxky Aio
359	Aquaninonocke
112	Aquehongian
481	Aracoma
562	Arawak
369	Arcoon
323	Arrowhead
436	Ashie
193	Ashwanchi Kinta
563	Atchafalaya
264	Attakapas
185	Atta Kulla Kulla
477	Aw Wa Ge
061	Awase

B

538	Baluga
313	Bison
281	Black Beaver
467	Black Crescent
482	Black Eagle
023	Blackhawk
094	Blackhawk
210	Blaknik
349	Blue Heron
026	Blue Ox
453	Bo Qui
087	Bob-White
381	Braves of Decorah
129	Broadwinger Hawk
527	Buckongehannon
412	Buckskin

C

537	Cabrosha
149	Caddo
126	Cahokia
127	Cahuilla
166	Calcasieu
219	Calusa
511	Canaku
090	Canalino
373	Carcajou
115	Cascasquia
459	Catawba
097	Cha-Pa
052	Chan-O-Wapi

483	Chanco
015	Chappegat
183	Chatoka
204	Chattahoochee
165	Chautauqua
229	Chawtaw
021	Checaugau
154	Checote
503	Chee Dodge
031	Chemahgwa
226	Chemokemon
194	Chequah
050	Cherokee
116	Cherokee
424	Cherokee
369	Chi Sigma
546	Chi Sigma
180	Chickagami
406	Chickasah
293	Chickamauga
202	Chicksa
406	Chicksaw
255	Chief Cornplanter
171	Chief Crazy Horse
341	Chief Lone Wolf
408	Chief Pomperaug
120	Chief Shabbona
397	Chilantakoba
523	Chilkat
242	Chimalus
440	Chinchewunska
524	Chippecotton
029	Chippewa
229	Chippewa
425	Chippewa
391	Chiriqui
467	Cho-Gun Mun-A-Nock
514	Choa
193	Choctaw
304	Chumash
283	Cimeroon
259	Cole-Snass-Lamatai
137	Colonneh
254	Comanche
279	Consoke
009	Cowaw
224	Cowikee
213	Coyote
171	Crazy Horse
117	Croatan
446	Cuauhtli
218	Cuwe
017	Cuyahoga
304	Cuyucos

D

561	Dala Ishadalakalish
155	Dan Beard
138	Daw-Zu
244	Day Noomp
256	Deer Rock
043	Delmont
164	Doog Gni Tuocs
429	Dzie-Hauk-Tonga

E

382	Eagle Creek
358	Echeconnee
200	Echockotee
552	Eckale Yakanen
129	Egwa-Tawa-Dee
520	El-Ku-Ta
037	Elauwit
059	Eluwak
046	Eriez
531	Esselen
560	Eswau Huppeday

G

547	Ga-Goh'-Sa
374	Gabe-Shi-Win-Gi-Ji-Kens
477	Gajunka
555	Gamenowinink
417	Ganeodiyo
159	Ganosote
025	Garrison
339	Genesee
378	Gila
214	Gimogasm
223	Gischingan
423	Gitche Gumee
106	Glihikan
313	Golden Eagle
492	Golden Sun
344	Golden Tomahawk
034	Gonlix
298	Gorgonio
086	Great Horned Owl
317	Guneukitschik
255	Gyantwachia

H

387	Ha-Kin-Skay-A-Ki
544	Ha-Wo-Wo-He-Que-Nah
554	Haleakala
028	Half Moon
047	Hanigus
578	Hasinai
554	He-Dia

456	Powhatan	334	Shin-Go-Beek
557	Pupukea	490	Shingebis
169	Pushmataha	497	Shingis
		360	Shinnecock
	Q	363	Shoshoni
309	Quanopin	024	Shu-Shu-Gah
160	Quapaw	080	Silver Tomahawk
316	Quekolis	073	Sinawa
166	Quelqueshoe	312	Sinawa
400	Quetzel	062	Sioux
325	Quilshan	377	Sipp-o
479	Quinipissa	377	Sippo
		019	Sisilija
	R	052	Siwinis
145	Raccoon	064	Skanondo
004	Ranachqua	256	Skanondo Inyan
403	Red Feather	442	Skyloo
209	Red River	270	Skyuka
282	Royaneh	212	So-Aka-Gha-Gwa
		447	Souhegan
	S	249	Spe-Le-Yai
108	Sac-N-Fox	207	Stanford-Oljato
130	Sagamore	342	Stanislaus
187	Sah-Dah-Gey-Ah	114	Stigwandish
287	Sakawawin	049	Suanhacky
573	Sakima	342	Sumi
551	Salado	011	Susquehannock
388	Samson Occum	039	Swatara
298	San Gorgonio	263	Swegedaigea
002	Sanhican		
116	Santee		T
010	Sassacus	502	T'Kope Kwiskwis
504	Saukenuk	474	Ta
130	Scarouady	488	Ta Tanka
472	Scaroyadii	138	Ta Tsu Hwa
535	Schiwa'pew Names	268	Ta-Oun-Ya-Wat-Ha
109	Scioto	032	Tahawus
475	Scouts of the Mountain	247	Tahgajute
260	Sebooney Okasucca	348	Tahoma
281	Sekettummaqua	383	Tahosa
311	Sel-Koo-Sho	127	Tahquitz
239	Semialachee	173	Takachsin
085	Seminole	533	Talako
394	Seneca	070	Tali Taktaki
184	Sequoyah	293	Talidandaganu'
548	Sha-Cha-Quoi	084	Tamrack
061	Shaginappi	147	Tamegonit
038	Shaubena	225	Tamet
051	Shawnee	339	Tana Wis Qua
109	Shawnee	067	Tanacharison
192	Shawnee	389	Tanawisqua
452	She-Sheeb	439	Tanawisqua
258	Shenandoah	016	Tankawampus
276	Shenshawpotoo	313	Tankiteke

228	Walika	167	Wolpenk
274	Wangunks	501	Wolverine
451	Wannalancit	347	Wopsononock
053	Wap-A-Ha	021	Wukakamike
448	Wapagoklos	140	Walapeju
367	Wapita	039	Wunita Gokhos
243	Wapsu Achtu	121	Wyandota
322	War Eagle	018	Wyona
474	War Eagle		
288	Washita		Y
319	Watatic	328	Ya Ha Klack Co
2690	Watonala	066	Yah-Tah-Ney-Si-Kess
055	Waukheon	465	Uahnundasis
197	Waupecan	278	Yo!Se-Mite
400	Wawookia	506	Yokahu
010	Wawonaissa	138	Yoqui
366	Wazhazee	303	Yowlumne
290	Wazi Yata	385	Yustaga
517	We-U-Shi		
273	Wehadkee		Z
023	Wenasa Quenhotan	352	Zhingwak
227	Wetassa	123	Zit-Kala-Sha
272	Wewanoma		
182	White Beaver		
343	White Buffalo		
322	White Fang		
499	White Panther		
013	Wiatava		
086	Wiccopee		
035	Wichita		
113	Wihinipa Hinsa		
234	Wihungen		
361	Wilgus		
534	Wincheck		
030	Winingus		
453	Winnebago		
158	Winnepucket		
432	Wipala Wiki		
558	Wipunquoak		
170	Wisaka		
190	Wisawanik		
247	Wisawanik		
351	Wisie Hal'A Con		
478	Wisumahi		
044	Witauchsoman		
431	Witauchsundin		
346	Wiyaka		
403	Wiyaka Luta		
106	Wiyapunit		
322	Woa Cholena		
471	Woapalane		
343	Woapeu Sisilija		
167	Woapink		
416	Wolf		